Letters to Earth... The Future Is Yours!

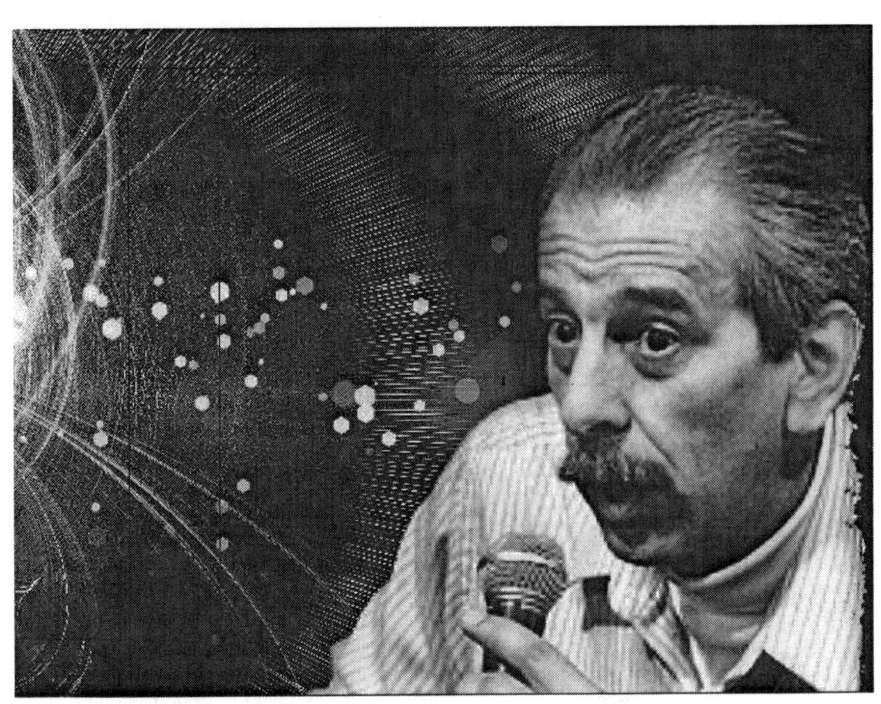

By Peter Kling

LETTERS TO EARTH: THE FUTURE IS YOURS!
previously released as "Letters to Earth: You Can Survive Armageddon!"

Re-Published & Revised in 2016 by Neely Worldwide Publishing
Cover Art Designed by Katie Neely

ISBN-13: 978-1-635358-08-7 (Digital)
ISBN-13: 978-1-635358-10-0 (Paperback)
ISBN-13: 978-1-63535-066-1 (Hardback)
Library of Congress Control Number: 2016916818

This is a work of non-fictional research. The ruminations and opinions expressed in this book and in any articles (within) hereto before or hereafter published, are solely those of the author and do not necessarily reflect or represent the official policy or position of any agency of the U.S. government, or any entity of the U.S. Government. This book is an expression by the author to generate discussion, knowledge and awareness, truth exposed and interest. This book is not, and never has been, intended as a validated source of discoveries or processes and, it does not meet any established criteria of the community required to be accepted as fact. Any republication or quotation of the expressions made herein by the author as being a " a fact"; "a source"; "a discovery"; "a revelation"; "as conclusive of"; "as evidence of" or, in any form representing these expressions as being truths or facts accepted by the community or any research specialty therein are strictly prohibited. The author has made every effort to ensure the accuracy of the information within this book was correct at time of publication. The author does not assume and hereby disclaims any liability to any party for any loss, damage, or disruption caused by errors or omissions, whether such errors or omissions result from misrepresentation, any misunderstandings or any other cause.

All documented facts were researched and obtained via The Freedom of Information Act (FOIA), 5 U.S.C. § 552, is a federal freedom of information law that allows for the full or partial disclosure of previously unreleased information and documents controlled by the United States government.

The publisher does not have any control over, and does not assume any responsibility for, the author or third party websites or their content.

www.peterkling.com
www.neelyproductionsinc.com

Tell us what you think...
We appreciate hearing reader opinions about our books. You can email the authors directly or you can email us at publishing@neelyproductionsinc.com (when contacting us be sure to state book title and author).

The authors welcome comments from readers. You can find their websites and email

Addresses on their bio pages www.neelyproductionsinc.com

Contents

CHAPTER 1
HOW DID WE GET HERE?

A few years ago we entered a new millennium, Y2K never happened, the planets aligned and the end of the world did not come. We lived through 911 and the world lost a little more innocence. It was now apparent that terrorism was going to be part of our lives, not just something that we hear about in the news. With all of this, our lives became busier and a bit more complicated, but nonetheless, life finds a way and moves on!

When we reflect on the last 100 years, we can plainly see that as a people we have accomplished many amazing things! Take the history of flight, 100 years ago, we could hardly fly 100 feet and by the end of the 1960's we put a man on the moon. Now we have developed aircraft that fly far beyond the speed of sound and are invisible to radar, aircraft that can touch space itself and return to Earth safely.

We have seen advances in technology in every corner of our lives. In fact, we would be very hard pressed to find a part of our lives that technology does not affect in some way. Science has opened vast volumes of knowledge to us in every discipline under the stars from the start of life on Earth, to the unbelievable vastness of space. Science has attained the ability to clone life and even D.N.A. has given up its secrets to us. We have mapped the human genome. We have wiped out diseases, extended the human life expectancy and for the most part have improved the quality of life for most people on the planet. We are in fact genetically engineering the world around us, from advanced medicines right down to the food we eat. We do our best to cure the sick and feed the hungry. In fact it is said that the United States grows enough food every year, to feed the world's population!

Computers have changed all our lives in many different ways. Not a day goes by that we do not interact with a computer in some way. Computers have done something amazing for the world. Not since the fabled days of the "Tower of Babel" has the world started to speak one language again. Through the world of technology, we can communicate with almost anyone on our planet at any time. Communication has been a driving force in our lives. Look at cellular phone communication; this was just an infantile industry in the 1980s. Cellular or mobile phones were only reserved for the rich or executives of companies. Today you can enter any city in the world and it looks like everyone, from children to grandparents, all have their own cell phone and everyone is talking to everyone else. Something that most people never had a few years ago is now a necessity of life! We communicate not just within our own circle of friends, but we communicate with people around the world, and we do so on a daily basis. So our world has become much smaller and language is no longer the barrier it once was.

Yes, there is no doubt that we push back the frontier of science a little more every day and become more knowledgeable of our world and the universe. As they study the stars and the universe around us, astronomers are finding that there are what seem to be endless galaxies; in the never-ending expanse, we call the universe. In fact, it is said that there are more stars in the universe than there are grains of sand on every beach and every desert on the Earth! What is more is that we are finding that many stars have planets orbiting them. It is believed that before long we will find planets, like our Earth, that are capable of supporting life. On the darker side of things, they have also found rogue asteroids and it is believed that it is only a matter of time before an asteroid of considerable size hits our Earth and forever changes our lives, or the lives of the survivors, if there are any. Because of this possibility, governments are spending millions of dollars for scientists to come up with a solution to address this problem.

There is no doubt that science and technology have become a part of our everyday lives, and without its benefits, most people's lives would be very difficult and very inconvenient to say the least. Still with all the advancements that we have seen over the past 100 years, we are no closer to answering the basic questions of life, such as: "Why are we here?" and "Where did we come from and where are we going?" "Does God exist?" "If he does exist, does he even care about us?" Many people have thought about questions like these, many times in they're live, but still have no hard answers. What is worse is that religion, which is suppose to represent God, has no answers either. It is all a mystery to them, or they invent things that sound good to their parishioners. How can they really offer any help to those who look to them for the answers of life's questions? Still, science seems to be more reliable than religion. Science looks for the pure answer to the question and deals with facts as they are understood. Therefore, when science examines the accepted clues to our origin, the fossil record, the conclusion is that life on earth somehow started when "something" shocked some simple proteins into becoming a living working organism and that "evolved" into life as we understand it today. As for the existence of "God", well, we really cannot prove scientifically that he exists, but we cannot prove that he does not exist either! So we form our own ideas and opinions, we choose to have a god or not to have a god and we decide if he is a good and loving god, or a god who demands sacrifices and who burns "wrong doers" in fire forever. Whichever we decide is what we believe and life continues.

The questions of the ages never get answered to our satisfaction. We are happy to accept the things our parents have told us and we make those things our personal beliefs and accept the traditions of our family, or the community we are part of. We become educated, polished and enter the work force as a small cog in the big machine that is our world. Like the worker ant, one of millions scurrying across the face of the Earth, coming into and slipping out of existence without really being noticed! Our goal in life is to attain "more", to have more than our parents did, to have more than our neighbors do. We want more wealth, more honor, more happiness, more love, more everything, more than everyone else! So we bury ourselves in our life's ambition. One day runs into the next and really, how often does anyone have the time to sit and contemplate his or her own life, or reflect about the world around us? Every day demands are made of us. At times there are so many demands made of us that we can forget who we are and what is important to us and the only question we want answered is "Why?"

There are so many "whys" in our life, that to start to answer them is a major undertaking! However, for us to really understand our lives today, the questions of "why" have to be answered. Without those answers, we are no better off than a worker ant, which is hardly noticed, passes into yesterday and is quickly forgotten! To get a clear and accurate answer to any question, it is best to reduce things to their most simple form and start from there. The more complicated something becomes the more difficult it is to understand. The more difficult something is to understand, the easier it is to confuse someone. When one becomes confused, it is easy to get lost, so how many people live their whole lives lost and confused? Their lives are the same today as they were yesterday and they will be the same tomorrow, without meaning, happiness and satisfaction, just like the worker ant! Too many of us live our lives this way, from cradle to grave, one foot in front of the other, day after day, year after year and then we die and with what hope?

WHERE IS HERE?

To answer any question accurately, we have to gather as many pertinent facts as possible and start from the beginning. So where is here anyway? We find ourselves in a three-dimensional world, on the third planet from the star we call Sun, in the galaxy we call the Milky Way. Our planet, the Earth, is just the right distance from the Sun to have produced an abundance of life on it. We find that life exists in the harshest conditions on earth, from blistering hot deserts, to thousands of feet below sea level; we find life in boiling hot springs, and the ice-encrusted poles. Yes, everywhere we look, we find life on our planet, even in places that we have polluted, or destroyed with nuclear radiation, life somehow finds a way!

For thousands of years man has placed himself at the center of the universe; the Sun, the planets and the stars all revolved around the Earth. Naturally we know differently now, but we still want to be at the center of at least our "own" universe. Nonetheless, our planet Earth is our home and a very unique one it is at that! Everything we need to live is provided to us from the Earth. It gives us fresh water to drink, it grows our food, and supplies us with the materials we need for shelter and warmth. When we compare the Earth to other planets in our solar system, we can plainly see that we live on the "gem" of all planets, the others are totally incapable of supporting life, as we know it! They are all pocked marked by meteors. If there is any atmosphere at all on our neighbor planets, it is a deadly mixture of gasses, one that would kill us quickly! So there is no doubt that the Earth is our home. It has everything we need and we are well taken care of here. But the Earth does not just give the necessities of life; on the contrary, there is an abundance of everything!

WHY ARE WE HERE?

What is the purpose of our life? Every generation that has gone before us has pondered this question. For some reason we want to believe that there must a "higher" purpose to our life. We are born from pain, we enter a world that at times can be very vicious. We spend most of our life working to make the lives of our children better than ours and then we die! The really sad thing is that this has been pretty much the way life has been throughout history. Every generation before us has faced pretty much the same thing, however it is our generation that is exhausting the resources of our planet and leaving a wake of pollution and death in our path.

For centuries, we have accepted that man was "created" by God. Religion has taught us that we have a spiritual connection with a supreme being and that he loves us, cares about us and watches over us. But that still doesn't tell us why we are here. If there is a God who cares about us so much, where is he and why doesn't he show us that he cares about our lives? You would think that if there were really a loving God that watches over us and cares about us, and our future, he would have some kind of communication with us. Maybe this is what gave rise to the slogan of the 1960's that "God is Dead!"

The sixties were a very interesting decade. They started off with the election of the young and handsome president Kennedy, the space race between the United States and the Soviet Union, and the Cuban missile crisis that brought the world to the brink of nuclear destruction. However, turmoil soon shook the world with the assassination of President Kennedy, and the unrest that was soon to follow would change the world forever. We lost our innocence and as the "Press" stated it "Camelot was lost!" The changes that took place in the 1960s changed the world forever! We saw the "Civil Rights" movement, the Vietnam War, the "Peace movement", the "Woman's Liberation" movement and these "protests" changed the way we view the world. Liberalism was changing our lives at every point and we believed that our "rights" and "personal freedom" were growing and becoming stronger everyday. We put a man on the moon and life was beautiful, or was it? We saw political turmoil, the oil embargo and interest rate hikes of the 1970s, runaway military spending and the fall of Communism, with the destruction of the Iron Curtin and the collapse of the Soviet Union in the 1980s. Then there was the "Dot Com" era, "Globalization" and the prosperity of the 1990s. But what cost did we pay for the twentieth century?

The twentieth century started off very unassuming, at least that was until 1914 and the start of what was to be World War One. It was called the "Great War" at the time; I guess that was because we did not expect that we were going to have to number them. Along with the First World War came the Bolshevik Revolution in Russia and the Murder of the Czar and the royal family. The Russian monarchy was replaced with the first communist government, which we now know becomes a major world power. Peace was not only torn away from the world, but death was being served up in wholesale fashion, by the first "mechanized" war to besiege the world. However death would not be satisfied by just war. Famine spread through Europe and several parts of the world and then the "Spanish flu", one of the worst epidemics to have ever struck our planet, left more than twenty million dead in its path and some estimates are twice that amount.

With war, famine, plague and death ravaging the world all at the same time, one could really ask, had the four horseman of the Apocalypse been turned loose on the Earth? Never before had we seen such problems on a worldwide scale and to the extent that they were happening!

The Spanish influenza we could do little about, but world leaders thought they could do something about keeping world peace and never letting another world war take place again. To this end the League of Nations was born. A group of nations formed to provide an open forum to discuss world differences and problems in a peaceful way and avert war. What a noble idea! U.S. President Woodrow Wilson fully supported the idea of the formation of the League of Nations and wrote the charter for the League. However, he could not convince the U.S. Congress that joining and supporting the League of Nations was more than just a good idea and in the best interest of the people of the United States but was a necessary step to prevent war on a global scale again! As we know, the League of Nations never did get the support from the United States and in 1939 the world found itself in the grips of Global conflict a second time.

While it would not be for a few years that the United States would be dragged into the war on the side of the "Allies", major investments and support were given to both Axis and Allied sides of the conflict. After Japan attacked the United States at Pearl Harbor, the "sleeping giant" had been awoken and manufacturing and production took center stage. Factories would work around the clock turning out supplies for the war effort. Not only were supplies being produced for the war, but in fact whole factories were being produced and then shipped to England and Russia, so goods could be manufactured for the "War effort" in those countries as well. The resources and the manufacturing might of the United States really won the Second World War, but that manufacturing might, would not last forever!

World War Two showed us just how cruel we could be to our fellow man. Well over fifty million people died in just a few short years! We even invented a completely new method of killing and a new terminology to go with it: "Thermonuclear Warfare". But nothing was going to prepare us for the total shock of the Holocaust! Over 6 million people murdered because they did not fit a mad man's idea of what a "pure race" should look and be like! Imagine being rounded up like cattle, forced to work while you starved to death, and in the end led to a slaughter house to be put to death. Your body discarded or burned like yesterday's garbage all because of your race, religion, or personal beliefs. Yes the Holocaust was horrific and many have pledged their lives to see that nothing like that ever happens again! But what many people have no idea of is just how many people were put to death by the mad dictator of the Soviet Union as it was purged of "dissidents". It is said that Joseph Stalin was responsible for as many as fifty million deaths, but the real number may be much higher because "official" records were not kept of all the murders. When it comes to mass murder Stalin makes Hitler look like a choirboy!

Out of the Second World War, was born the United Nations. This organization had the same agenda as the League of Nations: to preserve world peace! At least the United States would become a member this time. In fact the United States and England have been and continue to be strong supporters of the United Nations.

When you ponder the massive carnage that has piled up in the twentieth century, you must be sickened by it and have to agree that the "Horsemen of the Apocalypse" were riding! If the Horsemen of the Apocalypse are riding, then Armageddon will soon be upon us! Belief in the prediction that we are going to be facing the end of the world in the year 2012 is becoming more popular. The Mayans, Nostradamus and others have dire predictions for the year 2012, even a secret code found in the Bible says Armageddon is coming and the people of the world will see a comet strike the earth. Is God's War of Armageddon really coming? If so will there be any life left on this blue planet we call home? What can we do to survive Armageddon?

CHAPTER 2
WHAT IS GOD?

Everyone wants to start at the beginning of a story but no one ever really does; they just start at the point they want you to know about and not before. Maybe sometimes it really doesn't matter, but at other times, like this, it could be life impacting. One never really knows what things are to come from truth and knowledge, once they are revealed. Even when someone wants you to know the truth, it is really their truth they want to tell you. It is kind of a "need to know" truth. The whole reason for the writing of this book is to look for the truth and expose the lies that we have had forced upon us from our birth! The human race has been lied to from the beginning and we, who now live in the 21st century, are lied to all the time. The reason is control! As a race, we humans love to be lied to! Example, one of the most loved presidents of the latter part of the 20th century was Bill Clinton, "Slick Willy". Some wondered if he even knew what the meaning of the word "truth" was, but we Americans really didn't care. The economy was good and everyone was making money, so make me feel good and tell me lies! Lies are much easer to accept than the truth anyway. If we know the truth about something, it usually hurts us and no one likes to be hurt. The truth also forces us to have to deal with the reality of life and who wants to deal with reality when fantasy is so much more fun and easer to take?

But to find truth, we have to search for it and examine what we find! We must search all that we "believe" is true and use benchmarks and reference points to uncover the deception where it is found and reveal the truth. It is time to stop believing the lies we are told by those who would control and oppress us into doing their bidding! So in an attempt to uncover truth and stop the lies it is important to find a reference point that is accepted as true. Here is an example of a good reference point! We know that energy cannot be created or destroyed, it can only be transformed. The sun gives its energy to the earth; plants use this energy along with carbon dioxide and water and transform it into food. Other living things then eat the food and the energy is transformed to nourish animal life, humans included. We use this energy and transform it to power our bodies; our bodies give off heat as they function, again another transformation of energy. But our bodies give off things that are much harder to measure than just heat; they also give off electrical energy via thought process and the aura that surrounds us and all living things. Here is another reference point; all living things as we know and understand them have two main things in common, water and DNA / RNA. If it was ever alive on this planet, or ever intends to live on this planet, more than likely it is going to contain water and DNA if it is going to live and reproduce. It also needs a source of energy to convert to food for itself, and in turn, it transforms this energy and passes it along in the process.

If we really are interested in the truth about our existence and why we are here, we need other reference points; reference points that can be taken as benchmarks for our progress as a civilization. A really good source for a reference point is the Bible; after all it was inspired by God, right? But is it really truth, or "need to know" truth? For instance, it starts, "*In the beginning God created the heavens and the Earth...*" Well that may be the truth, but this is clearly a case of "need to know" truth. The real truth is that in the beginning, there was only God! God is an interesting concept. Does man really need a "GOD"? In addition, who is this God anyway? A better question is "What is God"? Before we can come to know who God is, it would be helpful if we knew "what" God is!

So how do we figure what God really is? We can make a real good argument that man, through out the centuries, has contemplated God to the point that he could no longer fathom who or what God was, and because of not being able to understand God he just started to worship the things he found in his world. This was much easer to understand and who cared if it was true or not, man could rely on and understand these things, because they were simple and they affected his every day life. The sun no doubt is the widest and most important god that was ever worshiped. Sun worship started before the first world power, Egypt, and is still worshiped to this day with the now worldwide celebration of Christmas. Yes, look around the world and Christmas is celebrated by those who could care less about Christianity, Christ, or any of the things he taught! Look up the origin of Christmas for yourself and you will find that it is a lot older than Jesus and had nothing to do with him or his birth. Christmas is taken from the Roman holiday of Saturnalia, a celebration or the return of the sun god. But the Christian religious leaders insist that it is the birth of Christ they celebrate, another lie! Well the sun worshipers may not be too far off track when it comes to understanding God. If you take into consideration that you can neither create nor destroy energy, and this is true, then God must be energy. What kind of energy? Just what is he made of and how much energy is there in God? One may ask, "Well how much energy is there in the entire known universe?" and "How did it get there?" Scientists turn to the "big bang" theory and claim that about 10 to 15 billion years ago there was an explosion so massive that it created our universe as we understand it today. But wait a minute; let's consider what kind of energy is really needed to create so much matter across billions of light years. Well maybe we can't fathom such a great energy source and if there really is this great source of energy somewhere out there, why can we not see it? There are more unanswered questions and even more beliefs as to what God is, so we get into the esoteric to try to explain God. Ask ten people about who is God and most likely you will get ten different answers, from there is no God, to God is all around us and in all living things.

So let's start at the real beginning! If at one time there were only God, then it would be safe to say that there would be no need for time as we understand it, because if there was only you and nothing else, then you would have no need for anything! So it is pretty safe to say that if there was only God, he would have no need for anything, there would only be God and only be the need for one dimension of life and understanding. We can call this "God Dimension". Why? Because it is the easiest and most simple thing to understand! Let us take it to a really easy concept to understand, a single cell. If there is only a single cell of life and that is all there is, then there is nothing but that single cell. There is no time, no space, just one single cell of life! However, just as cells divide and reproduce themselves, this "God" cell must have done the same thing! Again, we need a reference point. There are several references that this "God Cell" did divide and created another cell. We can find these references again in the Bible, where we are told that God had a "first born". He is given different names, but the most common is "Jesus"! I am not saying this is true or not, I am just referring to what we are told and what is written in the Bible for our understanding.

I really need to make a personal disclaimer here. It is my opinion that the absolute worst thing that ever happened to the Bible is that religion got involved! The reason I say this is every major so-called Christian religion has twisted the Bible to fit the teachings and traditions of that religion! When one examines the teachings of religions through out the world and compares it with the teachings of the Bible, you will find that religion does not really teach what is in the Bible. They are teaching the traditions of man and weaving pagan beliefs in those teachings. A prime example of this is Emperor Constantine in the third century. What he did was little more than marry the pagan Roman religious beliefs and the teachings of the early Christian church which, by the way, was becoming vastly corrupted together. This became what today is known as the Catholic and Eastern Orthodox Churches. The start of the "Holy Roman empire" and the start of "Christian" lies to further enslave mankind to the teachings of the lies of the upper class theologians, who were "learned men" taught in religious seminaries to continue these lies to further enslave the common uneducated man to blind religious faith! So if you now really question the validity of this statement that is fine, because one should question everything when looking for the truth! But ask yourself, if the Church really wanted to teach mankind the truth that was written in the Bible, why were so many people burned alive, with the blessing of the Church, for reading or just possessing the Bible? It is very obvious that the Church wanted to enslave man with the lies that they propagate! Furthermore, for centuries, everything spoken in the Catholic Church was spoken to the common people in Latin. This continued until the later 1960's when protest was raised because only a very small percentage of people in the world could speak Latin. The only people who could really speak Latin were the "church leaders" who were starting to lose their grip on the populous of their flock! The real reason for the change of not speaking Latin anymore was very simple, money! The common people could not understand what they were being told. It was difficult at best to support something you cannot understand and with dwindling coffers the "Church" was forced to do something! Another problem was "higher" education. More and more "common people" were getting a college degree and in teaching more about the scientific world around them and the "scientific process" The "Church" was loosing its credibility! The common person was now starting to question the religious idiosyncrasies as pure nonsense! Please. You mean to tell me that God tells us that if we are good we go to heaven to be with him and the other angels and get to play harps and sing songs and if we are bad we get to spend eternity with the Devil and roast like little pigs forever in a fiery hell? Do you really want me to believe this? What does the Bible say? In Genesis 3:19 we read that God tells Adam that he would eat bread until he returns to the ground, God said "For dust you are and to dust you will return." Now, at this time, God was really pretty upset with Adam. Adam had just derailed God's purpose for mankind! So why did God not say to Adam, "You disobeyed me, now you will burn in a fiery hell for all eternity!" He did not say this to Adam because there is no fire in hell! Hell is just a place where we throw a dead body to become food for worms and other living things. The energy that was once living, breathing tissue now gets passed on to other living organisms. One of the wisest men ever to live was the Hebrew king Solomon and he said at Ecclesiastes 9:5 *"As for the dead, they are conscious of nothing at all."* So whom do you want to believe; the religious leaders who want to enslave mankind or God?

So let us look at this God more closely. Now that this "cell" divides and we have two "intelligent" life forms, what has to change? Well, there is the start of time; a birthday if you would like and there can no longer be only a "God dimension", there now has to be more detentions! It would be logical that there had to be more than two dimensions, because now there was "God", "Jesus" and the dimension of "time" but calculated not by the same way that time is calculated here on earth. Time would have to be measured much differently than we calculate time and we are talking about three different dimensions here at this point, but are they the same as our three dimensional world, no! They really can't be because our world, our universe was not yet brought in to existence; the "Big Bang" was not yet on the list of things to happen, at least not yet! So what does happen next and even a better question, why?

Let us look at the "why" of things first! You may ask' "So what happened, did God get tired of being by himself?" Most likely, he did not! A conscious decision had to be made to reproduce, but to do this in a way that intelligent life could be passed on and duplicated. However, not just intelligent life, "life force" it self would also need to be passed on and duplicated too! This is just the first understanding of a intelligent life force, giving a similar life force its start. Kind of sounds like having a baby to me! However, we are not talking about a 3 dimensional life force here, as we commonly understand it! This is "God dimension" starting to multiply in to other necessary dimensions to replicate and duplicate life. A life slightly different from the form and life force we understand as "God". There is a different name given here, hence a different species. This species is referred to as the Archangel Michael in the book of Jude: 9, *"We have known him as Jesus, God's son"*. Just think of this, if Jesus really was the Son of God, then we really killed E.T. Boy I bet his dad is mad at us! Let us return to logic here. For this to occur, we have to take into account that it is first possible! We are told that all things are possible with God! So let us show a little emotional here. Think about the bonds that surround a new family. In a perfect setting, we have a man and a woman meet and fall in love, their love grows and they want to get married. As we are told, the two become one; one mind, one sprit and before long, a child is conceived in love! Two intelligent, living creatures have biologically reproduced, in a manner that has been going on here on the "blue planet" from time in memorial. That is except for one thing, love! Love, as far as we know, is something unique to the higher intelligence of mankind. There is very little love that is involved in cellular division. How much love do bacteria have? How much love do salmon express as they are drawn up a river to start life in the same place where they started life and how much love do animals express as they carry out the reproductive process? Their sexual activities are driven by a release of pheromones, a chemical signal to engage in sexual reproduction. At least that is the way it happens here on Earth, right? Well we are not seeing a three-dimensional life form reproducing here. This is a one dimensional force becoming, changing and creating new life forms and new dimensional "play grounds" for them to "play" and live in. 1 John 4:8 tells us that God is love. It does not say that God has love, but God is love!

Love in itself is an interesting quality, a very powerful emotion and one that can be felt on many different levels. The love we feel for someone special to us, the love we have for our friends, our family, or things we enjoy doing. We humans use the word love in many ways to describe a number of levels of feeling and direction those feelings from everything from the foods we enjoy, our favorite clothing, to ourselves and those we hold the closest to us. Just how powerful is this feeling of love that we have? Does love carry power of its own, or is it just an emotion that we feel at times of contentment and enjoyment? We know that love itself must be at least a catalyst that can stimulate power within us. Many years ago a story was related to me. A man was in a hospital on his deathbed, his diagnosis was in and he was terminal. With some of the last of his strength, he talked to his wife who he loved so dearly and asked her to please not marry again after his death.

As much as she loved him, she could not grant his last request. She was still young enough to marry again and start a new life with someone else and she did not want to lie to her husband, whom she loved very much, but who was at death's door. The fact that she could not make him this promise did something to her husband. The thought of his wife giving her love to another and not return his love anymore, started him back on the road to recovery and before long he was back to full health. I am sure we can find many accounts of how love overcame insurmountable odds and conquered all. The Bible has many accounts of different types of love and it's power. In 1 Corinthians 9, is a whole chapter talking about the qualities and power of love. So what happened with God? Did he just decide one day that the love within him needed to get out? We do not know. However, one thing is obvious about love to us humans, it is never consistent. It changes in type, form and intensity and it always feels good!

CHAPTER 3
MULTI-DIMENSIONAL LIFE

Scientists tell us that billions of years ago there was a large explosion of matter, a "Big Bang" and our three-dimensional world was born. It was a new world for a new intelligent life force to inhabit! The three dimensional world! We are at least told that the Universe started with a "big bang". One big three-dimensional universe made up of both solid and gaseous matter with gravitational forces so great that we can hardly calculate that high without the aid of super computers to do the math for us. The more we learn about our universe the more complex it becomes. Once we only knew about the stars and planets that we could see, then other galaxies and massive gaseous nebulas were found. We have built a variety of different types of telescopes to unlock the secrets of the heavens and the three-dimensional universe that we live in. However, is what we see, all there is?

STRING THEORY AND A TEN DIMENSIONAL WORLD

Really though, how many dimensions are there? This was really an unknown answer until mathematicians and physicists, who were working on a unification theory to tie all forces of energy together, came up with the answer. It is called "M" theory or "String" theory. Simply put, String theory states that all energy is made up of "strings" that vibrate at a specific speed. It is very much the way a string works on a guitar. When it is plucked a note is sounded and depending on the speed of the string vibration you will play a note. So for everything that exists in our world, there are sub-atomic particles that vibrate at a predetermined speed. This gives that element, or compound it's characteristics. Hard or soft, visible or not, all things are ultimately made up of "strings", including us!

In doing the mathematics to tie all this together, something very interesting was discovered. In order for our three-dimensional life and all we know to exist, there must be at least seven other "dimensional plains"; one of those being time. Some who have been researching "string theory" suggest that there may be eleven or more different dimensions, but in order for the math to work there must be at least ten dimensions.

We know that energy cannot be created or destroyed but only transformed. This must mean that all energy is made up of the same substance, regardless if it is the energy given off by an atomic explosion, or the energy given off by the process of thought, both of these energies can be detected and measured. Here is an interesting note. Mental energy can transcend time and space! Studies of physics indicate that mental transmission during the thought process happens in an instant! The theory goes like this: If you had two physics on opposite ends of the galaxy, they could communicate with one another in an instant. If this is true, then your thoughts can also transcend dimensions in an instant, because we know that time is a dimension. So with "string theory" all energy is the same and what makes it react differently is vibration. So as we think, we release strings of energy that vibrate at a certain speed. On an atomic level the atoms are made up of densely packed particles of energy, vibrating at a preset speed which make up the structure of the atom and therefore giving it it's own characteristics.

So really, how many dimensions are there? Personally I like the number 10, but there is no reason to stop there. Here is how it would break down. First, we live in a three-dimensional world. Everything in our world has height, depth and width. It does not matter how small it is or how big it is, everything we can quantify physically has those characteristics. Well where do the other 7 come in? For some reason this intelligence we fondly call God likes the number 7 because it signifies spiritual completeness, or spiritual perfection. The number 6 on the other hand, shows spiritual incompleteness, or spiritual imperfection. Hence the proverbial 666 from the book of Revelation is a number that most humans do not have a good feeling about. It is sometimes related as the "Devil's" number, signifying spiritual incompleteness to the third power. It is the mark of one of the wild beasts of Armageddon. So what about the number ten? It shows or signifies earthly completeness or the completeness of mankind. You know ten fingers, ten toes; our whole life is biased on the number 10. My thought is God lives in a 7 dimensional world, we humans live in a 3 dimensional world; let's do the math! Here is something else to contemplate, if this is correct, then our minds or thought process can span the seven spiritual dimensions while our bodies are stuck in a 3 dimensional world. At the present time none of this can be proved, but when you analyze it, it does make sense! We all have a spiritual side that we understand very little about, but without it, it's obvious that humans would be very different then we are now.

But does all this make a difference? Yes! Here is why. Every year we spend millions of dollars looking for E.T. using giant radio antenna telescopes. We have the most complex equipment and some of the greatest minds looking for intelligent life in outer space! In three-dimensional outer space! Well if you are looking for intelligent life in a three-dimensional outer space and are using equipment that only sees in a three-dimensional universe and intelligent life is four-dimensional or higher, I really don't think you are going to find much of anything useful in your quest to find intelligent life in our part of the "dimension system". Now I am sure that all the people that work with or directly for S.E.T.I. are just thrilled at my comments, because that just makes all their hard work totally useless and futile, sorry guys! The only intelligent life in our three-dimensional universe is us! Now before we get all upset and throw the baby out with the bath water, I am convinced that there is life in "outer space", but the life that is there is much less intelligent than we are. I doubt that it is much more intelligent than a chimpanzee and that might be stretching it! We will discuss the possibilities of additional three-dimensional life forms throughout the universe a bit later.

With our technology it is impossible to detect just how many dimensions really do exist. We can only do this with the science of mathematics and then it has to be "translated" into a language that we can all understand. However, if there are at least 10 dimensions as "M" or "String" theory indicate and we live in three of them and use one to keep time, this leaves six other dimensions that we know almost nothing about except that in order for us to exist, they have to exist too! So how do we know that some sort of life form doesn't call those other six dimensions home? Chances are if there are other intelligent life forms, they don't live in our three-dimensional universe and are not governed by the laws of the three-dimensional world in which we live.

Humans are biological carbon-based life forms. We live in three-dimensional world, mostly made up of atoms packed with "vibrating strings" giving them their own unique characteristic properties, which we have all become familiar with. Regardless of how we use the elements of the world around us, or what compounds we turn them into, those elements always keep the same properties because of the speed of the vibrations the "strings" are set to. But what would happen if you changed the speed of the vibrations of the "strings"? Then you change the properties of the element and you have something else. That cool glass of water you are about to drink isn't water anymore, it could be something that will kill you on contact, or it may turn into a gas and boil away, or it may become solid. It would all become something much different than what it was before we changed the speed of the "strings"!

Ask yourself, "What would happen if we could control the speed at which a string vibrates?" Could we not create anything we wanted? There would be no shortages of any kind. Run out of something? Just make more! Yes I know it is not that simple, but what if you could? What if you could you change the speed of the strings that make up the molecules in your body so they vibrated at such a speed that you would no longer be in a three-dimensional world, but "cross over" into the other six dimensions and exist in a world that is made up of energy, but organized in a much different way than our world. (Time is a constant between dimensions, only calculated differently. For example, a "light year" in our three- dimensional world could be equal to a year in the other six dimensions. The Bible records that a day with "God" is as a thousand years to mankind.) What if you could control the energy of the atoms that make up our bodies? What would we be able to do? Where could we go? What things could we see and learn? These are all interesting questions, but they all center on the question, "What if". Two things are for sure, if you could control the speed of the strings that make up the energy your body is made of, you would not be bound to the three-dimensional world we live in and you would not be human!

Why all the "what if" questions about String theory? Throughout our whole existence, man has only known a three-dimensional world. This is where we live. Everything in our world we can touch, feel, smell, see, or hear. It is the only world that exists for us and throughout the whole existence of man, we have made a life long study of our world and the universe that surrounds us. Indeed it is very safe to say that we have come to learn more about our world by scientific means in the past hundred years, then in all of recorded history and now we learn about the existence of other dimensions beside our own. So why would it be foolish to think that intelligent life forms may live in those other dimensions? That is like thinking the earth is flat!

We know that our universe had a beginning, the "Big Bang". Eventually, through time and chemical processes we know that life came to be formed, because we are here. We don't know what existed before the "Big Bang", as far as we know there was nothing! Science can agree that there was an explosion casting matter and energy across the universe. In fact our universe is still expanding and going through changes everyday as matter expands into the emptiness we call space. So where did the energy come from to set off the "Big Bang"? Could it have come from a seven-dimensional world that existed long before our world of three dimensions?

If we go back to one of the first rules of physics, which is that you cannot create or destroy energy, you can only change its form, then we can all agree that the energy that makes up our universe came from some place, but where?

This is pretty much where science stops and faith in a higher power starts. We cannot see past the three-dimensional world that we live in, but through mathematics and physics we can calculate that more exists than just three dimensions. Could the personage we call "God" live in the other six dimensions along with his "angelic family"? (Remember time is a constant and its own dimension.) We would have to say that there is a possibility that this could be in fact true. We search the heavens for signs of intelligent life forms, but we find nothing! What if we could search other dimensions? What would we find?

EXTRA TERRESTRIALS, DO THEY REALLY EXIST?

All throughout recorded history man has been involved with other life forms. The Bible speaks of three other life forms beside "God"; there are seraphs, cherubs and angels. However, we know very little about these life forms as only very basic things that are told to us in the Bible. We also have recorded, through the history of the world, mankind's involvement with gods and spirits. All cultures and all peoples throughout history have had a connection with some sort of extra terrestrial life form. Some of these cultures, such as the Egyptians, Babylonians and the empires that stretched throughout South and Central America, such as the Incas, Aztecs and Mayans, all achieved feats in their civilizations involving technology, that many have suggested came from "extra- terrestrials" because the knowledge and the technology is considered too advanced for the peoples living at those times.

As we get closer to the twenty first century, we find that the "gods" have lost their grip on civilization. Even in lands where people have worshiped many gods for centuries, modern life has minimized spirituality, and science and technology are replacing or at least minimizing the gods. Even in "Christian" countries, between the pace of life and the scandalous acts of the "Church's clergy", many people in today's world have had their fill of religion, God and all that goes with them. There is no doubt that religion is losing its grip and control over the populous. Everyday more and more "places of worship" such as churches and temples are closing their doors because of the lack of interest in God and spirituality. While many still feel the need to worship a "higher spiritual power", today's clergy are not filling the need of the people who are looking to them for answers.

Is it really any wonder that people have lost their interest in religion? For the last hundred years we have been taught that man evolved from lower life forms, which eliminates the "need" for a higher power to answer to. In fact, even though evolution is still a "theory", in the United States of America it is illegal to teach the opposing viewpoint that life on earth was created by a higher life form we call "God"! So in essence we have made science our new god and we look to it to solve all our problems from personal health issues to saving the environment of the earth we live in. But then again, isn't "science" responsible for many of the health and environmental issues we have today?

As religion loses its influence over the earth's population there is a phenomenon that is coming to replace it very quickly; the belief in "extra terrestrials" and "Unidentified Flying Objects! In fact, more people in America believe in UFOs and "extra terrestrials" than go to church!

One minute here! Are we to understand that "ET" is replacing "God"? Well it does seem that way, but what if "ET" is God? Well maybe not "God" but what if they are the "gods" that have influenced man from prerecorded history?

Aircraft pilots from both allied and axes powers during the Second World War recorded an interesting phenomenon. While in flight, some pilots reported seeing "balls of light" that would surround and maneuver with them as they were flying. They called these balls of light "Foo Fighters". There was no real explanation for what was seen there, but after the war, in Roswell, New Mexico it was alleged that a crashed "flying saucer" had been recovered by the United States military. While first reports by the local military authorities supported this discovery, they quickly changed their story and reported that it was a weather balloon used for research that had fallen back to earth. Accusations of a cover up of the truth by the United States Military arose and UFOs and ETs were now a part of earth culture. As time passed more and more reports of UFOs were reported and people came fourth and claimed that they were abducted by "aliens" and had experiments carried out on them. While the super powers kept quite on the subject, other countries released reports of engagements with their air force and UFOs.

Now I am not here to say that UFOs and aliens are real, however people who claim to have had encounters think they are real! After reviewing the data, at the very least, one must admit that there is some kind of phenomena occurring that cannot be explained by what we know and understand about the natural world around us and the sciences that we have developed.

Here is something that I can say with confidence because it is true! At the start of the Twentieth Century almost all people went to "church" or some religious place of meeting on a regular basis, mostly at least once a week. Almost all people had a very strong belief in god and no one believed in UFO's or aliens. At the end of the Twentieth Century, most people do not go to "Church" on a weekly basis, some questioned the existence of "God" and most believed in "extra terrestrial life forms" or "aliens" and the existence of UFOs. So what happened? Where did the "gods" go and where did the "UFOs" come from? Could they be one in the same? In America we went from a very religious country to a very scientific country in less than one hundred years! So have the gods of our forefathers become the extra terrestrials we have come to "know and love" today?

THE PARANORMAL

While I really do not wish to spend much time on this subject, it does need to be talked about. It covers many things that we cannot explain, but it seems most of the paranormal revolves around "poltergeists", or "ghosts" or the "spirits of the dead" who for some reason are bound to this world and will not "pass over" as it is referred to.

Volumes of books, movies and TV programs have been written on the paranormal and it seems that "evil spirits" and ghosts have been with us forever, in one form or another. The Bible talks about evil spirits and it has been recorded that Jesus and his disciples cast out "demons" from people whose body they had taken over. We have all heard tales and legends of haunted places from castles of Europe to American Indian burial grounds. For many years these reports and stories were scoffed at as urban legends and just good ghost stories to be told to kids around campfires, but is it all just innocent fun and legend? No! In fact the second largest celebrated holiday in America is "Halloween". A day where "ghost", "demons", "witches" and the "undead" are imitated by and inculcated into the minds of our children and for dressing up as the "undead" we reward them with candy!

Have you ever wondered how a holiday that celebrates the devil and all his evil hoards made it in to Christendom? When the Romans conquered the British, they found themselves around a people called Celts. Both the Celts and Romans had holidays that were in the fall of the year celebrated after harvest time. The Celts held the celebration of "Samhain" a day where the spirits of the dead were allowed to crossover into the world of the living. The Romans celebrated the holiday of "Feralia" a day to give peace and rest to the dead. Over time, the traditions intermingled somewhat, but it was still a very pagan celebration of the dead. By the time the seventh century came around, "Christianity" had been spread through Celtic lands, but the Celts still kept their holidays including the "Celebration of the Dead", so Pope Boniface IV introduced "All Saints Day". The day is intended to honor the saints and martyrs of the Church and replace the "Celebration of the Dead" by the Celts. Pope Gregory III moved the holiday to November first, renamed it and the customs were accepted by the "Church" and handed down from generation to generation, just as we hand this tradition to our children. There was president for accepting another cultures holidays and traditions and giving it a Christian name. In fact Emporia Constantine gave many of the pagan Roman holidays "Christian" names when he made Christianity the national religion of the Roman Empire in the third century and converted himself before his death. Well imagine that, Christians are Pagans in disguise! Who would have guessed?

The point here is that there is yet another form of life that is not bound to the three-dimensional world as we know and understand it. Though for years scientists would have nothing to do with or say about paranormal events, today is quite different. Now many are taking a "scientific view" of the paranormal and the strange events that they "conger up" and are doing their best to record, measure and understand "events" that in other words are "unworldly".

OUR TIES TO THE SPRIT WORLD

Humans have a very long history of involvement with a "spiritual world". Somehow, we feel a connection to something that we can't touch, see, feel, hear, or smell, but we still know it is there. We feel a need to love and be loved and yet there is a spiritual side of love that makes us look to the heavens from time to time and feel a connection to a "Higher Power" and for some reason we feel compelled to love and worship this higher power. The vast majority of people who have lived on this planet earth of ours have worshiped "God" or "gods" at least at some level. Many have died for their love of the god that they worshiped. Throughout history there are countless cases of religious wars, or accounts of those who were martyred for their beliefs and the love of their god. Most likely the stories we know best, are the stories of the martyrdom of the early Christians, who were fed live to wild animals, used as torches to light the night sky or cut in half or "quartered", all because they would not compromise their love for the god they worshiped.

Regardless of the education of the civilization, or where people are located on this planet, we all have one thing that makes us humans different from every living creature we exist with and that is the ability and the need to love and feel loved. Deny love to a child long enough and it will start to develop emotional problems and the longer love is denied the deeper the emotional problems become until the child becomes completely dysfunctional. There are many documented cases of offended and abandoned children in the country of Romania, who left without love and attention for years, started to cause bodily harm to themselves, some going as far as gouging their own eyes out! Why? All because of a lack of love!

Somehow this emotion of love seems to be "hard wired" into us. We cannot help but to love someone or something and if we are normal and healthy, we want to be loved too! So where did this emotion of love come from?

The Bible book of Genesis chapter 1 verse 26 reads in part, "*And God went on to say: "Let us make (genetically engineer) man in our image, according to our likeness"* and the book of 1 John 4: 8 reads in part. *"God is love." So if we were "made" or "genetically engineered" in God's "image" and "likeness"* and as we read in 1 John "*God is love*", then it is most likely safe to say that we are "hard wired" to love, we really don't have a choice in the matter!

DO SPIRIT CREATURES EXIST?

If we can trust what is written in the Bible, and there really is no reason that we shouldn't, archeology has proved the Bible right time and time again. Then you have to ask to whom was God talking to when he said "Let us make man in our image"? No doubt there were other intelligent life forms there to communicate with. The Bible tells the basic story of good and evil and how one day God's war of Armageddon will destroy the evil and reestablish God as rightful ruler and all mankind will be blessed! It also tells a story of a "heavenly revolt" where the leader of the revolt turns a third of the population of "Heaven" against God and then does his best to control the hearts and minds of men and women, a new intelligent life form that inhabits the third dimension.

With all that we have considered thus far, understanding about "String Theory" and how the speed of the vibration of the strings determine the properties of everything in our world, we also learned that in order for our three-dimensional world to exist, there must be seven other dimensions, one of them being the constant of time. We talked about the possibilities of life existing in the other six dimensions. We have discussed the fact that some other types of life forms have had an influence over the lives of our ancestors and they worshiped them as gods. Now that we have become "educated", the gods have seemed to become "aliens" or "extra terrestrials". Let's not forget about the poltergeist, spirit creatures that do their best to "haunt" mankind, pretending to be the "undead" spirits of our ancestors.

More importantly, we explored an area that affects all of us. It is the emotion of love and the spiritual connection that we have to a "Higher Power". From the evidence we looked at we were most likely genetically engineered that way. We all want to be loved by someone, we want to love others, and love has so many different forms.

When we examine all the evidence that we discussed here, we must admit that humans have a connection to a spiritual world beyond the three-dimensional we live in, a world we cannot touch but we can feel. We must also admit that some intelligent life form or forms have an interest in us humans and have throughout our existence. You have to ask why? What is their interest in us? Why is it so covert? Why do they not just show themselves? Could it be for our control? If they can control our minds, or what we think about by means of world events and intimidation, they control us. Look around in the world today and ask yourself how many "layers" of control do we have in our life? There is the control that exists with in the family. If you are like most people in the world you have the control of religion. Then you have elected officials at the local, state and federal government levels. We also have layers of police control from town police to county sheriff, state police, to the national police force such as the FBI. Let us too not forget The United Nations. You may laugh now, but wait! The United Nations will soon have more control over our lives then most people will think is possible. Research the "Law of the Sea Treaty" and see how it will affect your life. Add in the control that we have from our jobs, insurance companies, the bankers and paying taxes and we realize that we have almost no control over our own lives at all. Have you ever wondered how all this control got here? Here is a better question, why do we allow it? Yes allow it and at times even welcome it!

Look what happened after the World Trade Center bombing on "9-11" 2001. In order to be able to detect and stop terrorists before striking again, The Congress of the United States of America passed the "Patriot Act" which gave the government a greater control over the people within it's borders and American citizens lost a little more "freedom" and gained another layer of control over their lives.

In Genesis chapter 1 verse 28 we read in part, *"Further God blessed them"* and God said, *"Be fruitful and become many and fill the earth"...*" In the Bible book of Matthew, when asked what the greatest commandment was, Jesus replied in verse 37, *"You must love Jehovah God with your whole heart, your whole soul and your whole mind."* The only command or law that God gave man was to reproduce and have enough children to fill the earth and do not eat the fruit from the "Tree of Knowledge of Good and Bad". Jesus told us that we should love God completely. So what kind of control did God put on us? To have kids and love him. How much more freedom could you have?

Humans are "free will" life forms. In other words, we are free spirits who can choose what we want to do. We are not "preprogrammed" to act a certain way and nobody can really force us to do things we do not want to do. No one can get you to do anything that you do not want to do, unless you let that happen, or you are under someone else's control and are fearful of the consequences of what they will do to you if you do not submit to their control.

So if we are created as free will life forms and were not given any other rules then to love and reproduce, why do we have so many rules, laws and levels of control heaped upon us today? If God is not responsible for us being enslaved to the systems of this world, then who is?

CHAPTER 4
THREE-DIMENSIONAL LIFE

HOW DID IT START?

Everything in our world has three surfaces, length, depth and width. It really does not matter what it is, from the largest mountain to the smallest microbe, even down to the sub atomic level, it really is what we are. However, science tells us that the most likely way that our three dimensional "world", started was with a "Big Bang"! It was an explosion of matter that was most likely hydrogen. That matter spread across the universe over billions of years and with the tremendous amount of processes that took place since that "Big Bang" now makes up what we know as our world and everything around us as we understand it. But do we really understand it?

The people who dedicate their life to science are truly great people! They have an interest in the world around us and they will spend their whole lives researching just one small part. They learn everything that is possible to learn and then pass that knowledge onto others. They push back the frontiers of their disciplines as they learn about our world and we have benefited in so many ways!

Most of us get up in the morning, wash and dress, eat and go to work. We get in a car, drive to an office, factory, or job sight and do something of value for others, so that we can earn a living and feel successful. Wait a minute! Let us look at this process a bit closer. Most likely, you live in a house, or an apartment, which is temperature controlled. It is using energy in some form to raise and lower the "comfort level" to that which you like the best. This is a simple process that most of us take totally for granted, but if it were not for dedicated scientists, we would be sleeping on the ground, in trees, or maybe a wood and thatch hut. We would have to walk down to the lake or river to wash and then start our day by finding some nuts or berries, or maybe there is some dried smoked meat that we could eat. Then it's off to work, finding more things you could eat so you could live another day and in your process you would hope nothing would eat you!

I guess when you think about it, things have not changed very much, have they? Yes we fill our lives with the most modern conveniences to make things easier in our lives, or to give us pleasure of some sort, but almost everything we know and have today is because some scientist some place has dedicated his or her life so our lives can be easier and more enjoyable.

Science has given us our education system that has taught us and our parents and will teach our children. The question is, "What are they teaching and what are we learning?" Are scientist always right? No not at all, sometimes they are far from it. Almost all knowledge has been replaced with new understanding. The scientists of tomorrow will no doubt learn things that will invalidate what we accept today as fact. It happens everyday as we learn more and more about the world we live in and the universe that surrounds us!

Okay, so what does science says about us? How did we get here? Maybe a better question is, "Why are we even here?"

DID WE JUST EVOLVE?

From the time of Charles Darwin writing his theory of evolution, until today, there probably has not been a more studied subject than evolution! Evolution is a very interesting subject and hard to disagree with, because all the evidence is written in stone. Granted, the many fossils that are recovered are nothing more than a "snap shot" of the past. It is the only information that we have and while that information is hundreds of millions of years old, it does show us what lived on earth before we did and it gives us a very good idea what was involved in the process of the development of the hominids and the life form that we now believe is us!

Even though evolution is still just a theory and Charles Darwin had a strong personal belief in God, science and most scientists view evolution more as a fact then a theory. Why is this? Maybe it is because it is much easier to tell a story about something you have found and have people believe it, then to logically and scientifically try to explain that something you cannot see, feel or touch, created us and placed us on this planet for some kind of unknown purpose. Really, which is easier for you to believe, that we were just placed here by some supreme being for unknown reasons, or that over millions of years and changing environmental conditions we changed from some pond sludge to the intelligent life form we are today? Well to tell you the truth, neither of these explanations are ones that I particularly like! The problem is how do you argue with something that is written in stone?

EVOLUTION VS CREATION

Very few issues divide people as much as evolution verses creation. If you took both sides and looked at them at a glance this is what you would see. One side holding up "rocks" (fossils) saying that it took hundreds of millions of years for our environment and us to develop to the point that we have attained today! On the other side, a group holds up a book called the Bible and argues that a supreme being created all of this in six days and now it is the seventh day and he is resting, that is why he is not around! This argument has been going on for over a hundred years and there is not much that is going to bring these two sides together on any issue until God shows up and settles the argument.

The idea of creation is worldwide and spans every culture and every land. Some place in the history of all peoples there is a story of how some "Supreme Being" or "Beings" caused a cosmic event and our world was then created! This idea has been set in our history and it is not going to go away! People are willing to die for what they believe in and the idea of some sort of "Supreme Being" is almost "hard wired" in to our psyche. In fact it seems that with each generation before us, that wiring becomes harder and harder and for thousands of years it was a fact that "God" created the heavens and the Earth and all we know and understand! It has only been in the last century that the "Evolutionists" have attacked the idea that God created everything. It is very difficult for logic to attack faith and win, but it is not impossible!

Let's look at our two sides here. On one side we have an "inspired book" written by God, or more correctly, a group of "inspired books" written by man at the direction of God and compiled and presented to us today to help build our faith in God and live good productive lives. On the other side we have a pile of rocks! So which do you believe in, the book or the rocks?

We need to be fair here and be as open minded as possible, because we are going to compare the evidence logically, much the same way a jury would do and do our best to find who is correct here, or at the very least find the truth!

One of the biggest problems with the argument of evolution or creation is just that, it is an argument with neither side willing to listen to the other for very long! So I have no argument here, I am only going to do my best to present the evidence in a logical way. You will have to make up your own mind as to what really happened!

If we look at the "rocks" we are going to want to look at the earliest ones that we can find because there will be the evidence as to what happened here on Earth. For that we need to go back to what is called the Precambrian period and see what we can find. The Precambrian period covers what happened here on earth between 4.5 billion and about 542 million years ago. Basically this is the time that the earth was cooling down from a molten state, developing a crust and our seas were born from the massive amounts of water vapor that had been developing. As the water fell over the newly formed and still forming land, it became mineral and chemical rich, forming what scientists call a "primordial soup". It is in this "soup" that we find the first evidence of life on earth. Simple single cell life forms start to fill the new oceans.

What does the Bible say about this that causes such a problem? Let us look! Genesis 1:1 reads, *"In the beginning God created the heavens and the earth."* I really did not read how long this process took, that information was omitted for some reason. Maybe God really did not think it mattered. I have to believe that if science tells me that the earth is about 5 billion years old and "God's Word the Bible" doesn't say, that science is most likely right in this case.

If "God" started all of this and he is still around today, I have to believe that he does not keep time as we do, what do you think? Genesis 1:2 reads *"that the earth was a formless waste and there was darkness on the surface and God's force was active over the surface of the waters."* As we read verses 3, 4, and 5 it appears as though sunlight has reached the surface of the earth and the end of the first day.

For the sunlight to reach the earth's surface, most of the water vapor had formed into heavy clouds. When the rain started, it rained so hard and so long that the vast oceans we have today were created and a simple atmosphere containing gasses incapable of sustaining life as we know it, was formed. However the oceans were full of microscopic bacterial life, so what started it? Was it God's "Active Force"? Well science comes up a little short here because simply, they don't know! The best scientific guess is that life started close to underwater volcanic vents. Between the heat, bubbles and chemically laden water, a reaction somehow started and in time simple single cell life forms appeared. These life forms were able to replicate themselves and still live with us today. Bacteria are, without a doubt, the oldest and most prolific life form on earth. In reality, life on earth could not be possible if it were not for bacteria.

From what we know, about 3 billion years ago there was almost no oxygen in the earth's atmosphere. About 2.4 billion years ago the seas were releasing oxygen produced as a by- product of photosynthesis, by cyanobacteria. Somewhere about 800 million years ago, the oxygen levels hit about 21 percent and that allowed complex life forms to appear.

In Genesis 1: 6, 7, and 8, it sounds like a more complex atmosphere is forming and the rain cycle is obviously in place and we end a second day. From what we see here, it looks as if the

Bible and the scientist pretty much agree as to what happened, except for this: Scientist do not know what started life on earth. The Bible says it was God's "Active Force". Science tells us this process took over 4 billion years to happen. The Bible says it only took God two days, however it does not say how many earth days or years it takes to equal one of the days that it took for God to do all this work. When you examine the verses, God only works to create the heavens and the earth and it was His "Active Force" that moved over the water. After that he is giving commands or orders, but who is he giving them to? So by the end of the Precambrian era we have used 2 "creative days" of God, or about 4.5 billion years.

Now to all of you who claim that God did not need 4.5 billion years to accomplish this, but did it all in two twenty four hour earth days, all I have to say is it is very arrogant to think that God runs on your time! Think about this! You are talking about an entity that, by his words, is the *"Alpha and the Omega, before me there was nothing and after me there will be nothing."* How do you reduce that down to a twenty-four hour day? Please tell me! If your reply is, "Well He's God, He can do any thing!" Yes I agree, but which is more logical, that an entity that is not bound to time as we know it and has been around forever, set off a series of natural processes to "kick start" life on this rock which took hundreds of millions of years, or He did it all in two earth days? Which is more logical to you? Remember we are very egotistical little creatures in this universe. We use to believe that the sun, planets and the rest of the universe revolved around us!

Genesis 1: 9 and 10 tells us that the water was separated and land appeared. Could this be Pangaea? Verse 11 tells us that grasses shoot from the earth, vegetation bearing seed and then fruit trees, all according to their kind, and at the end of the third day the land was now covered by vegetation. So the elevated oxygen levels produced by the cyanobacteria and algae allowed the next process to take place starting with the more simple grasses and ending with fruit trees. There is an interesting thing to notice here. God said "each would produce of its own kind." So where does the evolution come in? Here is a fact! For life to exist on this planet, it needs two things, 1) water, 2) DNA. We have learned volumes about DNA in the last few years. In fact it has led to a whole new science, the science of genetic engineering. Not only is it a science, but genetic engineering is a very big money business! From proving paternity or tracking down criminals, to manipulating genetic information and creating new life forms. Yes, we have learned volumes about DNA and there is still so much more to learn! Wait a minute, did I say we could manipulate genetic information and create new life forms? Why yes I did, remember that information!

WHAT DOES THE FOSSIL RECORD SHOW?

The Cambrian period from 542 to 448 million years ago was witness to the largest explosion of different life forms this planet has ever seen. Scientists are at a loss to explain the biological diversity which just seemed to explode! The earth must have been at its most fertile time ever for life to take hold the way it did. The species that left their evidence behind as fossils are fantastically numerous and many of their descendants are with us today! In fact, hominids are among the descendants of the survivors of the Cambrian period. Chordates were the first animals with backbones. In addition, common during this time, are the brachiopods, which are shelled animals such as clams and the arthropods, which make up most of our insect species on earth today. Among the arthropods are the trilobites. Trilobites are among the most diverse species of the Cambrian period with over 17,000 different species ranging in size from one millimeter to over two feet long.

So I ask again! How did all this biological diversity just explode all over the earth? How did all that genetic information change so drastically, from simple single cell organisms to complex multi cell animals? Here is a better question for you! Where did the DNA come from to allow these changes so quickly? Follow this line of logic for a moment. The oceans of the earth are full of life. The problem here is that it is the simplest life form, only one cell. There is no DNA information for a brain because one is not needed. There is no circulatory system because there is no blood to circulate. There is not a skeleton internally or externally and there are no organs! So where did all the information come from to make these changes?

Here is another way of looking at what is happening here. Take a pair of roller-skates and let us say that these roller skates are the life forms that are in the oceans at the end of the Precambrian period. Then, at the start of the Cambrian period, we still have these single cell "critters", our roller skates, but now they are surrounded by trucks, buses, sports cars, heavy equipment, trains, planes and ocean liners. That is really what we are talking about here. So I once more ask. Where did the DNA, yes the "blue prints", come from for some of the roller skates to turn into motorized vehicles of all different kinds?

We can deny that these complex animals, complete with brain, nervous system, circulatory system, digestive system, sensory system and a skeleton, existed as we have their fossilized bodies with us today. I just don't know how they all exploded onto the earth at the same time and scientists don't have the answer either. They only have a guess and at this point their guess is as good as yours and mine!

Let's see what the Bible has to say about this. If we read Genesis 1:19, the fourth day ends and the earths' "systems"; atmosphere, rain cycle, and tides, are pretty much in place as they are today. Skies are clear, because the sun, moon and stars can all be seen, and God says it is good and ends his day. It is also the end of the Precambrian period.

COULD THERE HAVE BEEN OUTSIDE INFLUENCE?

The Precambrian period is over and the Cambrian period starts with an explosion of complex life forms and no one has a clue as to how they got there. There is no fossil evidence of any kind of progressive change in life forms during this time period. It is a biological explosion of extremely diverse life forms. My favorite fossils from this time period are the trilobites. With more than 17,000 variations of this little, or in some cases not so little critter, it is a great example of the diversity of life in our early oceans. Think about this! Look around you on earth today and find something that has over 17,000 different variations. There are not too many, but they are there.

Okay, we need some information here. How did all these different life forms just spring in to existence? Scientists already admit they do not know. So back to what the bible has recorded in Genesis. This time Genesis 1: 20, 'And God went on to say: *"Let the waters swarm forth a swarm of living souls..."* Wait! Are we to understand that God did this? He made all the life forms that inhabit the ocean? Is that what we are to understand? I guess this is one of those places that we have to give some thought. The scientists do not know how this happened and the Bible says that God is responsible. So what do you think happened? I guess this is time for a little faith here!

We have to look at the facts and how a tremendous amount of genetic information was now upon the earth. In fact, there was probably more genetic information in just one of the species of the Cambrian Era than the combined DNA of all the species that lived in the Precambrian Era. Remember, we went from "roller skate" to "jet fighter" in no time at all!

There has to be a good explanation for where all the genetic information came from and science doesn't have the answer. We have to look elsewhere for the explanation and we don't have much to go on. The only information we have comes from Genesis 1:20 and the fossil record. The fossil record pretty much speaks for itself so let us examine Genesis 1:20, it says, *"God went on to say..."* We can understand that God was talking to someone, but to whom was he talking? Could God have been talking to other sprit creatures similar to himself? Most likely this was the case. The Bible has numerous accounts of man's interaction with extra terrestrials called "angels". Now let's not get all religious and think of a bunch of winged, male-looking creatures flying around the earth. We are talking science and logic here, not religion!

DID ET AND GENETIC ENGINEERING HAVE A ROLL IN LIFE ON EARTH?

Several times in Genesis, God is talking to someone and giving a command. Only four times is he directly involved in the creation process. The first time is at the very start as Genesis 1:1 states, *"In the beginning God created the heavens and the earth."* Today we call it the "Big Bang". The second time is in Genesis 1: 2 when his "Active Force" moved over the water covering the earth. The third time is in the creation of man, Genesis 1:27 *'And God proceeded to create the man in his image; in God's image he created them male and female.'* The fourth time is in Genesis 2:22 *"...God proceeded to build the rib that he had taken from the man into a woman..."* Wait just a minute. It really says that "God" took a tissue sample from the man, Adam, and built a woman? Yes it does and that means that "God" knows genetic engineering! Think about that for a minute. The entity that we refer to as the "Supreme Being", "God", "Jehovah", "Allah", whatever you want to refer to him as, knows genetic engineering and if he can take a tissue sample from a man and "build" a woman, he obviously knows much more about genetic engineering than all of our top scientist combined could ever hope to learn. You know, I wonder how many people have read Genesis 2:22 and make the connection that what is actually happening here is "God" is genetically engineering a human female from a tissue sample taken from a man.

I once had a very interesting conversation with two ministers, "learned men of the cloth". We talked about several things before I pointed out to them that their teaching was limited and walked them down a "conversational path" to Genesis 2: 22 and pointed out that what "God" was actually doing here was indeed genetic engineering! After eyebrows were raised and chins were grabbed, their heads started to nod and they said, "You know, you're right!"

Chapter 4 ~Three-demensional Life

It is okay! Their lack of knowledge is not their fault. They look at everything through clouded religious eyes. The scientific community is not any better since they look at everything with blinders on. This gives them tunnel vision and they can only see as far as their expertise in the area of their discipline. It is a real shame that they cannot see eye to eye and give a logical explanation for life on this planet, or the purpose of man!

Here is a question for you to think about. If "God" created man in his image, what did he use to make him with? Genesis 3:19 says in part, *"from the ground you were taken, to the ground you will return..."* So Adam, the "First Man", was made from the elements of the earth, but how is that in Gods' image? How was Adam different from Cro-Magnon or Neanderthal man? What is the image of "God"?

Now back to the Cambrian era. With such an explosion of different life forms all coming about in such a relatively short time, is it possible that genetic engineering played a major role? Genetic engineering would be a really good explanation of why there was such an explosion of different life forms all at the same time! Am I saying that "God" genetically engineered everything here on earth? No, he had help! What I am about to say is no doubt going to upset a lot of people, but if you think about it for a minute, with an open mind, you will have to agree that it is a very logical explanation to how life came about on earth.

Let us talk about something that most all of us can relate to. That is the erecting of a building. It does not matter much what kind of structure it is, the same steps have to be taken to complete the building. The first thing you need to do before anything else is know your outcome. What kind of building is this going to be? For our example, we are going to use an apartment building. The first thing that has to be done is the design. The owner of this future building will first choose an engineering company for the design and blueprints. Next, you are going to need a work force with the knowledge and the equipment for each part of the building project. First, the building sight has to be cleared, next the ground graded and the foundation is dug out. After that, footings are put in and concrete poured as the framework for the building starts to be erected. The floors go in, the sides go up, the roof goes on and the utilities installed. Each apartment is built, decorated, and ready for occupancy. Why would we think the earth is any different? Each step that was taken in the development of this planet had to take place before it was ready to be "occupied" by humans.

It would be logical to think, just as it takes many skilled people with knowledge of different trades to erect a new building, the same would be true about the earth and the vast amount of different life forms that inhabit it. If it were "God's" purpose to expand intelligent life, would he not know what he wanted as an outcome or result? Would it not be logical to think that there was some plan or "blueprints" used so that the finished product matched the design? Would it not also be logical that many skilled "people" or intelligent life forms, may have also worked on engineering life on earth?

The term "artistic license" is a great term. It gives someone the freedom to be as creative as they like, as long as they stay within outlined parameters or specifications. Just think about this. If you had advanced knowledge of genetic engineering, and you liked flowers, how many different flowers could you make? How tall would they be? What colors would they have? What would they smell like? How many combinations could you come up with? Really, you would only be limited by two things: your imagination and the amount of DNA code you have to work with.

Believe it or not, this is already happening! We have made tobacco plants that glow in the dark and goats that produce spider silk. So why would it be so strange to think that this could not have happen before? Are we so almighty and self-centered to think that we are the most intelligent beings ever? If so, it is only in your mind and on this planet! When we have the ability to transcend time and space, then we can tell each other how great we are. Until then let us stay humble and remember that all of us are here by someone's good graces.

So when you examine the evidence set before us in a logical way, one must admit that it is possible that life on earth could have been genetically engineered by a group of "life forms" at the direction of a "Supreme Being". Really which is more logical? That everything we are and know just happened randomly by chance, or that we, and our earth, are the product of design and engineering?

HOW DO YOU BUILD AN ENVIRONMENT FOR MODERN MAN?

Have you ever thought what would be involved in taking a planet, a little more than a rock, and turning it into a living organism with a vast variety of life forms on it and make it inhabitable for man? NASA has. At one time travel to mars was just a dream. The technology did not exist to justify working on such a project! That is not true any more! Worldwide there are hundreds of scientists and technicians working on that technology right now. Is the goal just to get to Mars? No! The goal is to inhabit Mars much the same way that we inhabit earth. The term used is "terra farm". Processors would be built on Mars to create an atmosphere. The goal is to make a Martian atmosphere much like the one here on earth. There are some real problems with this. Beside the problem of getting all the equipment to Mars and setting it up, so it operates as designed, what is going to keep the solar winds from blowing everything away just as it did with the original Martian atmosphere? However, let us say that all the conditions were just right to terra farm a planet. Let us say that this planet already has water and an atmosphere containing some oxygen. So what is the first thing you are going to do? Grow bacteria and algae in the water. The next thing would be to set up processors to pump water vapor into the upper atmosphere and hopefully create a rain cycle. Additional bacteria and other microbes would have to be grown and implanted into the soil of our new planet, and as long as the rain cycle was intact, you would expect that soon you could start growing simple mosses and eventually ferns. As each step was a success, you could go to the next step, until you had planted a massive variety of plants to cover the land. These processes took hundreds of million years to happen on Earth, but with constant work and attention, along with the advancements in technology, we should be able to accomplish the same task in only a few thousand years. In reality, this is all still a dream. None of the technology to do this even exists, but scientists believe it can and must be done if we are going to advance and survive as a civilization.

HOW MANY PLANETS ARE THERE?

I am sure we have all looked up at the sky on a dark clear night and pondered about all the stars we have in our Milky Way galaxy. If you are fortunate enough to live some place where there is very little light pollution, or have visited such a place, you look up at the stars and realize there are so many there! It is almost as if you could reach up and touch them. Is it any wonder that all those stars capture our attention and make us think about life? Maybe you have thought of how insignificant we are, or maybe you wished that you could travel among the stars? Maybe you even thought that with all those stars, we can't possibility be the only intelligent life in the universe! Perhaps, you just looked up and said, "Wow!"

Yes, for thousands of years man has looked to the stars and contemplated life. The study of the stars, astronomy, is among the first sciences. The stars and their movements were studied to such an extent that it was, and still is, believed that the stars rule our lives. Astrology is the study of the stars and planets and how their movement affects our lives. It is believed that you can foretell the future by studying the movement of the stars. I do not understand how this works, but millions of people throughout the world will not step out the door in the morning without reading their horoscope first. However, we are not interested in how the stars "rule" or "direct" our lives, we want to know about the stars themselves. It was not too long ago that we did not have any idea if other stars had planets revolving around them, but because of what we now know about our own solar system, astronomers believe that most stars would have planets. However, they had no proof! It was not until the stars were watched very closely and a simple little "wobble" was noticed. As planets revolve around a star, their gravitational pull tugs on the star and makes it move a little, or wobble. So the key was to find stars that have a wobble to them and they are the ones with planets! The Hubble telescope has aided in this search and now we know of over 200 planets outside of our solar system. No doubt this amount will grow as we spend more time looking at other stars. Because of what we know about our own solar system, astronomers can assume that all solar systems similar to our own are going to have planets around them. So how many stars are there in the Universe? Astronomers tell us there are more stars in the Universe than there are grains of sand on the Earth! Think about that next time that you go to the beach, or see a picture of the Sahara Dessert! So how many planets are there? Billions and billions of planets!

CAN OTHER PLANETS HAVE LIFE ON THEM?

Life here on Earth is so abundant! Really though how many times do you stop to "smell the roses?" Our life is so hectic that when we do stop to rest we find that we are just exhausted! So how are we going to examine the world around us if we are too tired to do anything? But really life is all around us and it astounds scientists at just how prolific it really is and what's even more amazing is that it is found in the most hostile environments here on earth!

Therefore, the real question should be, "Why wouldn't other planets have life on them?" We have discovered life around volcanic vents thousands of feet below the surface of the oceans, in hot springs where the water is almost boiling and locked in ice in the arctic. Almost every place we look here on Earth, there is life! From what we know, you need water and DNA to have a life form. So why could not every planet that has water on it, have life on it? The truth is that it could! To think that of all the billions and billons of planets that could exist, there has to be some that are much like the Earth, would only be logical!

If a "Supreme Being" created or caused the "Big Bang" and then an "Active Force" moved over the water of the Earth, why could that same energy not be used on other planets throughout the Universe that had water on them? We know the "Big Bang" started our universe. From a single explosion of matter that started our three-dimensional world, a shock wave extended across the emptiness of space and no doubt is still expanding. So why couldn't that "Active Force" have behaved in the same way? If a shock wave traveling behind the "Big Bang" by a few billion years, energizing all water it came in contact with had the right conditions then bam! Life starts!

About 95 years ago a meteorite fell in Egypt and was only recently discovered that it was a piece of Mars. What is even more incredible is that this rock has microscopic holes in it that resemble the same holes made by bacteria when they are on a "feeding frenzy". Unfortunately, scientists are thus unable to recover any DNA evidence of the existence of bacteria. However, let's keep in mind that this rock, 1.3 billion years old, was blown off the surface of Mars, traveled through space and got pretty cooked when it entered the Earth's atmosphere. So extracting DNA from a rock that had a history like the "Mars Rock" would be incredible at best! But the information found in this rock raises more questions than answers. This rock would have been from the same time as the Precambrian period here on earth, a time when the oceans would have been teeming with bacteria!

IS THERE OTHER INTELLIGENT 3 DIMENSIONAL LIFE?

Just by the possible number of stars, like our sun, that exists and based on what science knows about life on our own planet, surely life has found a way on other planets as it has here on Earth. Remember there are more stars in the universe than grains of sand on the Earth! How many have life on them?

Chapter 4 ~Three-demensional Life

S.E.T.I. Search for Extra-Terrestrial Intelligence was founded to do just that, search for other intelligent life forms! The S.E.T.I. Institute was founded in 1984 and it's mission statement is to "explore, understand and explain the origin, nature and prevalence of life in the universe." (I hope they read this book and take notes!) Many of us have heard about S.E.T.I. and we know of their work and the result they have had thus far.

S.E.T.I. has been using radio telescopes and listening to outer space for a signal from another life form. The thought is that radio transmissions travel through space at the speed of light forever. So if our "cousins" from the other side of the universe have "evolved" to our level or beyond, sooner or later we should hear something. Really, we should be able to hear their first transmission, the same as they should be able to hear us, should they even care.

ARE HUMANS ON EARTH THE FIRST?

With all the planets that may exist that scientists believe there is life on, there is no way that we are the first or only! Or is there a way we are the first? We cannot answer this question with scientific facts! The reason is very simple. There is no scientific evidence to support that there is intelligent life any place but here on Earth. Everything else is just supposition, theory, or worse, denial! Denial, either way, that we are or are not the only intelligent life forms in the universe, is the worst because when you are in denial you end any and all other possibilities!

Let us take a logical view of this. The only record we have of anything as far as life on Earth is the fossil record and what the Bible has to say. As Genesis 2:22 indicates, "God" "genetically engineered" a female human from a tissue sample taken from the man's rib. The Bible also keeps a chronological history from Adam down to Jesus, so it is possible to track the history and age of modern man. I repeat "modern man" "created in God's Image", not Cro-Magnon man. When calculated out, from Adam's age, 1975 marked modern man's six thousand years from being "genetically engineered" or as the Bible calls it "created". Interesting fact! The history of civilization is about six thousand years old.

So what are we to take from all of this? If "God" genetically engineered "man" only six thousand years ago and He lives forever, what has "God" been doing with his time? Well on the seventh day the Bible says He "rested". But why could He not be making intelligent life in other parts of the Universe? The truth of the matter is the Bible does make many references to other life forms. The most common are the "Angels" and other life forms called seraphs and cherubs. They are each given different jobs and or assignments, but are they 3 dimensional life forms? We do not have any evidence of that. In fact the evidence, what there may be of it, is quite the opposite! But is there another intelligent, three-dimensional life form in our Universe? As much as S.E.T.I. has listened for other intelligent life forms and from the evidence we find in the Bible, we have to believe we are the only intelligent life forms in the three-dimensional universe we live in.

WHAT IS OUR PURPOSE?

The purpose of man is something that we have wondered about and contemplated as a society and individuals for what seems to be before recorded history. Philosophers, world rulers and religious leaders have all wondered as to our true purpose! No doubt, at one time or another, you yourself must have wondered, just why are we here?

Man does obviously not have an answer for this question. Does "God"? Well, yes he does and it is found recorded two times in the Bible. The first time is in Genesis 1:28, which reads in part, *'Further, God blessed them and God said to them: "Be fruitful and become many and fill the earth and subdue it..."'*. The second time is at Genesis 9:1," *And God went onto bless Noah and his sons and to say to them: "Be fruitful and become many and fill the earth."* That is it? Fill the earth and become many? The short answer is yes! It must have been important if "God" gave the same command twice. However, is having children all we are meant to do? No, but that is the main purpose of man or at least it was the purpose when the command was given.

If we look at the original command and the circumstances under which it was given, we find that the first man and woman were perfect in design and were not meant to die. If we look at the number of eggs a woman is born with in her ovaries, about 450,000 (yes that is a correct number), and if a woman passed one egg a month, she would have to live over 3000 years to use them all if she did not get pregnant. Start adding in pregnancies and, well, you get the picture. To design a woman with that kind of reproductive system and design a male reproductive system that never stops producing sperm, I would have to say "God" was serious about filling the earth! This is the purpose of man! However, is it our only purpose?

CHAPTER 5
WHO IS E.T. UFO?
WHO WERE THE GODS?

The Twentieth Century was indeed a century of enlightenment. The technological advancements we have seen come out of the Twentieth Century were truly amazing! We saw the early days of flight that led to supersonic aircrafts, to space flight and landing on the moon. We saw the first telephones all connected by wire to cellular communication. When computers were first invented, they were as big as a truck and only did simple mathematics. Today we have hand held computers that will keep track of our lives, and when connected to the internet can track down any information that we need. And the deadliest advancement of the Twentieth Century, the Atomic bomb!

But the Twentieth Century gave us something else! A phenomenon we do not understand at all! It has left us scratching our heads and led to accusations of a government cover up and divided many people as to the answer. That is the phenomena of UFO's and aliens.

UFOs were seen and recorded for the first time during the Second World War. They called them "Foo Fighters". At first, all that was seen were bright lights of varying color, but then "metallic objects" were seen. Soon the phrase "Flying Saucers" was coined and the term stuck! Over the years more and more sightings were recorded and stories of abductions started to become "public". An unexplained phenomenon along with personal testimony, fired up by an alleged government cover up, has practically turned UFOs and aliens into a cult. If nothing else it has become big business. The fact of the matter is more than 50% of the population of the United States believe in the existence of UFOs and aliens!

What do the governments have to say about all of this?

Well, what the government says and what the reality perceived by the public is, are two different things. One thing is for sure, the governments of the world have spent billions of dollars to investigate UFO's and yet very little information is available to the public. In fact, the most reliable information is from incidents that happened in "Second World Countries" whose governments have much less to hide.

It is not my intent here to fuel the flames on the UFOs debate! However one cannot deny that "something" is there that is not from this world. You really have to wonder though, with S.E.T.I. searching the heavens for a signal from another world and documented reports of pilots who encountered UFO's that are sighted on radar, what are we really talking about here? We know the governments are not talking. Are S.E.T.I.'s ears deaf too?

FIRST CONTACT. WHEN?

Most UFO experts will tell you that first contact took place in July 1947 in Roswell, New Mexico, USA. It is alleged that the US Military recovered what may have been a "flying saucer", but a cover up quickly followed, when the alleged flying saucer turned into a weather balloon, which only lends support to this story. But is this really the first time?

As we look back through history, there are writings that man had contact with extra-terrestrial "Beings" as far back as recorded history. The first evidence of this in the Bible is in Genesis 3: 1-5, with the account of the "Serpent" seducing Eve. The Angel Lucifer plays the part of the "Serpent", better known as the "Devil". The word devil means "deceiver" and the name Lucifer means "light bearer". There are several places in the Bible that talks about this fallen angel as once having a very high rank among the "Sons of God", but was cast out or down. It is very possible that if other "life forms" were involved with the vast engineering of this planet, Lucifer might have been the "overseer" or "foreman" of the "Earth Project". There has to be a logical reason for someone with high rank, a "Son of God", to rebel.

Chapter 5 ~Who Is E.T? Who Were the Gods?

The Bible is only one place where there is evidence of contact with "Extra-terrestrials". Earth's history is full of what appears to be evidence of contact with extra-terrestrials through oral traditions, writings on cave walls, petroglyphs, stone tablets and monuments and art forms of all type.

WHY THE INTEREST IN MANKIND AND OUR WORLD?

It is clear that there has been a relationship between "extraterrestrial" beings of some type and man for as long as we've existed. The most direct relationship is recorded in the Bible and in the book of Enoch. The Book of Enoch was found among the Dead Sea Scrolls and was used by different religious sects before the time of Christ and by the early Christians until about the third century. The Book of Enoch was never canonized and lost popularity after the "Council of Laodicea".

Enoch was the son of Jared and the great-grandfather of Noah and the writings of what had happened at this time were most remarkable! The Bible does not say very much about Enoch, however the most important thing is that he was *"walking with the true God and then he was no more, for God had took him."* The only indication this leaves us with is that he had a close relationship with God and God took him someplace.

The Book of Enoch explains exactly what was going on in the world at that time and gives great insight into a time period when extraterrestrial contact with humans was an everyday occurrence! We do get some insight in Genesis about what was happening. Genesis 6: 1-7 explains that the "sons" of the "True God" had taken notice of women and how beautiful they were and they took wives for themselves "all that they wanted" and produced hybrid males called Nephilim. (Think of Hercules, a super strong man. His father was Zeus, king of the gods and his mother was a mortal woman.) Nephilim means "fellers of men", so they were not heroes but giants and terrorists! Things had gotten so bad in the world that the scriptures read that "God felt regret" that he even created man and that "He felt hurt at his heart" over how bad things had gotten on earth and wanted to destroy it all! It kind of makes you wonder what He is thinking now with the conditions we have on earth.

In the Book of Enoch, in chapter 6 of "The Watchers", Enoch records that there are 200 "Watchers" that are conspiring to leave their assigned position and engage in sexual relations with women in order to have their own children.

"The Watchers" were a group of "Angelic Overseers" extraterrestrials that were assigned to watch over the development of mankind. They were not to have direct involvement with man and the fact that they engaged in sexual intercourse with women was an abomination! It was inter species breeding and the children that were produced from this relationship were the Nephilim.

Chapter 7 of the Book of Enoch, tell us about "special knowledge" that the watchers gave to their wives about the earth. Enoch said that *"they taught them charms and enchantments and the cutting of roots and made them acquainted with plants. They became pregnant and they bore great giants..."* Chapter 8 gives us information about how the knowledge of metalworking was given to men and they were shown how to make weapons. They were taught about astronomy and astrology, different signs to look for in the heavens and on the earth. All of this was knowledge not meant for man to have and it was imparted to man by extraterrestrials. Could we be getting specialized knowledge from extraterrestrial beings today? With the advancements in technology that we have seen in the past years, you have to wonder! It is said that during an interview with Dr. Christiaan Barnard, the surgeon who performed the first successful human heart transplant, he said he felt as if his dead father had helped guide him through the difficult operation by telling him what to do. It may have been Dr. Barnard's own mind giving him the information he needed to complete the operation successfully, or maybe it was some other source of "Higher Intelligence".

In Enoch 17:1 & 2, Enoch reports that he was taken to a "place where those were like flaming fire, and when they wished, they would appear as men". Enoch saw what? He saw flaming fire turn to the form of a man? No, they would appear as men, but they were not men! Let's think about his report. He saw a "life form" that looked like "flaming fire". Could we use the term "pure energy" here? Is this like "Beam me up, Scotty" where a man turns to energy and then is transported to another location? Not likely. The life forms encountered here were already in their natural state and turned to men as they wished. Imagine a life form of energy that has the ability to materialize into a man at will. If it were these same types of life forms that impregnated the women of earth, would it be any wonder that you would have hybrid giants roaming the earth?

DID WE CREATE THE GODS?

It is obvious that throughout all of recorded history, from the beginning of civilization until our day today, that in every land, in every people, from the smallest tribes to the largest cities, we are surrounded by gods! "The gods" are everywhere we look! In reality we have put them on monuments, in artwork, as decorations on buildings, in museums, and as decorations in our home. We watch them on TV and in the movies. We even go as far as to put them on our money! "In God we trust". While many people believe in one god, a "Supreme Being", there are others that believe in many gods. So who is right and who is wrong? Well I guess you might say everyone is right, and everyone is wrong!

The people in the "western" part of the earth mostly believe in one god and are monotheistic. The people in the "eastern" part of the earth are polytheistic and have many gods. But the people in the west like decorations of eastern gods and symbols and the people in the east celebrate Christmas. One of the most interesting things is that in Europe and the United States, more people believe in "aliens" than go to church. The fact is that interest in "religion" is down all around the world and has been for some time, (excluding areas of religious fanaticism).

So where did all these gods come from? Did our ancestors just invent them and because of tradition we have kept them with us? Well, we didn't quite invent them as much as they live with us. I know that is a bold statement, but it is true. We get a little insight to this in Genesis 3:15 where we find the first prophesy of the Bible. God is talking to "Satan" and says "And I shall put enmity between you and the woman and between your seed and her seed. He will bruise you in the head and you will bruise him in the heel". The woman talked about here is not Eve, but is "God's" "Heavenly Organization". Evidently "God" feels the same way about his "Heavenly Organization" as a husband feels about his wife. The seed of the "Serpent" is Satan or "Lucifer's" Organization". The "He" in this prophecy is Jesus who is the same "entity" as "Michael the Archangel". The "bruising in the heel" happened when Jesus was put to death in 33 CE. This was a heel bruise because while no doubt it was very painful, it did not end Jesus' life, only his life on earth. He returned to "heaven" again as "Michael". The bruise "in the head" signifies a "death blow" that will be delivered to "Lucifer" and his organization at a future date, but soon!

By understanding that there is a major issue here that split the once "happy family" of the "Sons of the true God" into two opposing factions that are indeed organized, it allows us to start to have insight to the reality that we are involved in a conflict that goes beyond our three dimensional world.

WHO IS THE PRINCE OF PERSIA?

In the Bible in the Book of Daniel there is a very interesting account regarding "extraterrestrial" life forms. In the 10th chapter of Daniel, there is an account of three different life forms that are opposed to each other. What actually happens is that a message is being sent to the prophet Daniel and a "life form" by the name of Gabriel is the one who is to deliver it. The problem occurs when another life form called the "Prince of Persia" stops Gabriel and prevents him from getting through. Gabriel has to call for "back up", because after twenty-one days Gabriel still can't get past. Then a "life form" by the name of "Michael" comes to help Gabriel get past to deliver the message to Daniel. The account is in Daniel

10: 13 which in part reads, *"But the Prince of the Royal Realm Persia was standing in opposition to me for twenty one days, and look! Michael, one of the foremost princes, came to help me..."* Gabriel delivers his message to Daniel and in the 20th verse Gabriel tells Daniel that he has to go back and "fight with the Prince of Persia" and that the "Prince of Greece was also coming". The "Prince of Persia" was most likely Ahura Mazdah ("Lord Wisdom"), the chief god of Persia. The Persians like other peoples of their time had many gods. No doubt these gods were "fallen angels" who became part of "Lucifer's seed" or organization and were given different positions.

If we look at what was happening in history at this time, we find that the fourth World Power, Medo-Persia, is ruling. They have just defeated the Babylonians and had released the Jewish exiles there to return to their homeland. Daniel was a Jewish prophet who held a very high rank in the Babylonian government and was now living in Persia. He was in his mid-eighties when the Jewish refugees went back to their "homeland". He stayed behind in Persia, because he thought he could do more to help his people by using his influence with the Persian government. Evidently he was successful. The Jews were fully repatriated to their homeland and King Darius even helped finance the rebuilding of the Jewish temple in Jerusalem.

MYTHOLOGY AND RELIGION

Scientists and archeologists are finding every day that there is less myth in mythology and more truth in history! Archeologists have uncovered many locations once thought to be "mythological" and artifacts that support writings that have only single source information such as the Bible. The more we dig, the more we learn, the more clearer picture we have of our past and myths turn into things that we can identify and categorize and put in museums.

Some artifacts have been turned into religious icons because of the "myths" surrounding them, such as the "Shroud of Turin" or the spear that allegedly pierced Christ at the time of his death at the hands of the Romans and Jews. The sale of "religious artifacts" was big business during the time of the Crusades. The "Church" wanted as many artifacts related to Christ as could be found. No doubt the Knights Templar filled this need quite nicely, by literally sending boatloads of Middle Eastern artifacts deemed to be religious and used by the early Christians or maybe even by Christ himself.

Two of the most desired mythological religious artifacts, the Jewish "Arch of the Covenant" and the "Holy Grail" or "Cup of Christ", have been sought for hundreds of years and are still not found. Did they ever exist? The Bible says they do! Moses was given the instructions as to how the "Arch" was to be built and there have been many accounts throughout the different books of the Bible that support the premise it did once exist. It "vanished" at the same time that the Babylonians laid siege to Jerusalem around 607 BCE. The story of the "Cup of Christ" is a bit vague. Jesus did use a cup to start a covenant with his 11 faithful Apostles and commanded them to "keep doing this in memory of me". Allegedly, it was this same cup that later caught some of Jesus' blood when he was executed. Were they the same cup? I doubt it! Jesus being Jewish celebrated the "Passover". He instructed two of his disciples to get things ready and that they would find an upper room in the house that they were sent to and they would use it for the celebration. The room was furnished and. I am sure. had all the utensils that would be needed for the Passover meal, including the cups! Do you really think that someone would take or steal a cup from the owner of the house and later use it to catch Jesus' blood in? How likely is that? If the cup does exist how could you ever prove it?

It really does not matter that almost every religion on the face of the earth has its relics and icons and is steeped in mythology either by their teachings or the holidays they keep. If you think I'm wrong examine the most celebrated holiday on earth, Christmas. The holiday has very little to do with Jesus or his birth, but comes from the Roman holiday of Saturnalia, the worship of the sun.

Chapter 5 ~Who Is E.T? Who Were the Gods?

HOW MANY GODS ARE THERE?

The Egyptians had gods, the Syrians had gods, the Babylonians had gods, the Persians, Greeks, Romans and all the peoples they concurred had many, many Gods. The Greeks even erected a shrine to an "unknown god", just in case they missed one. The only people that had one god were the Jews or Hebrews. The idea of one single, all-powerful, supreme "Being" was handed to us by the teachings of Jesus. It is these teachings that Christians today believe they are following, but here is an interesting side note. The Christians, Jews and Muslims, all claim to worship the same god. As a matter of fact, the Muslims share their lineage back to Abraham the same as the Jews do so yes, Abraham was father to both peoples. So if they all worship the same god, why is there so much hatred there?

I really don't know if you could count all the different gods are worshiped throughout the history of the world. The Hindu religion is said to have over three hundred thousand gods and that is just one of the many polytheistic religions of the world today. If you could count all the gods what would it matter? The reason that I bring this point up is two fold; first, if there is only one "Supreme all powerful, all knowing Being" that wants us to worship only him, why are there so many other gods? Secondly, where did all these other gods come from and why are they there?

First, we know the Bible talks about other "life forms" but does it say how many there are? Not exactly but it does tell us in Revelation 5:11 that there are "myriads of myriads". A myriad is ten thousand, so there were ten thousand, multiplied by ten thousand, so it could well be that there are as many as one hundred million or more intelligent life forms that exist, other than the human population here on earth. Revelation 12:3 & 4 also tells us that "a fiery-colored dragon" "drags a third of the stars of heaven and hurled them down to earth". This "fiery colored dragon" is none other than Lucifer or Satan himself and the "stars" are the "life forms" that sided with his cause. So there must be hundreds of thousands, if not millions, of these "fallen angles" that are now confined to the earth. Revelation 12: 9 tells us that *"the one called Devil and Satan was hurled down to the earth and his angels were hurled down with him".* If Lucifer and "God" were at odds with each other and Lucifer had "control" of the earth, would he not do everything he could to "distract" man's attention to a "Supreme All Mighty God"? If Lucifer or Satan did have control of the earth, would he not set up his own hierarchy, give his closest and most powerful friends leadership positions and appoint them as gods to be worshiped or "princes" to rule over parts of the earth? Here is an interesting note. Sun worship is probably the oldest and most prolific religion ever. All peoples of all nations and tribes throughout history have worshiped the sun and it is still with us today! The holiday we hold for the sun? Christmas! Could Lucifer have set him up as the "Sun God"? Most likely yes! Lucifer does mean "light bearer" and the sun is what makes our life possible here on earth. Without it we would not exist! As you look at the conditions we have here on earth today, would you say they are more god like, or more satanic? Who among us wants to be happy? Who among us really is?

WHERE ARE THE GODS TODAY, WHAT ARE THEY DOING?

What happened to the gods? Do we see them around us today? Yes in art and in other forms as we discussed earlier. But are they active in our world today? Not sure? If you are wondering about the "Prince of Persia", he is a star among us today and has several video games named after him! He is just one of the many "gods" that our children fight for or against in the endless stream of video games. If you check for yourself, you will find that many of the names used on or in the games that our children are playing have ancient pagan gods attached to them. If these "gods" are real "life forms" and are part of Lucifer's organization, are we not paying homage to them today by making them part of our children's lives?

Let's look at the bigger picture. Not too long ago I was in Ukraine, part of the former Soviet Union, and while I was there I found very handsome and congenial people that were friendly and ready to share their way of life with me. I have a special fondness for the people in Ukraine and I have many friends there. To think that at one time we had nuclear missiles pointed at each other ready to go off at the push of a button is almost inconceivable to me now. But with all the propaganda that our government has fed us, at one time we wanted to see these people destroyed! So what was it that started all this hate in the first place? You might comment, but the "Cold War" is over, everything ended peacefully, doesn't that show love for our fellow man? No it saved the earth from nuclear destruction. There is no doubt that if we did have a nuclear exchange with the Soviet Union and the earth became uninhabitable, whom would the gods rule over? As we look at our world today it seems pretty peaceful. Yes there are areas of concern with the Middle East perhaps being the biggest problem today with its export of terrorism around the world. It makes me wonder about the "Prince of Persia" and what his plan is.

Most of what we hear about wars center in the Middle East and are "religiously" inspired, however, as of the time of this writing there are thirty two major wars or conflicts world wide! Here again most of these "conflicts" have less to do with geo-political issues and more inspired by religious or ethnic differences. We see a major trend here, which is religious beliefs play a major role in war and always have throughout recorded history! So could we say the gods are alive and well? It would appear that way! Here is something to consider. If you took a map of the Middle East today and laid over it a map of the Persian Empire, you would see that it would cover Syria, Iraq, Iran, Afghanistan and Pakistan. The Biblical "Prince of Persia" covered all this area and was doing his best to defend his interest when his conflict with the "life forms" Gabriel and Michael took place. You would have to reason that he is still doing his best to rule over this area and he is using religion as a tool to insight the population to arms. The center of the "Persian Empire" is Iran. The whole world is worried about the Iranian nuclear program and Iran's involvement with terrorism. So would you say this "life form" known as the Prince of Persia has been busy? It does seem that way.

However if we examine society around the world, we see that there are hundreds of issues all over the world. Today, Africa is considered a continent lost, war has ravaged many countries, famine and food shortages have struck a major blow and those left over have been struck by disease with AIDS leading the way! While not all countries in Africa are ravaged by AIDS, some countries in Africa are going to lose a major part of their population. Swaziland is leading the way with more that a third of its population infected with AIDS, and three other countries have over a twenty percent infection rate. This is astounding! Think of your own country. What would happen if twenty percent of the population was sick and dying? What kind of economic problem would that cause? How do you deal with a social problem of this size? Let's bring this a bit closer to home. If there are five people in your family, one is dying of AIDS! Look at your extended family including grandparents, aunts, uncles, cousins, nieces, and nephews, and there are fifty people in this family group. Just think, between ten and fifteen of your relatives have AIDS and are most likely going to die!

Another major problem that governments are having difficulty dealing with and that has affected all of today's society is "gangs". In every city and now into the "suburbs", gangs and gang warfare have caused major problems all over the world! In the United States, according to the Department of Justice's 2005 National Gang Threat Assessment, there are at least 21,500 gangs and more than 731,000 active gang members. They are responsible for half of all the homicides committed in major cities. Gangs have changed much over the years to the point they have become "Global Guerrillas" who's goal is to infiltrate and take over whole countries by whatever means possible!

There is no doubt that our world today has become blood thirsty! During the twentieth century literally hundreds of millions of people were killed in wars or conflicts and related circumstances! In fact the world spends about $25,000 US dollars every year for every man, woman and child on the face of the earth to kill them! That is correct! If you totaled all the money that is spent by the governments of the world on arms, you could give everyone in the world about $25,000 US dollars. What could you do with an extra $25,000 US dollars this year? If you belonged to a family of four, two parents and two children, that would give you an extra $100,000 to live on and do you know what else it would give us? PEACE! Is that we see today? No, not at all and if we look back through history, it is full of blood thirsty gods that demanded human sacrifice. Maybe the ones we know the best are the gods of South America. Huitzilopochtli was the Aztec god of war and sun. His temple was on the Main Pyramid at the sight of what is described as “fearsome sacrifices” of prisoners that were captured by Aztec warriors. It is believed that as many as six million human sacrifices were offered up to this “sun god” . Moloch was a god that was worshiped in the Middle East by many people including early Jews. Moloch required the sacrifice of human children, babies! A fire was built in the lap of Moloch sitting at his throne and babies were thrown into the fire alive as drums beat loudly to drown out their screams, what a loving god! These are just two of the many blood thirsty gods that are recorded through history. Really, do you need to question if these gods are with us today, tearing apart our society, causing the death of our children and loved ones, when all we want is to live in peace?

WHAT DO THE GOVERNMENTS KNOW AND WHAT IS THEIR INVOLVEMENT?

Over the years many groups and organizations have been claiming that the US government has been covering up that we have had contact with “extraterrestrials” and that many of the advanced technologies we have are because we have “reverse engineered” alien technology that has been captured or found at “crash sights”. I am not here to comment either way on this subject, but there are some very interesting “breakthroughs” in the scientific world that you have to stop and wonder, how do they do that? One has to ask, why does it seem that most of these major "scientific breakthroughs" all happen in the realm of warfare? We learn how to split the atom and what do we do? Go kill people! We learn how to make an airplane travel several times faster than the speed of sound and appear invisible and what do we do with it? Go kill people! Why do the governments spend all the money they do to kill us? Who really wants us dead so badly, that they are willing to spend so much money to do so?

We will most likely never know if any direct contact is being or has ever been made between government or military leaders and "extraterrestrial life forms", but what has been documented is the involvement between government leaders and "fortune tellers" and "astrologers" and what is commonly known as the "occult", in order to gain an advantage or make an important decision. If the ones that gave this information to man were the "fallen sons of the True God" as the Bible calls them and as we are told in the book of Enoch, then why would we not think it reasonable that these "life forms" are using this occult technology to guide the leaders of the world? Given the evidence at hand, it is more than possible!

There is a private resort in the state of California called Bohemian Grove. There are about 2700 members, all men and all very powerful in their position in the world. It is interesting that Bohemian Grove is covered by the 1947 "National Security Act" to protect the secrecy of any goings on there. Every republican president from Herbert Hoover to George W Bush has been a member or a guest at Bohemian Grove. President Hoover is quoted as saying "It is the greatest men's party on earth". No one who is not a member really knows to the full extent what happens at this "resort", but over the years many accusations have risen that there are occult and pagan practices going on there including murder and human sacrifice to Moloch! Investigation of any wrong doing reported to the authorities is blocked by the "National Security Act" of 1947, so if these things are going on there, it will never come to light. But you might say that our leaders today would never do things like that! I am sure you are right and Hitler was a choirboy and never killed 6,000,000 Jews and Joseph Stalin never ordered the cleansing of the Soviet Union which never led to the killing of as many as 100,000,000 Russians. Our leaders could never do that! Regardless of what occult, pagan, or other rituals go on at Bohemian Grove, one thing is certain, the power brokers of the world are helping each other gain more power and more control over the people that they are suppose to be serving.

The expression that "power corrupts and ultimate power corrupts ultimately" might apply here, because of the alleged goings on at the Bohemian Grove. Just think, you are one of the most powerful men in the world and you are at a 2200-acre private resort where "anything goes" and nothing can be exposed because of "US Federal Law". You are there with about 2000 other members and their guests and among the most powerful men in the world. So what do you do for entertainment? I guess anything you want, even if it included human sacrifice.

DO THESE "EXTRATERRESTRIAL LIFE FORMS" HAVE AN IMPACT ON OUR FUTURE?

Just by the very fact we have a history that is littered with life forms that are not human, which obviously have influenced our ancestors, we cannot simply say that they have no influence over us today. Just by the fact that we have found evidence of their existence has already influenced the archeologists and historians to study their findings and look for more information that will hopefully lead them to a better understanding of a people whose lives have been literally covered over by the sands of time!

We also have a group of very dedicated people that are looking totally in the opposite direction. We even have a new word for them, and it is "Ufologist". These people dedicate their lives, the same as historians and archeologist dedicate theirs, to looking for evidence of the "gods" or "extraterrestrial life forms". They do this by gathering information of unidentified flying objects, either by photographs, video recordings, "personal encounters", "declassified" government documents, and from any and all sources they can find. Interestingly they get more reliable information from second and third world countries, which have much less to hide than the "major powers".

Today, with all the information that is currently available to us about almost any subject, and the fact that more people have personal video recording devices than ever before and the internet, it is difficult at best to keep anything a secret! There is so much information regarding our world leaders and their involvement in "secret societies", the occult, pagan rituals, and even devil worship, it only lends credence to the bazaar stories that are reported, such as those that come out of Bohemian Grove. It is a sad state of affairs when we, as a society, no longer believe what our "leaders" and "elected officials" tell us, and we only feel that we are being lied to again! However if the things that are reported on about involvement in the occult and pagan rituals by our 21st century elected and appointed officials are only half true, than no doubt these "extraterrestrial life forms", "the gods" of old, are directly involved in our present day lives and no doubt will effect our future lives as well.

It became public knowledge in the second term of President Ronald Reagan that his wife Nancy was consulting an astrologer to help guide her husband, the President. Mrs. Reagan claimed that she used this occult information to find the best days and times for President Reagan to hold his appointments with other "heads of state" to give him the best advantage. Mrs. Reagan never admitted any other involvement than just finding the best day and times for meetings! Is that so?

President Reagan came out with some very interesting programs during his administration. The "Star Wars" program is a good example of this. The idea was to develop a "defensive" weapon system that would detect the launching of a Soviet nuclear missal and destroy it before it would reenter earths' atmosphere and hit it's target. Billions of dollars were poured into this program and the Soviet Union took this as a major threat, but there was nothing that they could do about it. While the United States was working on the "Star Wars" program, President Reagan was holding meetings with the Soviet Prime Minister to first limit nuclear weapons production, and then reduce the number of nuclear weapons that both governments had "pointed" at each other. This process finally ended with a major blow to "Communism" and the fall of the Soviet Union!

Mrs. Reagan's astrologer must have been pretty good at "consulting the stars" for the President to have had the result he did. After forty years of arms build up and the development of thousands of nuclear missiles destined to end life as we know it, President Ronald Reagan and his diplomacy, along with specialized "occult" information, brought the biggest enemy the United States had to an end without firing a shot!

Did President Reagan just put faith in the "stars" to guide him? It is alleged that while Ronald Reagan was an actor in California, he and Nancy had an "encounter" with a UFO while driving along the California coast on their way to a dinner party. This must have had quite an impact on the future president, because during his presidency, in three speeches President Reagan made statements about an "extraterrestrial" invasion of earth. In fact he brought this to the attention of Soviet Prime Minister Gorbachev during a five hour private meeting in Geneva. Gorbachev confirmed this himself on February 17, 1987 during a speech in Moscow when he addressed the Central Committee of the Soviet Communist Party. On page 7a of the 'Soviet Life Supplement' we find the following statement:

"At our meeting in Geneva, the U.S. President said that if the earth faced an invasion by extraterrestrials, the United States and the Soviet Union would join forces to repel such an invasion. I shall not dispute the hypothesis, though I think it's early yet to worry about such an intrusion..."

Gorbachev must have taken Reagan's words seriously to report them back to the most powerful people in the Soviet Union! It is said that the real reason for the Star Wars Program was to protect the earth from an "alien invasion" and not from Soviet missal attack, but when the Soviet Union collapsed, the money for the development of the Star Wars program dried up.

Reagan did not stop with the Soviets. President Ronald Reagan, on September 21, 1987 in an address to a full session of the General Assembly of the United Nations, made the following statement:

"...in our obsession with antagonisms of the moment, we often forget how much unites all the members of humanity. Perhaps we need some outside, universal threat to make us recognize this common bond. I occasionally think, how quickly our differences worldwide would vanish if we were facing an alien threat from outside this world. And yet, I ask, is an Alien force not already among us?"

Where did the President get his information from regarding aliens and the possibility of an "alien invasion" of earth? If Ronald and Nancy Reagan did indeed have a personal encounter with a UFO, it would have had a dramatic affect on them and no doubt probably left them with more questions than answers. When Mr. Reagan was elected to the office of President of the United States of America, it gave him access to classified and top secret information that was compiled by the military and the Central Intelligence Agency. In his speeches where he talked about an alien or extraterrestrial invasion of earth, was he "spilling the beans" so to speak about what he had learned from "classified top secret" government files? Or did he get his information from an astrologer?

It is also reported that President Reagan had meetings with very prominent religious leaders. What was the topic of conversation? Armageddon! While Ronald Reagan was not a minister, he knew his Bible and Bible scripture and he certainly knew about "God Almighty's" "War of Armageddon", that is why he sought out the counsel of prominent religious leaders. With all that was going on in the Middle East and his belief in an "alien" invasion on earth, he wanted as much insight as he could get on the subject! Maybe he thought he could stop Armageddon from happening or maybe he wanted to be as prepared as possible. One thing is for certain, President Ronald Reagan believed in extraterrestrial alien life forms and they caused him great concern!

IS E.T. LIKE MAN?

Just what are we talking about when it comes to these "extraterrestrial life forms"? What are they like? Are they "little green men"? Are they the "Arians", the "Grays" or "Reptilians" as the cult followers of the Ufologist would have us believe? Really just what are they? What are we dealing with here?

For the longest time, history has referred to these creatures as "the gods". The "gods" that we most likely know the best are the Egyptian gods and the Greek gods. The Greek gods were probably best brought to our attention by tales of Hercules as told by Hollywood writers, directors and producers.

Hercules is a great story. His father was Zeus, king of "Mount Olympus" which was home to most of the Greek gods. Hercules' mother was a mortal woman. Hercules himself had super human strength, far beyond what was normal for an average man. Evidently Zeus had many sexual encounters with goddesses and mortals and he either tricked them, or just outright raped them, as he chose.

Interestingly enough this story resembles the same account we read about in both the Bible in the book of Genesis, and in the book of Enoch as we discussed earlier in this chapter. So here in "Greek Mythology" we have a third account of a "god like" life form having sex with a human woman and producing a hybrid offspring of enormous strength! Really there are stories in most all cultures of antiquity that describe "god like" life forms engaging in sexual intercourse with women and it is recorded as a matter of fact and in some places a matter of great concern!

If we take what is recorded about these life forms, it seems they looked like men, most likely very handsome men that were extremely powerful! In the book of Enoch, he made reference to life forms that appeared as a man and could change to fire and back to a man at will. The Bible, in the book of Genesis, tells us that the sons of the "True God" took many wives for themselves, all they wanted!

Evidently we have no idea what energy these "sons of God" are made of, but they have, or at least did have the ability to control that energy and change it into a human male form capable of reproduction. And reproduce they did on all accounts!

What was it though that made some of these life forms "cross the line" and breed with human women? Was it "lust" or "love"? Genesis 6 tells us that as women grew in number the "true sons of God" noticed how beautiful they were. They had emotions and they let those emotions run away from them the same as what happens to us humans sometimes. Who of us hasn't been infatuated with a member of the opposite sex at one time or another in our life and wanted to have intercourse with them? I guess you could say it was lust more than love, but this does prove that angels are "emotional creatures". They must have cared for these women to some extent, because as we have learned from the Book of Enoch, the "Sons of God" taught their wives "specialized knowledge" which gave them an advantage in life. We still have the remnants of it with us today in the beliefs and teachings of "Wicca" and "Mother Earth". The book of Genesis also tells us that the "Sons of the true God" took "wives for themselves". We can figure that they must have had some feelings of love for their "wives", because neither accounts found in the Bible nor the Book of Enoch, refers to any kind of forced sex or rape. We can pretty much conclude that indeed the "angels or sons of the true God" have feelings much like our own which makes sense because "God" said "Let us make man in our image". We all reflect the same emotional feelings and thoughts and that is what connects us all together and one of the reasons why they are involved in our lives today!

IF NOT WHAT IS THE DIFFERENCE?

Obviously, there are major differences between humans

and these "sons of God" but not quite as many as you might think! The Bible book of Hebrews gives us some insight here. At Hebrews 2:7 we are told, God made man *"... a little lower than the angels, with glory and honor you crowned him..."*. If we are designed, created, genetically engineered, or whatever the process was that was taken to make "modern man", we were created a little lower than the "life forms" than our ancestors called the "gods".

The two biggest differences are the age difference between species and that we cannot change our form. These "life forms" that the Bible calls angels do not operate on "our" time scale. Another thing is that the word "angel" means "messenger". Angels are not some manlike creature with wings coming off their back as the art world would have us believe. They are very dynamic life forms that somehow, as Enoch described, had the ability to change their form. They could change from some type of energy to a man and back at will. Is that possible? Yes it is, if you have the ability to control energy at a sub atomic level.

The idea to control energy at a sub atomic level is not a new one. Most of us today have heard the famous words *"Beam me up, Scotty!"* The idea of walking into some transporter machine that takes a solid form and transfers the form to pure energy, and move, or "beam" it to another location, fascinates us! I am sure that there are scientists and mathematicians trying to work out the solution to accomplish this task. There is a major difference here though, humans are limited to a three dimensional world. Even if we could transfer solid matter to energy, it would still be "three dimensional" energy. It does not make any difference if it were a radio wave or a beam or light that the matter was transformed into it is still "stuck" in the three dimensional world and limited to the "laws of nature" that govern the universe. In other words, we still could not travel faster than the speed of light and considering the size of our universe even moving at "light speed" travel is impractical outside our solar system. Then there is the idea or theory of bending or warping space, where we could take a "short cut" to get from one place to another. This would greatly reduce travel time because you eliminate time and distance, as we understand it. The term "Worm Hole" is used to describe this process. If you took a single sheet of paper and drew a line from the top to the bottom and this represented two places in the universe, millions of light years apart, instead of setting off to navigate all that distance, you would bend the paper or "warp space". When the two places lined up, you would punch a "worm hole" through the paper and that would be all the distance you would have to travel! The trick is being able to make the wormhole!

Whatever the energy is that these "angelic" life forms are made of, I seriously doubt that it is any type of "three dimensional" energy. With the speed that these life forms can travel, it must involve some sort of dimension change that goes beyond the forth dimension, time. Once you eliminate time as a factor in your travels, you could be almost any place you wanted in an instant, because you are no longer governed by the laws of time, at least not as we understand time.

Time is obviously a very big factor here when we consider that our earth is over four billion years old. We have no idea how old these life forms are when compared to our earth years or any other type of time measurements. If they were involved in engineering life on earth, they have been doing it for a very long time, so it would be obvious that these life forms are not governed by our three dimensional world and the laws that govern us, including time!

If you think about how much you knew at the age of five and how much you know now, I am sure you would say that there was a considerable difference in your level of knowledge, especially if you were a professional and held a PhD. Let us also say that you could live to 500 years old before you would start to get to the point of retirement. How much would you know by then as compared to a five year old? I think you can see the point here. If these life forms are indeed hundreds of millions, if not billions, of earth years old, what would their level of knowledge be? No doubt, the knowledge of these life forms would far out strip the total accumulated knowledge that our civilization has produced thus far. Then again, we could always wonder how much of our technology comes from them.

While there are some very major differences between humans and these extraterrestrial "sons of god" or angels, there are also very close similarities as far as our feelings and thoughts. The big differences are in physical make up and ability, the age difference of both our species and the level of our intelligence. But then again, we are the babies in the family!

CHAPTER 6
CIVILIZATION ITS START

WHEN DID CIVILIZATION START?

It is generally accepted, that civilization started on the plains of Mesopotamia about 4000 B.C. and this has Biblical support as well. In Genesis 10: 8 we are introduced to Nimrod, it says "He made the start in becoming a mighty one on the earth." In the 10 verse we read "And the beginning of his kingdom came to be Babel and Erech and Accad and Calneh in the land of Shinar." This land area of Shinar covered from just north of the Persian Gulf through the lower half of the Mesopotamian Valley. However, there are some signs of "civilized" people that date before this, before the "Flood of Noah's Day". I realize by using this "marker" in time I am lending credence that there was indeed a "Biblical global flood" and for good reason.

In his study of the Sphinx, Dr. Robert M. Schock a full-time faculty member at the College of General Studies at Boston University and who earned his Ph.D. in geology and geophysics at Yale University, found erosion on the Sphinx that would have to have been made by rain and therefore dates the initial construction of the Sphinx between 10,000 and 5000 B.C. This was long before Egypt became a world power. So who originally built the Sphinx?

In January of 2008 it was announced that an ancient city was found "off" the coast of India in the Gulf of Cambay. The find was unbelievable! It is a city five miles long and two miles wide and the unbelievable thing is that it is covered by about 36 meters (120 feet) of water. Artifacts have been recovered which include human bone and teeth that when carbon 14 dated it was found that these artifacts were about 9500 years old! But wait a minute, if you can trace Jesus' lineage back to Adam and calculate the years from Adam's creation until now, it would be about 6035 years. So how is it possible that uncivilized peoples, before Adam's creation, could create these structures? Is something wrong here? I really believe something is wrong not only here with these dates but with the Carbon 14 dating. For some reason artifacts that are carbon dated between 5,000 and 15,000 years ago seem to be out of place with the Bible record. So is the Bible wrong? Not likely! There is a factor that scientists do not take into consideration, the "Flood of Noah's Day". If a water "canopy" did exist around the earth it would have done a few things, one of which is moderate temperatures around the world so weather patterns would not be as "violent" as we have today. If there was a water vapor barrier in the upper atmosphere, the one thing it would have done would be to filter out much of the harmful solar and cosmic radiation that would have reached the earth and would therefore change the accuracy of carbon 14 dating. Obviously, something happened because Noah and his family were told that they could eat meat after they came out of the "Ark". Genesis 9:3 reads, *"Every moving animal may serve as food for you."* This was not told to Adam and was not recorded any place else prior to this. So something must have changed after the "suspended" water that was filtering the suns rays was no longer there. We obviously must have needed more protein in our diet now that we were being hit by more cosmic radiation. So it would only go to reason that if you were using a "dating" device that relied on the "half life" breakdown of carbon 14 and you varied the amount of radiation involved in the breakdown of that isotope, there is no way that you could get an accurate reading or date, unless you calibrated for that variable. But if you do not recognize that the variable even exists or existed, how could you calibrate for it? So if the flood of Noah's day did exist, the water that surrounded the earth in the atmosphere most likely reduced the amount of radiation breaking down the carbon 14, so it would have taken much longer for radiation to have the same effect before the flood as it does now. I am sure that if this were taken into consideration, the dates in question would be more in line with Biblical chronology.

Chapter 6 ~Civilization Its Start

Nimrod was a mighty hunter and warrior and he actually hunted men. Nimrod would launch raids against small villages, killing those he wanted to and then enslaving the rest to build his cities. The Bible also says at Genesis 10:9 that *"Nimrod was a mighty hunter in opposition to God."* Evidently there was even a popular saying "coined" at the time to reflect Nimrod's opposition to "God". Why did Nimrod find himself in opposition to God? Twice "God" gave the command to *"become fruitful and fill the earth..."*, first to Adam and Eve and then to Noah and his family. "God" wanted man to spread out and fill the earth, but Nimrod favored conquering peoples and built cities to keep them together so he could rule over them and obviously his hand was favored, but by whom?

WHEN DID RELIGION START?

If you are like most people you might think that "God" started religion, but did he? Obviously "God" had a personal relationship with Adam and talked to him regularly and directly, most likely the same way that you would talk to your children at the end of the day. Nowhere in Genesis will you find an account of Adam worshiping "God", even in the account of Cain and Abel. They both sacrificed some of their "produce" to "God" in a thankful manor, but evidently Abel picked out the best of his flock and Cain did not, only using a portion. Even when "God" counseled Cain about his anger with Abel, the conversation takes place in the "first person", which would give the indication that there was a "personal" relationship between God and Cain, but again, no real sign of "religion".

Even when the "sons of the true God" came to earth to take women as their wives, there was no talk of religion. These "life forms" were not worshiped, but were married. We really do not find any real reference to religion until we start to explore the start of civilization. Religion and civilization seem to go "hand in hand", why is that?

The Bible does not have much to say about just how

opposed Nimrod was to "God". You have to do some digging and when you do, you can understand the extent of Nimrod's opposition! Nimrod did not just set himself up as a mighty ruler; he also declared himself "Sun God" over his people and made his wife, Semiramis, "Moon Goddess" and "Goddess of Heaven". The story gets even better. After Nimrod died, Semiramis became pregnant and gave birth to a son named Tammuz. Semiramis made the claim that Tammuz was Nimrod "God of the Sun" reincarnate. Therefore, Semiramis, in giving birth to "god", made herself the first "Madonna" or "mother of god" and that same worship of the "Madonna" is carried out in the church today, even though there is no Bible basis for it. Why is that so?

You might wonder why Nimrod, who already conquered the peoples around him and ruled over them, now wanted to be their god. There is a clue to this in the "god" he chose to be. No doubt the "fallen angel" Lucifer had something to do with this. Lucifer had become "God's" adversary and was directly opposed to the will of "God". Lucifer also knew and understood what "God" had told him at Genesis 3:15. Lucifer had to "raise" up a "seed" or an organization. No doubt he influenced the angels who left their "post" and materialized to have sex with women and produce the "Nephilim". Revelation 12: 3 & 4 tells us that "the great Dragon" dragged "a third of the stars" with him, so since Lucifer had a following in "heaven", he now needed a "seed" on earth! So would it not make sense that he would "raise up" an earthly government and set up "false gods" to distract people's attention from the "True God"?

There is another reason though and it can be summed up in one word, control! If you are the ruler of a people you can control their minds. If you are a god over people now you control their minds and hearts! If you look at the world today, are not religion and government doing their best to control us? That control has lasted through the ages! Governments, or religion, or both have controlled peoples of all tribes, nations and lands throughout history! How do you truly control someone who is an agent of free will? You really cannot! "God" never tried to control Adam's actions.

"God" warned Cain not to kill Abel, but he did not stop him from doing it.

Really, if you think about it, "God" is like the best parent you could have. He is not going to interfere with your life. If you make a mistake, you can always tell him that you are sorry for what you have done and thank him for the lesson in wisdom you received. He does not stop us from doing well and he does not stop us from doing bad, he lets live our own lives. So why all the control over our lives now and why does the world governments only want more control over us?

THE FIRST COLLAPSE OF SOCIETY, WHY?

We've only skimmed over Nimrod and his accomplishments. He ruled over the entire Mesopotamian Valley and built cities from one end to the other, but in the first city he is said to have built Babel, a new construction project that was being started. It is unknown what involvement, if any, Nimrod had with the building of the "Tower of Babel" but it was planned to be a "show piece" that would keep the peoples together. We can read about the account in Genesis the 11th chapter, verse 4, where we learn the reason for the tower's building. It reads *"...let us build a city and also let us build a tower with its top in the heavens ... For fear we will be scattered over the surface of the earth."* This very well could have been Nimrod talking, considering a "city" was to be built and "also a tower". Regardless, the plan was to keep people together in cities and control and "reeducate" them as to all the choices of "new gods" they could have and be forced to worship!

So what was the problem with building cities with tall buildings? The intent of all this building work was to keep people together but "God" wanted everyone to scatter out and cover the earth. However, there is a much bigger problem here. Everyone at that time spoke the same language and communication was no problem so now you have a "central" point for the most intelligent minds in the world to work and live.

This whole problem caught "Gods" attention and according to the account in Genesis, He came to investigate what was going on himself and was angry at what he saw. In the latter half of Genesis 11: 6, we find out "God's" real concern, it reads, *"Now there is nothing they may have in mind to do that will be unattainable for them."* Just think what would happen if this "center for technology" were allowed to continue! It is quite possible that the "nuclear age" could have come before the time of "Christ". Here is a thought for you! Just think if Roman Emporia Nero had "The Bomb". Much more than Rome could have been burning!

You can understand "Gods" concern here. If Nimrod/ Lucifer's plan were allowed to be carried out, a "World Government" could have been formed much like the United Nations is attempting to do today, but with an all powerful despotic ruler who also sets himself up as "god" over all his earthly subjects. This has a very familiar "ring" to it. Could it sound like the "Anti-Christ" that many people are expecting to come and rule our world? It would have been possible to allow a seed to develop to bring the "Messier" or "Christ" and the world would have been ruled by a despotic anti-Christ all these years.

We will explore the "Anti-Christ" more in a future chapter, but for now it is obvious that this was a very devious plan and we have good reason to believe that the powers of the world today want to install a single "King" who would rule over the entire world and subject us all to a "one world" government. Do you really think this is impossible? Do a little investigating into the United Nations and find out what goals they have in store for mankind! Are you ready to give up your choice of religion or who governs you? Are you ready to live in a world that is much like communist China? Be prepared!

WHAT HAPPENED NEXT?

The Bible account continues regarding the Tower of Babel and those working on the tower in Genesis 11:7 & 8 and it tells us that "God" confused their language and scattered them and they stopped building the tower. However "scattering" these people did not solve the problem, only delayed it. Again look at the technological advancements made in the 20th century and before it was half over we learned how to split an atom and destroy ourselves. We learned it so well that we built enough nuclear weapons to destroy the earth five times over! There was another problem though, as those peoples scattered around the earth they took their "sun worship" and all their gods with them. That is why we see sun worship so prevalent in cultures around the world today!

THE WORLD POWERS

After Nimrod's kingdom fell apart nearly 1000 years had past before another powerful government emerged and this time it would be a "world power"! Their monuments have spanned the ages and are among the most recognized still today! I am referring to the very first world power.

EGYPT

Ancient Egypt, it is said, was ultra-religious! The Egyptians worshiped or venerated almost everything! Each village or town had its own "deity" that was entitled as "Lord of the City". Animals of all kinds were worshiped, including bull and calf worship. Hundreds of thousands of animals of all kinds were mummified and entombed. Many of the "major gods" of Egypt were animal's heads and men's bodies.

While the way the Egyptians worshiped was so diverse, the pharaoh who was reigning over the land and his personal beliefs set the major theme. Whatever the pharaoh believed he did his best to influence his subjects, but with so many gods in the land to worship, the pharaoh had a lot of competition.

There were three "gods" that are central in the Egyptian's beliefs and we still know them today as Osiris, Isis and Horus.

These three gods played a familiar role. Osiris is the "god of the dead" and he is married to Isis, his sister, and mother to Horus, his son. Here is the familiar part. Osiris is "reborn" or "born again" from the dead when Isis gives birth to Horus. Therefore, Osiris becomes a symbol for eternal life.

The "son god" Ra later became Amon-Ra, the king of all the Egyptian gods. Associated with Amon-Ra were his wife, Mut and their son the "moon god" Khonsu. In fact, in the tomb of King Tutmose III, a list was found with more than 740 "gods" with many of them depicted as being married to a goddess who had given birth to a son, thus completing a triad or trinity of gods. So much like the religion that Nimrod had started and became the center of pagan worship, the trinity of gods is carried on in Egyptian religion today, but to an extreme!

ASSYRIA

The Assyrians are probably one of the most blood thirsty and cruel peoples of the ancient worlds. Nineveh, one of the first cities built by Nimrod, was their capital city however they recognized the city of Babylon as their "religious center". The Assyrians were the ultimate terrorists! In order to keep conquered lands under control, they made "examples" of the prisoners captured in war. The way they dealt with their captured enemies, instilled fear and terror throughout the land. On wall carvings found in Assyrian runes, you can see many of the ways the Assyrians dispatched their captives. They flayed, dismembered body parts, built walls with heads of their enemies, impaled them, cut off ears and noses and put out their eyes, or any of the above combined. It obviously would have been better to die in battle than to be taken captive!

The Assyrians occupied the upper Mesopotamian Valley; the Babylonians occupied the lower part of the Mesopotamian Valley. Their frontiers shifted back and forth and something that was very common between these peoples was their religion. Again here we have very polytheistic peoples, with the emphasis in the belief that all living things had spirits. Their chief god was Asshur and he was depicted in a seal found in the runes of an Assyrian palace as a god with three heads. In fact, there were many "trinities" of gods worshiped in the Assyrian religion, as in the religions that came before them, so it is obvious that the "Christian" teaching of the "trinity" of the "Father, Son, and Holy Ghost" is not a new one but copies the idea of pagan peoples.

The Assyrian "Golden Age" ended when their neighbors to the south, the Babylonians, became a military might and conquered them as well as many other peoples to become the next world power.

BABYLON

If the Assyrians were known best for their bloodthirstiness and the terror that they struck in the hearts of their victims, the Babylonians were more known for their religious fervor. In fact, the name "Babylon" has been modified and the name used for this city by the Sumerian and Akkadian peoples meant the "Gate of god" or "Gate of the gods". Nimrod founded the city of Babylon and it is believed that he became the chief god of all Babylonian gods and was called or became the god Marduk. The city of Babylon had over 50 temples and countless idols. Numerous triad or trinity of gods was worshiped, but the most important triad was three gods that made up the "sun", "moon and stars" and the "earth mother". This triad is responsible for the "creation of the zodiac". Have you ever wondered where the expression "Mother Earth" came from? The Babylonians invented her, made her a goddess and worshiped her. In fact, almost all "pagan" religious beliefs as well as many so called "Christian" religious beliefs and traditions can be traced back to ancient Babylon. You may wonder how the pagan teachings of Babylon entered Christianity; we will explain this when we discus the Roman world power.

The Babylonians are responsible for destroying the Jewish temple that Solomon had built and took almost all the Jews captive in 607 B.C.E. The Jews were a monotheistic people who worshiped a single supreme almighty god. In fact, Christians and Muslims both claim to worship that same god. What is name? In English it is Jehovah. The Christians and Jews just call him "God" and the Muslims call him Allah. I find it quite remarkable, how three ethnic groups of people who all claim to worship the same god are bitter enemies today! It makes you wonder who their god really is!

Because the Babylonians captured "God's" people, the Jews, they involved themselves in many Bible prophecies that have had or will have an effect on our lives today. One of the better-known prophecies that apply in our day is one that talks about a statue that is made of different metals but with feet of iron and clay. A giant stone is cut from the "Mountain of Jehovah" and thrown at the statue, which destroys it. The statue represents the governments of the world from Babylon to the present and God will destroy them all! You can read about this account in the Bible in the book of Daniel 2: 31- 45. Daniel prophesied about many future events, including future world powers, the coming of the "Christ" or "Messiah" and "God's kingdom" established here on earth. One thing he foretold to the Babylonians was their overthrow by our next world power.

PERSIA

The Persian Empire was made up of two groups of people, the Medes and the Persians. The Persians worshiped over 50 major gods and as we discussed before Ahura Mazda was their chief or patron "god". No doubt the "Prince of Persia" talked about in the Bible in the book of Daniel, he was symbolized as a disc with wings. Interestingly, while the Persians were sun worshipers, they did not worship any major triad or trinity of gods and all their major gods were either good gods or evil gods.

The Persians themselves had an interesting view of right and wrong and the truth. The Persians prided themselves in telling the truth and one of their major gods was a "god of contracts". He was to watch over all contracts and ensure that the parties in the contract kept their word. In fact an agreement was found 18 years after it was to be placed into effect to return the Jewish people from their captivity in Babylon to their homeland. The Persians kept that agreement and did indeed not only returned the Jewish people to their homeland, but also helped finance the rebuilding of the Jewish temple.

GREECE

Probably one of the most influential world powers of history, the Greek culture has affected our lives today in ways we may not even realize. From the arts, to medicine, to philosophy, the ancient Greeks and the culture they brought to the world today have influenced much of our lives. The many stories told in Greek mythology have kept generations of people entertained right down to our day today. In fact, the Greek tale of Atlantis has launched many expeditions to find the great, lost city, which was alleged to be far more advanced than any other city on the face of the world.

The "gods" of Greece seemed to take a personal interest in their human servants. As discussed earlier, Zeus, the king of the Greek gods, had many sexual encounters with mortal women and produced offspring with them. There is so much detail in the information given in Greek mythology that archeologists, historians and scholars are starting to wonder how much truth may there be in these myths.

Sun worship was alive and well in ancient Greece with their worship of two gods, Helios and Apollo. Helios was the father to Zeus and grandfather to Apollo. The gods of Greece are divided into three groups. The Titans were basically responsible for the creation of everything; the Olympians were the "ruling class" over humans; and they were the Greek gods, better known ones and lesser gods, who had responsibilities but were not all that important in the religious teachings and stories of Greek mythology. The Greeks were extremely religious people, erecting many temples and altars in their cities. They even went so far as to erect an altar to an "Unknown" god so as not to offend one that they may have missed. It was the apostle Paul that capitalized on this and brought Christianity to the Greeks of Athens.

ROME

If there ever was a military power of the ancient world, Rome was it. Rome conquered all of the lands bordering the Mediterranean Sea, much of Europe and eastward toward Persia. Rome made the then known world it's master and many a "Caesar" brought the world's showcase to Rome for it's citizens to be impressed with the conquests of the Roman Empire. In fact, Rome became a "melting pot" of all the nations they conquered and besides Roman gods, the gods of the people of the Roman Empire also entered Rome and were worshiped there.

The Greeks had a large influence on Roman religion. Many of the Roman gods were the same as the Greek gods, only with Roman names, but with the influence of other cultures and their religions and beliefs there was no lack of gods to worship in Rome. However, in the third century, religion in Rome would change forever.

After three hundred years, Christianity had grown internationally. The belief of just one "supreme god" who gave his son to mankind to ransom us back from sin and death had taken hold in the hearts and minds of those who were controlled by many gods and the rituals and sacrifices those gods demanded. Now there was a religion that was based on love of "God" and your fellow man, what could be easier? If you "had" to be controlled by something what better thing than by love? That was and still is the basis for Christianity. You might wonder though, if Christianity is supposed to be based on love, why was so much blood shed and why were there so many wars waged in the name of Christianity?

So what happened in the third century to change the religion of the Romans? Constantine was marching his army to capture Rome when on one night he claims to have had a vision in which Jesus appeared to him as a symbol above the sun. Constantine had his army paint this symbol on their shields, and after their victory in battle, Constantine vowed to become Christian. He is considered to be the first Christian Emporia of the Roman Empire, even though he had very little understanding of Christianity and was not "baptized" until he was on his deathbed. While "freedom of religion" was accepted, the official religion of Rome became Christianity. However sun worship was most likely more widespread than Christianity at that time and the Roman pagan holidays were not about to be given up by those who loved and celebrated them. It did not matter what the "official" religion was, the people were going to worship the gods that they always worshiped. So really the Roman Empire became the Roman Catholic Church, complete with sun worship, a triune god, graven images and pagan holidays. It was the best of both worlds and the people of the Empire accepted their new religion.

As Roman political power started to fade, the power of the "Church" grew and before long the "Church" controlled the monarchs of Europe and their subjects, right to the point of the first rebellion against the church and the emergence of the last of the seven world powers that we recognize today and throughout history.

ANGLO-AMERICAN

King Henry the VIII decided he was going to do things his way and ran the Catholic Church right out of England and set up his own "Christian" religion. King Henry's legacy started England on its way to become a world power. It was once said that the sun never set on English soil and rightly so. England controlled countries and lands from the Far East to the Americas. England ruled the seas for over two hundred years before it would lose that privilege to one of its former colonies, the United States of America.

When the United States was formed it was to be a totally different country, one ruled by the people who lived there. Elected officials would represent the people who elected them, carrying out their wishes and needs through laws passed by those same officials. The country was governed by the people, for the people, and made "freedom" its cornerstone.

What America was really designed for was to be a capitalistic country, one set up for commerce. There were many natural resources across the country and a world market to sell them to. What we fail to remember is that the United States of America was founded by businessmen and bankers who were losing profits to England through competition and taxes. A revolt was sure to come because these businessmen stirred up issues about taxation and the control of the "Colonies" by a ruler who was depicted as a despot and could care less about his subjects in the Americas.

The United States did not really become a world power until after the Second World War. By that time no country on earth could match the military might of the United States! The United States had the largest and most powerful army, navy and air force in the world and they had the newly developed atomic bomb, able to destroy a whole major city with one blast! There is no doubt in anyone's mind, worldwide, that the United States of America is the world's foremost military power. And who is its closest ally? England. Hence you have the Anglo-American world power. The last world power recorded to come by the prophets of the Bible, save one!

THE NEXT WORLD POWER

With America and England at the top of the world's might, one may wonder, what do you mean another world power? Who can conquer mighty America? Can the Chinese or the Russians? Who could overthrow the United States and take control of the world? What country could possibly be strong enough to "dethrone" the good old U.S.A. as a world power? The truth is there is no country that will overthrow the United States! The United States of America will give its power freely to the next world power. As a matter of fact, the United States has been supporting this world power, breaths life into and eventually will totally submit to the will of this world power and a shot will never be fired! Who is this world power? The United Nations!

Before you start to laugh at the notion of the United Nations becoming the next world power, you had better read the "Law of the Sea Treaty". If you haven't heard about it or don't know what it entails, I strongly suggest you become familiar with it. When the United States ratifies this treaty and supports the United Nations laws, it will be giving up total power of its navy and make the United Nations the new world power! The United Nations will "rule" over seventy percent of the surface of the earth. The English used to brag, "He who rules the seas, rules the world" back when they ruled the seas. That is no longer the case. America rules the seas now, but not for long! Anything, I repeat, anything that takes place at sea, regardless of what it is, from shipping, to undersea mining or oil drilling, to commercial fishing, will be governed by the laws of the United Nations. The U.N. will be the ruler of the sea and I am afraid there is nothing we can do to stop that! One slogan that used to insight independence from England by the American Colonists was "Taxation without representation". How would you like to pay an extra ten percent for anything that was shipped across or taken from the sea? Under this treaty you could seriously be doing this. Just think, the fish you ate last night, the coffee you had this morning, and the car you drove to work in all cost more because you have to pay a tax to the United Nations and for what? So you can be controlled by yet another level of government! The United States could not throw a stone at a boatload of terrorists armed with nuclear weapons without the United Nations say so. So where does that leave the Untied States of America? Along with every other country in the world, under the rule of the United Nations, our next world power!

You maybe taken aback by what I say about the United Nations, because the United Nations appears to be almost useless and has virtually no power. Do not be misled! The United Nations has been working quietly "behind the scenes" to gain control of the population of the earth and a "blueprint" is already in place to change life as we know and live it! Guess what? We have a new religion coming our way too, developed by the United Nations. They have been working on a "world" religion from the mid 1950s and the finished product is a combination of Buddhism and American Indian Spirituality. Why these you ask? The answer is quite simple. The Buddhists are peaceful and respect life and do not arm themselves for war. The beliefs of the American Indians center on respect for "Mother Earth" and nature. So what better than a world of people who will not fight and will care for and respect our planet, our "Mother Earth"? Now you are thinking on a global level, but are you ready to give up your religion and beliefs? What if the government closed your church, temple, synagogue, or mosque and all religion was outlawed, except for the "global religion" of the United Nations? Would you comply and change your religious ideals? After all it is for the good of all mankind all over the world. Or would you say "I'll change and submit the day they pry my cold dead fingers from my gun?" Think if everyone around the world took that stand, what would you have? You would have the war of Armageddon? No, you have what Jesus prophesied when telling his apostles what would happen in the last days of this system of things. In the Bible at Matthew 24: 21 Jesus said, *"for there will be great tribulation such has not occurred from the worlds beginning until now, nor will ever occur again."*

WHY ALWAYS A POWER STRUGGLE?

All through recorded history we can see that man has tried his best to control other men and to what result? Sadness, pain and death! But is this just man's inhumanity to man? No and I say this with confidence, generally speaking all of mankind wants peace! It is obvious that outside forces are involved or we would have peace. Man was made in "God's image" and with "free will". "Lucifer" knows that and has spent thousands of years to turning mankind away from the face of "God". He has set up his "demon" hoards as false gods to distract mankind and we have had endless wars thrust upon us to keep us in submission! You disagree? Look at the facts that we covered and think again!

Chapter 6 ~Civilization Its Start

CIVILIZATION IN THE 20TH CENTURY

The year 1900 came and went without much fan fair. The aristocracy in Europe was happy, large and in charge. In America, we healed from the blood letting of the "War Between the States". There was nothing "civil" about that war. If you don't know the truth about the "Civil War" it was not a war to "free the slaves". It was a war to keep the ideals of the United States intact and destroy the aristocracy that was developing in the southern United Sates. I bring that up because the same forces that brought about the "Civil War" in the United States would soon do the same in Europe and for the same reason, to do away with the aristocracy! By the end of World War One, the ruling class in Europe was brought to their knees and the Czar of Russia and his family were dead. Out of ignorance they called it the Great War, but as we know there was a much bigger one to come. In fact, the twentieth century is the bloodiest ever! We saw death handed out at a "wholesale rate" and entire cities were destroyed with a single bomb. We have been surrounded by death as never before in history! Why?

To help prevent a world war from breaking out again, the "League of Nations" was formed after the First World War. Even though President Woodrow Wilson wrote the charter for the League of Nations, he could not get congress to ratify the passage of a bill that would make the United States a member of the League of Nations. The League of Nations received a "death blow" when the Second World War broke out, but returned as the United Nations. This time it would not be headquartered in Europe but in New York City and the United States of America was ready to be its foremost member!

Something else happened at the start of the twentieth century, something that had a huge impact on the world but went unnoticed by almost everyone. To learn what happened we have to return to the Bible, this time to the book of Revelation. In the twelfth chapter a war breaks out in heaven and Lucifer, or as he is called in Revelation the "Great Dragon", along with his demon hoards get thrown out of heaven and cast down to the earth. In verse 12 we read in part "Woe to the earth and to the sea, because the Devil has come down to you, having great anger knowing he has a short period of time." By Bible calculations this happened in 1914 so is it really any surprise that this century has been so bloody?

If you look at all the technological advancements made throughout 5000 years of recorded history and added them all up, they would not even begin to equal what mankind was able to do in the twentieth century. Just think about the history of flight. It took us 60 years to go from the Wright brothers with their wood and fabric "flying machine", to landing a spacecraft on the moon! Think about it for a minute, why have most of these technological advancements revolved around killing people? Why do the World governments spend $25,000 US dollars for every man, woman and child on the face of this planet each year on weapons to kill us? Is that not pure satanic? I rest my case! Let there be no doubt that this planet, this earth that is our home, is infested with life forms that want us dead! Ask yourself, why are there so many wars? Why is there so much killing? Why are so many people unhappy in this world? What is your answer?

WHERE ARE WE HEADED?

Have you ever just sat down, put your head in your hands and asked yourself, "Just where mankind is headed?" No doubt if you are an American, you may have very well done that on September 11, 2001, when a small group of terrorists attacked the United States. That one act of terrorism changed the United States and the people there forever. Americans willingly gave up a huge amount of freedom to stop terrorist attacks. The American Government grew larger and more powerful and now control all people with in its borders a little more closely.

The problems don't stop with terrorism! Everyplace you look today there are problems in the world; wars, food shortages, earthquakes, disease, pollution and now global warming! Where does this all end? In a word, Armageddon!

CHAPTER 7
THE DOMINATION OF MAN

WHEN DID IT START?

Anthropologists would have us believe that our ancestors were fighting with each other probably from the time they lived in trees. Indeed there is a fossil record that paints an interesting picture of man-type creatures down to Neanderthal and Cro-Magnon man. I will never argue the fact that our DNA is extremely close to theirs, but there is a difference between us and I believe that difference was additional DNA, which in part, hard wired us to love. Hence we were "made" or genetically engineered in "God's image". That would have separated us from all life forms that came before us and that would have made us truly different and also given us a spiritual connection.

If we were "created" as free will life forms, then we would not want to be controlled by anyone or anything! However, we are and as we discussed earlier, we have layers of control heaped upon us today. But when did it all start?

The earliest recorded account of "domination" over man would be the account of the "first woman", Eve, and the Serpent in the "Garden of Eden". Don't scoff or laugh! If we were genetically engineered, and remember evolution is still a theory, no doubt we would have been engineered perfectly. Think about it. Who would spend hundreds of million of years developing life on this rock we call earth, only to put on it an intelligent life form that would not even live one hundred years? Our bodies start breaking down in a little over 25 years, but we have a reproductive system and a brain that would out last many, many life times! So what happened?

The account is in Genesis the third chapter verses 1 through 5. Here we have Eve being approached by a "serpent", the most cautious of all the animals, and it talks to her. She was most likely pretty surprised. The serpent asks her *"Is it really so that God said you must not eat from any tree of the garden?"* Eve replies to the serpent, *"Of the fruit of the trees of the garden we may eat. But as for the tree in the middle of the garden, God has said, "You must not eat from it, no you must not touch it, that you do not die!'"* In verse 4 the serpent replies with the first recorded lie as he tells Eve, *"You positively will not die. For God knows that in the very day of your eating from it your eyes are bound to be opened and you are bound to be like God knowing good and bad."* Eve was totally deceived and thought she could be like God!

Evidently that fruit contained a virus that was deadly to mankind and it either attached itself to our DNA, or it erased part of our DNA. Either way because of eating the fruit from this tree that "God" had said not to, both Adam and Eve were now infected and were starting to die. The process was not a quick death. Adam was to have lived over nine hundred years before his body finally gave out. We today go through the same process in about eighty years.

Geneticists have learned that the DNA molecule has little "tabs" attached to it called telomeres. Telomeres have been compared with the plastic tips on shoelaces because they prevent chromosome ends from fraying and sticking to each other. If this happened it would scramble an organism's genetic information to cause cancer and other diseases, even death. Each time a cell divides the telomeres get shorter. When they get too short, the cell can no longer divide and becomes inactive or basically dies. This process is associated with aging, cancer and a higher risk of death. So if the telomeres never got shorter but stayed at their "original" length, would we ever die? That is a very good question and one I cannot answer. It has never happened before to the best of my knowledge, but it would be a logical assumption. Except for one thing! Both Adam and Eve disobeyed a direct commandment of "God" and he "cut" himself off from mankind because he does not have anything to do with imperfection. That is why Jesus was "sent" to earth to ransom mankind as the "Messiah" and the "Savoir" of the human race, or so the story goes.

Chapter 7 ~The Domination Of Man

WHY DID DOMINATION START?

What does "love" have to do with domination of mankind? Evidently the serpent in the story was "played" by the angel Lucifer, better known as Satan (slanderer) the Devil (deceiver). He wanted the love and worship of mankind for himself and in order to do that he had to ruin the relationship God had with mankind and then divert that love and worship to him. He wanted to set himself over mankind as their god and or father.

If "God" did have this planet earth of ours purposely "made" or "engineered" for mankind, no doubt it was like any other building project we would see today. If you were going to build a modern "high rise" office building, you would need a small army of workers with specialized skills. There would be crew chiefs, a foreman and a job supervisor that would make sure everything was carried out as indicated and specified in the blueprints. When everything was completed, the building would be ready for occupancy.

Evidently, Lucifer must have been very involved in the building or engineering of our home. He knew that the end purpose was to provide a home for a new intelligent life form that would be "hard wired" to love because they would be made in "God's image". Obviously, because of his involvement, he wanted that love that mankind was going to be giving to their true father and creator Jehovah, all to himself. He wanted the relationship that man was going to have with their father, for himself. In short it was as if mankind was "kidnapped" by someone who could not have children of their own. However, there is no real bond there like there would be between a parent and their child. So in essence, all of mankind was kidnapped and held for ransom.

There was only one problem at this point. Adam and Eve both knew that they had been tricked and were not about to replace what relationship they had left with "God" and start to worship Lucifer. In fact we do not find any evidence of anyone worshiping any other gods until after the flood of Noah's day when the Bible states that "Angelic" life forms came to earth to take women for their wives and fathered the Nephilim, as they were called, or the "Sons of God". Before the flood of Noah's day, the Garden of Eden was visible to all on the earth. No doubt the people who wanted to see the "Garden" could, but they were not allowed to enter! Therefore, it would only be logical that they knew the story of what had happened and still had a monotheistic belief in a "Supreme Being".

While at this point the only thing that mankind was dominated by was growing old and death, Wickedness had filled the then populated earth and God was "hurt to his heart" that he had even made man.

DOMINATION THROUGH HISTORY

The next account where man is dominated can be found in Genesis with the account of Nimrod, the mighty hunter. He mostly hunted men. By means of intimidation by death, Nimrod concurred, enslaved people, and put them to work building his cities. With cities came the control of "Government"; a set of appointed officials to keep order and rule over their constituents and press them into service to attain the national goals and ambitions.

Nimrod also gave us something else, another level of control, religion! The Bible makes the statement that Nimrod was opposition to "God". Why was Nimrod opposed to "God"? It is because God gave the command to man to "fill the earth". This would have meant that people would be spreading out across the land and moving into new regions. The more people spread out the harder they would be to control, intimidate and rule over them. So Lucifer, who also opposed "God", must have been "backing" Nimrod and his efforts to become the world's first ruler. In fact Nimrod set himself up as a "God" over his people and he was known as being opposed to "Jehovah God". In fact he was so opposed that not only did he make himself a "god" but he invented and encouraged the worship of many different gods. Whatever would divert worship away from "God", he encouraged. Worship of the sun, moon, stars, earth spirits, objects, animals and the gods who "ruled" over these things were all worshiped in Babylon and the other cities Nimrod had built.

You might ask how a man could have the backing of a spirit creature. So what if he did have Lucifer or Satan's backing? Does it really matter? To really understand if it matters or not we can look to the recent history of the twentieth century and at some of the obviously satanic rulers we have had to put up with and the genocide they brought to the earth. Pol Pot and the Khmer Rouge are responsible for over 2,000,000 deaths. Adolph Hitler and the Nazi regime caused the Second World War. They are directly responsible for the deaths of more than 6,000,000 Jews. Then there is my favorite despot, Joseph Stalin. He and his Communist regime are responsible for the deaths of as many as 100,000,000 people of the Soviet Union, they stopped keeping records of the deaths after they reached 50,000,000. Let us also not forget the innumerable deaths caused by religion and religious intolerance. If these aren't satanic acts heaped on mankind, then nothing is! And for what reason were these things done? To dominate, intimidate and control mankind.

As we examine history we find that mankind has been plagued by despotic rulers from the time of Nimrod right down to our day and what is worse is that there are more despotic rulers to come despite how civilized, educated, or cultured we think we are.

WAS MAN MEANT TO BE DOMINATED?

If we examine the fossil record of pre-modern man, or our "pre-human" ancestors, archeologists would tell us that they lived in a world of conflict with an "alpha male" at the head of the "tribe", much in the same way we see among the great apes. Troupes of chimpanzees have been recorded and filmed going out on "hunting trips" that led to the capture, death and eating of lesser primates. Chimpanzees have also been recorded capturing and killing chimpanzees from other clans, with no apparent reason than to exercise dominance and expand territory. Did our so-called pre-human "ancestors" do the same thing as we see chimpanzees doing today?

It is "believed" that there were conflicts between the clans of Neanderthal and Cro-Magnon man when they crossed paths. It is also believed that the two clans may have interbred when females of one group were captured by the other. Because there is no written record of what actually happened most of this is conjecture, more than likely based on our own "animalistic behavior" and what anthropologists have been able to uncover in the fossil record.

The Bible tells us that man was created in "God's" image. That image is more the qualities that "God" possesses and passed down to us and "hard wired" into our psyche and possibly even in to our DNA, rather than our "physical form" which is really more influenced by the environment we live in. As we have learned "God's" main attribute is love, so if we are given the power and emotion of love as our main attribute too, then we should only be dominated by love!

Really our lives and the world we live in, was intended to be ruled by the love that we "should" have for each other, much the same way you would have in your family, only on a world wide scale. If you remember a large "family get together", maybe a wedding or anniversary, or the "yearly family picnic", you most likely met relatives that you don't get to see very often, maybe aunts and uncles, or cousins, or maybe some you've never even met before. They are all your family and you have a love for all of them, because they are your family! After such a get together, you might reflect on the event and think how good it was to see and be with your family and how enjoyable it was to see those members that you have not seen for a very long time. Well think of this example on a worldwide scale! Let's say that you have to take a business trip to Tokyo, Japan. When you are told about the trip you get excited because some of your family that you haven't seen in a long time lives in Tokyo and now you get to visit with them. You can catch up on all the family news, see how your family has grown and best of all you get to spend time with people that you love and who love you!

Now ask yourself, how many laws does your family have? You might ask “Laws?” and reply that your family has no laws. There are the “rules” that your parents have given to you and you may have to live under the rules of your parents house, but those rules are mostly given for our protection the same as we give, or will give our children “rules” that will be for their protection. What parent wants harm to come to their children?

Every parent wants to see their children become successful and have good lives. No doubt parents do their best to guide and direct their children in a way that they believe is best for them. Sometimes though, you hear the story of the “demon child”, who despite being raised in a good family with caring parents becomes rebellious and defiant. They become opposed to anything their parents want for them, even if it is to get some kind of professional help from outside the family.

If we examine the Biblical account of how “God” dealt with Israel in the early days of the nation, we find that the Hebrew people had no king; they were instructed and led by “judges” and a “prophet”. The nation was the first monotheistic people in the world and for all intents and purposes they lived in a theocracy, a rule by “God”. The Hebrew people did not need a king to rule over them, they had their “God” Jehovah. He was their king and law giver, but they also had a special relationship with “God”, because of the covenant that Jehovah God had with the forefather of the nation of Israel, Abraham. The nation of Israel was God’s “chosen” people and they were like children to their “God” Jehovah. Because the nations around Israel all had kings, they wanted one too and even though the profit Samuel told them that they were making a mistake, that a king would only give them more rules and laws to follow and that they would have to support a king through taxes and tribute. The nation of Israel did not care they wanted a king to rule over them, someone that they could see with their eyes and so after the profit Samuel petitioned “God”, Saul became their first king. Because Saul did not follow the laws given by the “God “ of Israel he was replaced after his death by King David, the most famous king in all of Hebrew history.

The point of this is that while we do need instruction in our lives and guidelines to live by, even "God" knows that more layers of control and domination are not good for mankind and that a "family" type government based in love is much more conducive to our happiness!

THE BAD SIDE OF DOMINATION

In the Bible book of Ecclesiastes Chapter 8 verse 9 we read in part *"...man has dominated man to his injury"*. This was written over three thousand years ago and at that time, the wisest man on the earth recognized that mankind was being "injured" by other men. If that was three thousand years ago, how have things changed today?

In the United States as well as other "democratic" countries, we have elected officials whom "we" have put into their office of power to invent and pass new laws to put additional restrictions upon us. Are we crazy? For people who claim to value liberty and freedom so much we have let ourselves be dominated by a bunch of politicians who we know lie to us and allow them to pass laws to restrict our freedoms, take our money and force us under further submission to their rule over us.

While despots have ruled throughout history, that is not the general case today. Yes there are those dictators that still spot the earth, but they are becoming fewer. We think that the world should be a free and liberated place and all peoples in all countries should be free to choose the lives they want live. While that is the ideal, the fact is far removed. Even in countries that claim to be "free" and democratic, there is an underlying suppression of the populous in one way or another.

Society is broken down into many layers, starting at the country level; countries are broken down into first, second and third world levels. These first, second and third world countries are based on their technological advancement and "standard" of living. The problem is that about twenty five percent of the world's population is at, or below what is considered poverty level and what is worse is that about twenty percent of the world's population is malnourished! What is really shocking is that the United States alone could produce enough food to feed the world's population. So where is the problem?

I remember reading an article that showed a photograph of a quite obese grain merchant in a third world country. He was sitting on sacks full of wheat and dressed in what could be called "decadent finery". He was obviously very wealthy and decorated himself in gold. While he enjoyed the finer things in life, the majority of his countrymen were starving! What was this man's biggest problem? Rats! They were eating as much as twenty percent of his stock. He had little or no concern for those who were dying from starvation around him. His position was that he was a merchant and if people want wheat they must pay for what they get.

This was an example in a third world country. Surely, we would not see anything like this going on in a first world country. Oh really? A good example of oppression and domination takes place in all countries all over the world at all times, just in different forms that we don't recognize right away, if at all. What about the mortgage companies owned by large banks who invent new and creative ways to get people into the "house of their dreams"? They find after a few years that they cannot afford the payments because of rising interest rates and they lose everything they have worked so hard for, to the bank, only to be left with nothing at all! While bankers celebrate the success of the record number of mortgages they have written and give themselves millions of dollars of bonuses, in turn record numbers of people are losing the home they put their life and soul into and are left worse off then ever. Now they must first recover from the loss and then start to rebuild their lives all over again, only now they are worse off than when they first started! Again, we see "man's domination of man to his injury" and with no remorse!

Look around in your life, invest a few minutes and think about all the things that have control over your life, the things you like, the things you do, the things that you believe will protect you Is your life really free? Can you be the person of freewill that you were meant to be? Or do you have so many things that dominate your life that at times you feel as though you were carrying the weight of the world on your shoulders?

THE GOVERNMENT'S ROLE IN DOMINATION

In the year 1776, a group of rebels signed a document that declared them and the people that they represented, independent of and no longer subject to the rule of the King of England, and so the American Colonies were transformed in to the United States of America. "Freedom and Liberty" was the slogan of the day!

The interesting thing about the formation of the United States government, is that it was not going to be ruled by a king, but would have "elected officials" to rule or govern the people. This was to be the first "democratic" government ever on the face of the earth. The days of the monarchies were now numbered! What a novel idea; a government without a king, I wonder who came up with that idea? Really the idea most likely came out of a secret meeting held in Germany on May 1st, 1776, where a secret organization was formed with the intention of world domination. They are called the Illuminati. Very little is known about this group and we will talk about them in more detail in a later chapter. Evidently the Illuminati came up with a system of government that would be unstable in nature as compared to a monarchy and one that would be much easier to control. The people embraced it readily, because it did away with having a king rule over them and they had just gotten rid of the last king after a long hard war for independence. The new form of government was democracy!

Monarchies, are handed down from generation to generation, but remain in the same family. The only way to take over a country ruled by a monarch without going to war would be to marry into the family. Then you would have to be the child of a royal family yourself, and the process could take many of years and several generations to accomplish. However, if you introduced a method of government where the leaders were elected to office, you could have your own people run for office and with enough money you could pretty much ensure that your candidate for office would win. Now you can gain control of a country and the people within that country.

Evidently the Illuminati worked very close with a group known as Free Masons. The Free Masons were already a powerful group of merchants and government officials. It is believed that the Free Masons grew from the Knights Templars after they were outlawed by the "Church" at the urging of King Phillip the Fair of France, who owed the Knights Templars vast amounts of money.

When you look at the number of "Founding Fathers" of the United States of America who were Free Masons, it is obvious that this group helped found and at the same time gain control of a new country that had vast resources and wealth to be extracted and marketed around the world. Many early American families associated with the Free Masons became very rich and powerful by selling the natural resources of America and becoming politically involved in the rule of the United States of America. They could pass laws that would be beneficial to themselves and their friends. They would be able to make millions of dollars off the back of the common man because they were all powerful. He had the power of a personal "vote" to change what he did not like, just as today we have the domination of millions of people by the rich elite ruling class.

This "standard" is with us today. In fact the first President of the United States, George Washington, was a Free Mason. There have been numerous presidents who were Free Masons and the last President of the United States, George Herbert Walker Bush, is also a Free Mason just as his father is. In fact George H.W. Bush used the same Bible to be sworn into office as George Washington. Are we any less dominated today, than we were under the rule of King George when America was known as "the Colonies"? Fact of the matter is that the events that turned the Colonies against King George and England affected the common person very little. The slogan of the day was "Taxation without representation!", but who was being taxed? It was the merchants. They could not compete with the goods that were shipped to the Colonies because they had to pay a tax to the king. This cut into the profit margin of the merchants who were not happy about this and the revolution was on.

France would be the first country in Europe to revolt against the monarch and establish a democratic government. This was going to be a bit different than the American Revolution; it would wind up with an all-powerful "Emporia of Europe", Napoleon.

Napoleon had the financial backing of one of the richest families in Europe, the Rothschild family. In return for the Rothschild family's financial backing to wage war across Europe, Napoleon gave them control of the French banking system. A family now owned a country's bank.

As Napoleon set off waging war across Europe, leaving a path of destruction and death, the monarchies of Europe were becoming devastated. We all know that Napoleon was defeated by Wellington at Waterloo, but what most people do not know is that the Rothschild family had withdrew their financial backing from Napoleon and was now financing Wellington's army! Why was this? Napoleon had served his purpose. He had dealt the monarchy of Europe a devastating blow. There were many towns and villages that would have to be rebuilt and money was going to be needed to rebuild what Napoleon and his army destroyed. The idea was to remove the monarchies, not create a bigger one with Napoleon as emporia! This was not part of the plan, so Napoleon had to be removed from power and done away with and so he was! Napoleon did not remove the monarchies of Europe, but what he did do was put them in debt to "banking families" like the Rothschild's.

It is strongly believed that the Illuminati is made up of many large powerful banking families who today control about eighty percent of the world's wealth. So you could understand that a group this rich and powerful could dominate and gain control over whole countries. By controlling commerce and the money supply, you could do almost anything you want, even start a world war!

Chapter 7 ~The Domination Of Man

During the early 1970's Americans experienced their first oil shortage. This really unsettled the country. Long lines became normal at gas pumps. Signs reading "No Gas" were common. I personally remember my father having to buy "Black Market" gas during a trip in order to make it to our next stop and he was happy to find it and pay the price that was being asked.

What most people do not know is that a group of "European Bankers" had a meeting with leaders from OPEC who controlled the price and supply of oil. It is alleged that the bankers told the leaders of OPEC to stop shipping oil to the United States and raise the price on a barrel of oil. They were instructed to deposit the profits in specific banks and were told if they followed the instructions, the price hike on oil would be accepted and there would be no major repercussions. The rest is history!

Throughout these examples we see how our own governments have heaped additional levels of "man's domination of man" upon us. There is more here than meets the eye, because there is a sinister underlying domination going on as well and that is the domination of a group of very powerful and very rich individuals who seek to dominate and control the world and the people who live in it. Have you ever noticed how our lives revolve around the banking system? We cannot do anything in life without getting a bank involved and how many people in the world are deep in debt to banks? Too many people are! When you are in debt to someone, does that not dominate and control your life and actions? Yes it does!

Here is one more thing to think about. The government controls and regulates the banking industry, but who controls the Federal Banking System? If you do your homework, you are going to find that it is controlled by large international banks headquartered in other countries! Yes believe it or not, the United States Government as well as almost every democratic government in the world does not have control over it's own money. The same group of international bankers controls it all!

RELIGION'S ROLE IN DOMINATION

Good morning! It's Sunday, time to get up and go to church! For years and years and generation after generation, those words were spoken every week. So we get up from our sleep, get ready to start our day and we go to a fancy building and listen to a man in religious clothing talk about "God", say a few prayers and ask us for our money. It really doesn't sound bad to take an hour or so out of your week to attend a religious ceremony intended to save your soul, does it?

As we discussed earlier, religion had its start under the world's first ruler, Nimrod. He could control the minds of men by hunting them down and killing or enslaving them, but he could not control their hearts or the spiritual need they had by the same method. For that he claimed himself to be a god and gave the people all the different gods they wanted to worship. Now they had the spiritual connection they needed and Nimrod had another way to control his people!

Karl Marks made the statement that "religion is the opium of the people." No doubt he must have observed that religion had a vast control over the common man and dominated their lives, but gave nothing or very little back in return. No doubt he too saw the hypocrisy of religious leaders, the wealth of the "Church" and their deep involvement in governmental affairs. Karl Marks must have felt that just as if you were addicted to a hard narcotic like opium, you could not lead a productive life! If your life revolved around religion, it was just like being addicted to opium, you could not lead a full and productive life and therefore were a lesser citizen and not as valuable to the "State".

While I am not an advocate of Karl Marks by any means, the man did make an observation and a very astute one at that! Religion has done very little to bring peace to the world, instead you always see religious leaders, right up to the Pope, involved in governmental affairs. Many times the Pope will meet with world leaders, or address the United Nations directly. So-called Christians are not the only ones that are at the heart of war. The

Middle East has been a "powder keg" for years and Islam has taken its brand of warfare to the world and created terror in the hearts of many people worldwide. Jesus said that you would know his followers by the love they have among themselves. Really then, where are the people who claim to be of God? Where is peace? Where is the freedom? Where did the liberty go?

What does religion have to do with politics? It should have nothing to do with it, but it does! The American Civil Liberties Union has been doing it's best to remove "God" from government, down to the point that only evolution can be taught in schools. There are some that believe the word "God" should be removed from the "Pledge of Allegiance" and be taken off all money. These views may seem a bit extreme, but do not be surprised if one day soon they try to make "God" a thing of the past!

WHAT EFFECT DOES IT HAVE?

Most of us today live in a society where everything I have talked about so far is a normal part of everyday life. We live in a world where we are ruled over by politicians and religious leaders, or at least we believe we are. While some people may have reached the point in their lives where they have succeeded and have their own little "Kingdom", or have been born in to those families, the vast majority of people in the world are not that "gifted". Most people are living from month to month, or week to week, or in the worst cases they are not living at all, but starving to death! The bad news is that things will only get worse as time passes.

The more you oppress or dominate a people the closer you drive them to break down. Today there is no doubt that our lives have been sped up to the point that we have little or no time for ourselves. With the stress of everyday life increasing, day by day, year by year, there has been a trend over the past fifty years for the need of more and more "social workers" to take care of the needs of those whose minds are starting to break down. The fact is that "mental illness" is a multi billion-dollar business today.

Between social workers, psychologists, psychiatrists, and the drug companies with their anti-depressants and mood stabilizers and other psychotropic drugs that they produce and "push", being "mentally ill" and in need of professional help has become big business. What about those who cannot afford the help they need? We have dumped them on the streets of the world, to live life as homeless people and literally survive off the scraps of society.

We can all agree that everyday common men and women are carrying the burden of those ruling over them. While we work everyday to eke out a living, we find that more hours are spent working, but we don't seem to be able to really get ahead in life. How many times have you able to save up a nice sum of money just to have some tragedy take place and you need that money to pay to fix the problem.

Not too long ago I was watching a news report and they were interviewing a highly respected economist on his views of world events and their affect on Americans, his comment? He feared that the end of the "Middle Class" of America had begun and in time there would be only two classes, "the haves and the haves not." A very sad state of affairs is about to be thrust upon the "Middle Class" of the world, they are about to be squeezed out of existence!

ARE WE SLAVES?

When we think about slavery, if you are an American you will most likely think of the Old South, plantation owners and the Civil War. Maybe black men and women picking cotton in a field comes to mind or maybe someone being whipped into submission for trying to escape or breaking some rule.

The fact of the matter is that while there were slave owners that were very oppressive and cruel, most slave owners took good care of their slaves, making sure that they had plenty to eat, reasonable living quarters for the time and slaves had their own families that they raised. True they were slaves and had little say in their day to day lives, but they were taken care of.

Chapter 7 ~The Domination Of Man

If we go back and investigate slavery in Biblical times we will find things were very different than what we may think. Slaves were generally well treated and their position with their owners was more like an employer and an employee relationship, with many slaves holding important positions in their master's household or business.

So in respect to a slave in Biblical times our lives today are very much the same. You may protest that we live free and we are not slaves, we can choose what we want to do, we are people of free will and do not slave for anyone! Is that right? Ok you can choose your profession and you can choose who you are going to work for, but even though you may attain a very good job within a large prestigious company, after you put in your ten to twelve hour day and return to your home and family you find that your day is not even close to being over. There is house work to be done, meals to be cooked, children to raise, grass to be cut, repairs to be made, bills to be paid and when all is said and done you are worn out, stressed beyond belief and you have little or nothing to show for it! Are we not indeed slaves to this system of things we find ourselves living in? If you are still not sure, maybe you should ask your "Slave Driver" boss what he thinks.

THE GOLDEN RULE

Two thousand years ago, Jesus Christ gave us what was to be called the "Golden Rule". He told us to "do unto others as you would have done to you." For generations, honest-hearted people did their best to live by that "Golden Rule" and really, is it not very good advice?

It is a very unfortunate thing that this simple rule is not followed today. Instead, we have almost everyone trying to take advantage of everyone else and the old "Golden Rule" is now replaced with a new "Golden Rule" which simply states, "He who has the gold makes the rules!" Is that not true?

This shift in the meaning of the "Golden Rule" most likely happened in the later 1970's. Corporate executives were setting themselves up with what are called "Golden Parachutes". A "Golden Parachute" was a guaranteed "bonus package" that was given to top executives of corporate America, so when they "bailed out" of the company they worked for, they would be given a bonus of millions of dollars in cash, stock options, or other considerations which were agreed upon in their contract. This in itself was not so bad, but we saw scandal after scandal, where these people who were supposed to be managing major corporations, were doing nothing more than using them for their own personal gain. Company after company had the retirement funds of their employees raided and looted, leaving employees devastated and almost penniless. The money that they entrusted their company with for their retirement, was now all but gone, while top executives would walk away from the company that they just basically looted as multi millionaires. Is this not man dominating man to his injury?

After hearing of case after case of these abuses, the general attitude of people changed and while the American Government did try to put an end to this type of abuse, the attitude of the populous had changed and so did the meaning of the "Golden Rule". Jesus' words of "Do unto others as you would have done to you." became "Do it to others before they can do it to you!" and with time, only a few short years, Jesus' original command became "Do it to others and split!". As we got to the end of the "Dot com" era, billions of dollars had been invested and lost in internet businesses. The "Golden Rule" became "He who has the gold makes the rules!"

That is where we find ourselves today! Everyone wants to live a good and happy life, but what we feel we need to achieve that is much different than what our parents or grandparents felt they needed to achieve a happy life. Now all the attention is on money! How much do you have? What is your net worth? How big is your house? What kind of sports car do you drive? How impressive are the "toys" you own?

The media constantly shows and tells us that our life is incomplete if we are not millionaires, have the best of everything and are living our lives in a decadent way. We are bombarded everyday by the world we live in to conform to a life style that most people cannot afford. We are told we need the newest, the biggest and the best of everything, everyday of our lives. So to "fit in" we put ourselves into debt and "charge" the things we think we need on credit cards or get bank loans. All so we can impress those around us and have the nice things we are told will make us happy! Think about it! We have become slaves to a system that does it's best to dominate and control us any way it can. Either by government, religion, banks and "lending institutions", business or the "media", this world, or this system of things, does it's best to dominate our lives and keep us under control. Now ask yourself "Why?"

WILL WE EVER BE FREE?

Domination, domination and more domination! Our lives are filled with domination! We live in a country that was founded on liberty and freedom. Really, are we a liberated and free people? No! We have been enslaved to a system that is designed to dominate over our lives in a very insidious way. I use the word "insidious" because our domination is not open and obvious as it would be if we lived in a dictatorship or a communistic government. We are told that we are a free people and can choose the life we want and to some extant that is very true. But isn't the government in our lives almost from the time we are born? We are given a number to be tracked by all our lives; we are required to have specific drugs given to us as children before we are allowed to "socialize" with other children in schools. Rules and regulations start to enter our lives as soon as we can understand them. We are put into education systems that are failing to give its students an education. Then we are "thrown" into a world that does its best to dominate our lives and make us conform to a very stressful way of life and keep us under control!

One of the "Founding Fathers" of the United States of America, Thomas Jefferson, stated that the United States should undergo a revolution once every one hundred years; if that is the case we are two revolutions behind. You would have to admit that Thomas Jefferson was right because the freedom and liberty that he lived under and enjoyed was nothing like the "freedom" we have now. It would take a revolution to correct the problems that plague not only the United States but the whole world!

What would the "Founding Fathers" think of the United States if they were alive today? They no doubt they would start another revolution! But really how far do you think they would get? Under the "Patriot Act" passed into law by the United States Congress and President, chances are they would not get very far.

Today every communication that is sent, regardless if it is a phone call, fax, or computer transmission such as an email, is monitored on a worldwide basis by super computers. When certain trip words are used in a conversation, the super computer "pays attention" to the conversation and tracks the phone numbers that are involved. If those "trip" words continue to alert the computer, the computer monitors calls and conversations from these numbers more closely. Eventually a real live human will be monitoring the conversations and, if warranted, the authorities will be alerted and governmental law enforcement officials will start a full-scale investigation.

If our "Founding Fathers" were alive today and tried to start a revolution, the same as they did over two hundred years ago, more than likely the FBI would be monitoring all their communications. They would do their best to infiltrate the group, to gather as much evidence as possible and learn all who may be involved in the plot, where the money came from to the lowest "foot solder". Then at one of their "secret meetings", a S.W.A.T. team would burst in and arrest them all under numerous charges including sedition for plotting to overthrow the government. They would be enemies of the United States and most likely end up in a special extremely high security prison for the rest of their lives. Think about it, all those names that appear on the Declaration of Independence would have arrest warrants issued for them and those associated with them and why? For wanting to live free and with liberty and without being dominated by a large bureaucratic government, is that so bad?

IS THERE SOMETHING BETTER?

Could there be a better way of doing things where people actually cared about each other and had truly free and liberated lives? Apparently there is no type of government that we have found throughout history that has been able to address the needs of mankind without "ruling" over them and dominating their lives to every extent possible.

The closest a society came to living "free" were the early Israelites or Hebrews after residing in the "Promised Land" which is largely made up of the country of Israel now. The nation of Israel only had the Ten Commandments and the "laws" handed down in the Bible book of Leviticus. So in fact the nation of Israel followed laws given to them by a "Higher Power", their God Jehovah. As history records, when they followed these "laws" they prospered as a nation of people. When they didn't follow the laws, they had problems and were suppressed by other peoples and nations around them. The biggest problem that the nation of Israel had was keeping away from worshiping the gods of the peoples around them.

Because they were the first and only monotheistic people, they were set apart from all other peoples in the known world. They were "God's" "chosen people", His "Seed" from which whom the "Messiah" or "Christ" would come through. So it would only be reasonable that the laws that were given to them by their "God" Jehovah were for their benefit and only to serve as a protection for them. Certainly if the "Savior of the World" were to come through the nation of Israel, their "God" would want to protect them as a people.

So am I saying that we should become Jewish and follow Hebrew law? No not at all. If that were the case religion would already be answering the problems that are facing us today, but that is far from the fact! Religion, as we already discussed, is part of the problem and just another “Layer of Domination” in our lives. In fact Jesus himself called the Jewish leaders of his time “serpents and offspring of vipers” and that they “were from their father the Devil”. So obviously the Jewish leaders of that time were already corrupt and not caring for the peoples needs. So what is the answer?

EXPLORING A DIFFERENT CONCEPT

The real answer that will help all of mankind is recorded for us in the Bible at Matthew chapter 22 verses 36 – 40. Jesus was asked, “Teacher, which is the greatest commandment of the Law?” He said to him: “You must love Jehovah your God with your whole heart and with your whole soul and with your whole mind.” This is the greatest commandment. The second, like it, is this, ‘You must love your neighbor as you do yourself.’ On these two commandments the whole Law hangs and the Prophets.

If Jesus really was the Son of God, don’t you think he would know what was required for us to live happy lives? Notice what Jesus said here, he said you must “love” God in a complete way, with heart, mind and soul, this was most important. Notice He did not say you must worship “God” in any way, he said you must love “God”.

It is very obvious that this “Supreme Being” who calls himself Jehovah (He who causes to become.) wants us to love him! He wants a personal relationship with all of us. That relationship should be based on love not through some bizarre religious ritual as the clergy of the world’s religions would have us believe.

It can best be expressed and understood in this way. All of us have a grandfather, maybe one or both of your grandfathers are still alive and you have gotten to know them in your lifetime.

Chances are that you know your grandparents very well and love them very much and if they have already passed away, no doubt it was not an easy time for you and the loss was felt very much because of the love you had for them!

Chapter 7 ~The Domination Of Man

Personally, I have very good memories of both my grandfathers and knew them for almost 30 years. I was very close to my father's father and I have very fond memories of him. The memories that are the most impressive to me are the ones I have of my early childhood. My grandfather would take me places, do things with me and teach me things about many different subjects. He did things that I thought were special, just for me! When I think back about it now, they were just very simple things that he did, but he knew that they would make me happy. When I needed it, I was disciplined at times, but truth is I can only recall one time that he ever needed to discipline me. My grandfather and I had a great relationship, why, because we loved each other! I had his likeness or image just the same way we are "made" in "God's" image, as we are told in Genesis. My grandfather loved me long before I loved him. For me to love him I had to grow old enough to know who he was and to understand that he cared for me and I had to start to understand the concept of love.

Well in order to bring about any change in our lives, or change the many ways we are dominated, we need to go back to the very basic truth of life and change ourselves first and build a relationship with "God". If you think about "God" in the same way you think about your grandfather, you will have a much better understanding of the kind of relationship he wants to have with us. I am not saying that you need to "Find God" and be "born again" in spirit, or become religious in any way, because religion is part of the problem not part of the solution! Remember it was the Church that burned its own people at the stake for reading the Bible. Is that showing love and acting as "God's" representatives on earth? Please do not even answer that question! The Christians who were burned at the stake had the right idea. They wanted to learn how to build a personal relationship with "God" and the "Church" and knew that if they, the general populous, knew what the Bible taught, the "Church" would lose their domination and control over them. The fact is that nothing has changed; religion does not teach what is in the Bible and they never will! Do not believe me? Read the Bible and come to learn it, then when you have a question that you do not understand, ask your priest or minister to explain it to you so you can understand it. I would be willing to bet that they cannot tell you much more than "It's a mystery" and if they can give you an accurate and true answer, ask them to teach you more!

The second part of what Jesus said was to *"Love your neighbor as you do yourself!"* Hey what a novel idea! The truth is most of us today don't even know our neighbors, our own lives are hectic enough and to get involved with others and their problems, I am sure most will just pass on that. However there are places where people have come to depend on each other and because of one reason or another have formed close community bonds. Does this mean that they have love for each other? No it doesn't, it just means that they have a close community. But usually people who know each other better start to form relationships of one sort or another and are more inclined to look out for each other's interests.

But let us take what Jesus had to say and apply it in theory. The reason I say "in theory" is because we could never accomplish this under the conditions that we have in the world today. But what if we could all apply this simple rule in our lives, think about what would happen!

Look at the area in which you live. If all the people that lived in your neighborhood were your relatives, how quick would you be to lock the door behind you when you entered your home? If your children were going to play with the children down the street, would you really worry about whom they were with when you knew they were with their cousins over at your aunt's house? If all your neighbors were relatives, how much would you need to worry about some stranger coming to your neighborhood and breaking, entering and robbing your home? You most likely would not give it a lot of thought, because Grandma down the street doesn't miss a thing that passes her house.

While this sounds all very idyllic, what if we really could accomplish this? Think about if this scenario was expanded throughout the earth? What if everyone viewed everyone else as mothers, fathers, sisters, brothers, grandparents, aunts, uncles and cousins and we did this on a worldwide basis? What effect would it have? Let's think about it for a minute. Most likely crime would almost disappear; hence the need for police forces would be almost nonexistent. Think about it, you really would not want to hurt your family, so would we need armies? No, most likely they would be a thing of the past! We really would not want to see any of our relatives be killed now would we? Because we were all family, how much government would we need? Most likely none, we would live by "family rules" and if there was some kind of dispute, no doubt a family head would deal with it quickly so you most likely would not need a court or judicial system. Think about that a world without lawyers!

If you had a business or worked for a business, guess what, it is a "family business" so everyone works together and employee theft would not exist, nor would exploitation of employees. As for religion, chances are that you would only have one way of worship and most likely, you would have a much closer personal relationship with the "Higher Power" we call "God".

The most amazing thing about this scenario is the financial benefit that would occur! Considering that the militaries of the world spend about $25,000 US dollars for every man, woman and child on the face of the earth every year, just eliminating the world's armies would save us trillions of dollars. Eliminating the need for law enforcement and prisons, reducing the size of government drastically, would also save trillions of dollars worldwide.

In short, the population of the earth would be very happy and be able to live in relative peace for the first time ever! Social programs would ensure sicknesses and food shortages were dealt with quickly and in places where natural disasters occurred, you could be sure that there would plenty of family to help those effected, to console them and help get things back to normal.

Best of all the massive domination that we are all under by this system of things would be gone! We would no longer be oppressed by the world around us; instead we would be supported and loved by our worldwide family.

WHAT IS THE FUTURE OF THIS SYSTEM OF DOMINATION?

A worldwide family would be an unbelievable thing to have. But really are we all not human? Do we all not share the same DNA, the same genetic code? If you were lost in the jungle for several days, maybe even several weeks, how happy would you be to see another human? No doubt you would be very grateful that someone found you. You may be eternally grateful and have found a life long friend in the person that found you, even though your life style, background or race may be totally different. What really is the difference though? The fact is that one human helped another, much the same as one brother will help another.

Maybe at one time someone whom you did not know helped you, or maybe you helped someone in need that you did not know. Regardless, no doubt you felt good after the experience and maybe you even made a new friend in the process.

So why can't we experience the kind of peace and security we have in a family with all humankind? Are we not all the same, human? Are we not all part of the "Human Family"? Then what is the problem? Why do we not trust each other? Why are we ready to go to war with our brothers in other countries and why do we kill in the name of peace?

If "God" wanted man to live as a family and live in a peaceful world, what happened? Where did all the domination and control come from? Yes it would have to be from an adversary of "God" and who is that adversary? Lucifer, Satin, or yes the Devil.

The apostle John confirms this when he wrote at 1 John chapter 5 verse 19, *"We know we originate with God, but the whole world is lying in the power of the wicked one."* If Satan had control of the whole world in John's day, how much more control does he have today?

Any intelligent person can see that the world's systems are on the verge of collapse and it would not take much to make that happen. Every place you look today there is a major problem from financial instability, to government unrest and over taxation, social systems breaking down, food shortages, energy shortages, sickness and disease rampant in some underdeveloped countries, and terrorism and war spreading across the planet. Then there are the environmental issues. Pollution of the air, water, and soil by both businesses and individuals which leads to global warming, global warming leads to glacier melt down, glacier melt down leads to ocean levels rising and considering that eighty percent of the world's population lives ninety miles from the coast, they are all in harms way and eventually will lose their homes.

There is no doubt that the world system is on the verge of collapse both socially and environmentally and it will not last! There is a general consciousness that we are going to be facing major problems in the near future. The word "Armageddon", "God's" war, is on the minds of people today. We are told of the prophecies of Nostradamus, which contain disaster for our very near future. The Mayan calendar ends on December 21st 2012, which marks the end of a system and is believed that disaster will strike the earth. Wherever we look there is nothing but doom on the horizon.

In fact the domination we find ourselves under will soonend! There is only one way to clean up this satanic system we live under and that is to do away with it and destroy it, along with all those who support the propagation of this wicked system we are forced to submit to.

Make no mistake, our domination will not last! There are still major events, which must take place before the War of Armageddon will come upon us. In the coming chapters we will examine more closely those who are controlling world events and what they want to do to even control us to a greater extent. We will also learn what world events need to happen before "God's" prophetic War of Armageddon befalls the earth. Get ready; it will be upon us very shortly!

CHAPTER 8
RELIGION ITS START

You might think that religion had its start with the story of Adam and Eve and the Serpent in the "Garden of Eden" and in a way, you might be right, because that was when "God's" authority and right to rule over all intelligent life forms began.

It may be difficult to think that we humans are literally caught up in a dispute between far advanced life forms that we know very little about. What may be even more difficult to believe, is that in fact, humans are at the center of this dispute. Why you may ask? The right to rule over what was to become the most prolific intelligent life form ever created.

Lucifer no doubt was very involved with the development of life on earth and knew "God's" purpose for creating mankind. As we discussed earlier, the issue most likely had to do with love and if Lucifer could pass himself off as the god and creator of all things he could very well receive that love and devotion that would have gone to "God" Jehovah. He knew he could not convince the first few generations of humans, because of the relationship that they did have with "God" Jehovah, or what was left of it.

Even when Satan enticed the angels to leave their position in the world they lived in and cohabitate with earthly women, the Bible refers to these angels as "Sons of the True God". The women of that day knew whom these creatures were and I am sure that they felt very special to be chosen by one of the "Sons of the True God" and bear their offspring. There really was no doubt at that time that the "True God" was Jehovah. It would take a global flood and a few more generations of people to forget that Jehovah was the creator of mankind. It would also take the domination of man to turn their hearts against the "True God" and take up worshipping the sun, moon, stars and natural forces on earth. They also worshiped nature and animals; really anything that could distract men from worshiping "True God" was invented and worshipped.

WHO STARTED RELIGION AND WHY?

Nimrod, the first king of the earth was mostly responsible for the propagation of false religion, or paganism. The Bible records that "Nimrod was in opposition to Jehovah". God wanted man to spread across the surface of the earth and to fill it with more people, Nimrod wanted to capture men and put them to work building cities to keep people together. He well knew that domination of other men would be a lot easier if he could keep them together and that was what he wanted, to dominate others and rule their lives for his personal benefit.

The domination of man by Nimrod did not stop with him being king and ruler over his people; he also set himself up as a god. He was the first earthly "god-king" and the god that he chose to be was the "god of the sun", and so starts sun worship. Sun worship is the largest and most prolific religion in the world and has been throughout history.

As it works out, Nimrod is credited with the start of paganism, but more than likely he was more interested in hunting and conquering new peoples to bring under the domination of his rule. However, it is more Nimrod's wife Semiramis who seems to want to dominate the people with religious practices that are contrary to what the "True God" had instructed. She obviously enjoyed the idea of being a "goddess" next to her husband, a "god" among his people.

WHY ARE THERE SO MANY DIFFERENT RELIGIONS, CAN THEY ALL BE RIGHT?

How Semiramis actually became Nimrod's wife is unclear, but what is clear is her cunning and ambition. She started as a common woman, possibly even a prostitute. Some accounts say she was very beautiful and had blond hair and blue eyes. Whatever she looked like Nimrod must have been very taken with her, because she ascended to a god-like position over her husband's subjects. While Nimrod made the claim that he was "God of the sun", his wife, Semiramis, became "Goddess of the Earth". Ever wonder where the expression "Mother Earth" came from? It can be attributed directly to Semiramis! As a matter of fact her name has changed many times throughout history and she is still with us today. Where, you might ask? She stands at the entrance to New York City and today she is called the Statue of Liberty and holds the torch of enlightenment. The statue was originally intended to stand at the entrance to the Suez Canal, but it was rejected, so the statue was slightly modified and presented to America as the "Statue of Liberty". We will talk more about the subject of the "Statue of Liberty" in a later chapter dealing with Free Masons.

There is no doubt that Semiramis was strongly opposed to the "True God" Jehovah, just as her husband was, and both of them were key agents of the fallen angel Lucifer. After all it was truly Lucifer who was setting himself up as ruler and god over all mankind. All types of worship were encouraged and statues and shrines were built throughout the cities to induce the people to serve other gods. The biggest "obstacle" to "God" came when Nimrod started the project of building the "Tower of Babel".

The "Tower of Babel" was to serve a few different purposes. First was to keep the people of the then known world together and serve as a capital for a "One World Government". It was the intention to rule all the inhabitants of the world from one central location with Nimrod and Semiramis as king and queen, god and goddess. Both of them together were the physical representation of Lucifer. Together they carried out his will of domination upon the earth both politically and spiritually all in opposition to the true ruler of mankind, Jehovah God. Jehovah God intended for man to live free from domination. One of the main purposes that the "Tower" was to serve was as a refuge for the "ruling class" in case "God" should bring another global flood. The "Tower" was to have its "top in the heavens" and to be unreachable for a flood to cover. It was said that the tower was built to be to such a height that it would take all day for one worker to carry his bricks to the top and come back down.

With a building project this large, it is no wonder that it caught '"God's" attention and the Biblical account is recorded for us in Genesis 11: 7 & 8 which reads; *"Come now! Let us go down and there confuse their language that they may not listen to one and other's language."* Accordingly Jehovah scattered them from there over all the surface of the earth, and they gradually left off building the city. Notice the account says that they *"gradually left off building the city"*. The building work still went on for some time after the languages were confused; the use of sign language was employed for awhile, but the workforce needed was so large and it was only the work force that knew the sign language. Society started to fragment and people started to go their different ways throughout the earth, taking the religions and gods that they worshiped in Babylon along with them. That is why there are so many different types of religions throughout the world and why some cultures have so many gods. It also explains why sun worship is so widely spread throughout history and the world.

THE FIRST MADONNA

Semiramis is really the one whom we can thank for most of the religions on the earth today. She did her best to raise herself above all others on the face of the earth and while her husband's legacy has crumbled with the sands of time, Semiramis' legacy is still with us today, but not for long! Semiramis was not happy with being "Mother Earth". She also wanted a position in heaven and so she made herself "Mother of Heaven" and "Mother of God". This is how she went about doing it.

The accounts differ about how Nimrod actually died but one thing is clear, Semiramis was instrumental in causing his death! The most interesting account revolves around the "New Year" celebration of the returning of the sun. It was the custom for the upper echelon of Nimrod's empire and the high priests of the various religious orders, to gather at what was little more than a drunken orgy where they would rip apart a live lamb that had been raised all year for the occasion and eat it raw. It is said that at his last New Year celebration, while under the influence of wine and hallucinogens, Semiramis educed the attendees to substitute Nimrod for the "sacrificial lamb" and they did, ripping him apart piece by piece while he was still alive!

Shortly after Nimrod's death, Semiramis became pregnant. She was said to have a huge sexual appetite, so there is no telling who the child's father really was, but Semiramis claimed that the child was Nimrod "God of the Sun" returning from heaven and her pregnancy was a miracle, an "immaculate conception". She named the baby Tammuz and made him a god too. So now Semiramis was "Mother Earth", the "Mother of Heaven" and now the "Mother of God", the first" Madonna". She became in herself the first "trinity", but there was also the trinity of Nimrod, Semiramis and Tammuz. Modern day "Christianity" teaches the same thing as what was taught during the time of the building of the "Tower of Babel". In fact, I am sure that if you traced the origins of most of the religions of the world, they have their roots in Babylon.

The last thing that was built on the top of the "Tower of Babel" was a temple for Semiramis. She obviously controlled and dominated everything in her world especially the masons who were in charge of her building projects, including the "Tower of Babel" and they venerated her to their best ability. Semiramis has had many name changes throughout the millennia by the different peoples who worshiped her and still do. She has not gone away but is still very much in our lives today, regardless if she is referred to as "Mother Earth", the "Statue of Liberty" or the "Madonna" giving birth to "God" by means of a miracle, she is in our lives!

The interesting thing is the intention of Lucifer, or Satan the Devil, has not changed from the very beginning. He wants earth to be under a despotic "One World Government". He tried to do that with Nimrod and Semiramis five thousand years ago and he is doing it today with the United Nations! All the religions of Babylon are still with us today only they have different names. When you examine the evidence of who is controlling the world today, it is a very small group of men known as the "Illuminati", who control and direct the actions of the "Free Masons" and control government and business. Soon they will tire of the involvement of religion in their affairs and the governments of the world will turn on all religion and destroy it. We will learn more about this in a later chapter.

WHY DO WE NEED RELIGION?

After considering the origins of most of the world's religions, you may indeed ask, "Why do we need religion anyway if it is only another layer of domination upon us? While there is no doubt that religion has done it's best to dominate the lives of mankind from the very beginning, it does serve a purpose. "Religion" has tried to be a "pathway" to a "higher power". It has tried to connect us to a spiritual world that is far beyond our comprehension. Unfortunately, in most cases, the "higher power" that it has been connecting us to is not Jehovah "God" but his adversary, Lucifer or Satan!

Not all religion is, or has part in paganism; however most do in some shape, form, or fashion. Does this make them bad? No not in themselves, but you have to remember the issue at hand, does "God" have the right to rule over intelligent life forms? Eventually we will all be on one side of the issue of "rightful ruler ship" or the other, but now it would be a good idea to examine what you believe.

Many religious people today do their best to follow the dogma of the church that they attend. They are looking for a relationship of some kind with "God" and some people will tell you that "God" is in their hearts all the time and who are we to question that? The truth is that "God" does want to have a personal relationship with us and I am sure that it brings joy to His heart whenever someone is looking to have that personal relationship with him! What we need to be careful of is that we are doing things to help develop that relationship with the "right god"!

While Jesus was on the earth, He did his best to teach

people how to have that personal relationship with "God". He saw the people of that time as sheep without a shepherd. He healed their wounds and sicknesses, he fed them and he ministered to their spiritual needs. He gave guidelines for us to follow and live by which were based in love, not domination!

There is no doubt that many people throughout the ages have done their best to follow Jesus' example and have shown love and concern for their fellow man. Some have taken it upon themselves to become full time servants of "God" or missionaries to try to help and their fellow man and teach them how it is possible to have a personal relationship with "God". Do not most of us today look for a relationship of some kind with a "Higher Power"?

So we can see that we have a need to seek out a "Higher Power" in our lives. The problem is that there are many "higher powers" and we have to be careful that we do not seek out the wrong ones by mistake, because they will dominate our lives in a very unhealthy way! They will not lead us to the "True God", but will lead us faraway and put us in opposition of "God".

RELIGION'S ROLE IN HISTORY... HAS IT HELPED OR HURT?

When you examine the history of religion, you really have to ask, has religion helped or hurt mankind? There is a long history of religion's involvement with politics, but why should we be surprised about that? It was that way right from the very beginning! Semiramis' religion dominated Nimrod and his government and nothing has changed today. Religion is still doing it's best to dominate government.

You might ask yourself, if religion is here to help "connect" mankind to a "Higher Power" should not the clergy class be doing their job and not be involved in politics but be representing "God" and "ministering" to "The Flock"?

If we take the early Catholic Church, did the Church not rule over what was known as the "Holy Roman Empire"? Yes all monarchs throughout early Europe ruled by the grace of the Church and these monarchs supported the Church in a very handsome way! It was not until King Henry the VIII that the Church started to lose its grip on the monarchy of Europe. However it was the monk Martin Luther who is credited with the turning point of the "Reformation" of the "Church" and its loss of grip on the general populous when he nailed his ninety five theses to the door of the castle church at Wittenberg, Germany, on October 31st 1517. While the basic complaint of Luther was the selling of "indulgences" which were basically a "get out of hell pass", he said only "God" can forgive sins, not the "Clergy" or the "Church". With time and the teachings of other influential religious leaders, Christendom became fractionated to the point that is today. But have any of these "off shoots" of Christendom abandoned the false teachings that infiltrated Christianity over the ages? No, the same pagan traditions are held as "holy" and taught to people as they are fact and from "God", but they don't tell you the god is Lucifer! Don't take offense, do the research into the traditions of your religion, the "holy" things that are taught, find out their origin, see if they have their roots in the Bible or in pagendom!

IS RELIGION WORTH THE COST?

Religion has dominated politics for its own gain right from the very start and it is still deeply involved with the governing of mankind. Have you ever wondered why religious leaders of the world keep meeting with world rulers? It is to try to expand the teachings of Jesus? Or is it to have an influence in world affairs and to secure their position of dominance over the governments and their subjects?

Ask yourself how many wars have been waged over religion, or spurred on by religion. The most infamous are the "Holy Wars", 200 years of warfare to capture and control the "Holy Land", the birthplace of Jesus!

The Church commissioned the Knights Templars to travel to the Middle East and capture Judea. The Middle East was then and still is occupied by people who are Muslims and Jews. They lived together in relative peace at the time, but when the Knights Templars came war broke out in a very vicious way! When Jerusalem was captured, the Templars put to the sword every man woman and child and killed them all in the name of "God"!

It was over 200 years before the Templars were driven out of the Middle East, but during that time, both the Church and the Templars made out like bandits and accumulated vast amounts of wealth. In fact the Knights Templars grew to such power that they rivaled the Church itself. They became the richest political power in Europe at the time and the largest landholder right up to the point that the Church outlawed and disbanded the Knights Templars, took their land holdings and whatever wealth they could find. The Catholic Church now was the biggest landholder in Europe and even though they lost their grip on the Middle East, they tightened the grip they had over their subjects in Europe and ushered in the "Dark Ages".

There is no way of knowing how many innocent people were killed during the "Holy Wars" and in the name of God. We know that the Knights Templars were defeated and driven out of the Middle East or were exterminated. The Church, to whom the Templars served, accused them of "blaspheme against God" and tortured and/or killed all they could find. But evidently many Templars escaped and went into hiding taking much of their wealth with them.

The later part of the 16th century found religious wars in France between Christians. Catholics were warring against Protestants. There were numerous battles between both factions for over 30 years, with about three million deaths as the result. Whatever happened to the lessons that Jesus taught to "Love God and Love your neighbor?" Are not Christians to teach to promote peace and love? How could God who is "Love" even be involved in such bloodletting?

If we look at the twentieth century we can see that things haven't really changed much. Fighting between religions has not stopped but instead increased! Religion was a major influence in both world wars, but the Catholic Church rode Nazi Germany like it was a horse and with great anticipation that the "Third Reich" would provide a thousand year reign in it's domination of the world. Why do you think that the "Church" turned its head as Adolph Hitler proceeded to exterminate six million Jews? There were "pacts" between the "Third Reich" and the Catholic Church. The Pope and his "emissaries" were doing their best to secure the "Church's" position with Nazis should they win the war. If the Nazis did win World War Two, they would have rolled out their brand of government to the world and Catholicism would have been the "official state religion"! In fact the "Infamous Swastika" Adolph Hitler used on the Nazi flag came from the Catholic Church he attended as a boy.

The truth is, the "Swastika" has a history that is thousands of years old and it is used in sun worship as the symbol of the Hindu sun god "Surya"! You might want to ask yourself, "Why does a "Christian" religion use a pagan symbol of the sun as an ornament?" The fact is almost all of the "holy" symbols and icons of the "Church" all have their origin in the ancient world of pagan idolatry! It is time to examine what you believe!

World War II ended in 1945. As Allied forces vanquished Germany's army, the horrors of what was going to be known as the "Holocaust" were soon uncovered! If Jehovah God is a god of love, he must have been crying as this atrocity was going on! The surviving population of Germany could not believe what horrors were heaped upon the Jewish people, nor could the rest of the world! That is why the newly formed United Nations gave the Jewish people world wide a homeland in what is now Israel.

An apology did not come from the Catholic Church until March 12th 2000, fifty-five years after the fact, when Pope John Paul the Second made a very broad apology for the sins of the "Church" throughout the ages, including sins against the Jews. No mention was ever made about the Holocaust! The Church's "I'm sorry for our sins", I guess covers everything from the Crusades, The Inquisition, through the Holocaust. Many Jewish leaders thought that this apology was weak at best! They felt that the Pope had an opportunity to set the record straight and give a heartfelt apology about the "Church's" knowledge of the Holocaust and he missed it!

It is an unfortunate thing that giving the Jews a "homeland" started a whole new era of religious wars that still plague us today! There has been no peace in the Middle East since Israel became a country. At first it was just the Muslims against the Jews and contained to the Middle East. However as the Twentieth Century ended and the Twenty First Century started, the world came to realize it was involved in a "Jihad", a Muslim "Holy War", and no country would understand that better than The United States of America, when on 9-11-2001 the World Trade Center in New York City was destroyed by Muslim extremists! What was President George H. W. Bush's reply about the Muslim attack on the United States? He said that we were in a "Crusade" against these extremists! Interesting, another unholy "Holy War" and this time it was on a global scale! The years to come would bring war to the Middle East like it has never been there before!

So ask yourself. If we could remove religion from the world, would the world be a more peaceful place in which to live? If religion would just stay out of politics and looked after the "flock" as they were instructed to, would that make the world a more peaceful place? If the Churches of Christendom taught what Jesus told us were the two greatest commandments to "Love God" and to "Love thy neighbor", would that help bring peace to the world? When you look at the pain, suffering, and death caused by religion, either directly or indirectly, you really must ask yourself honestly, is it really worth it all?

WHAT DOES GOD THINK ABOUT RELIGION AND ITS ACTIONS?

If God is our "Heavenly Father" and we are told that his main attribute is love then how do you think he feels when he sees men killing other men? We have all had members of our family die, how did we feel? Didn't our hearts ache, didn't we feel sorrow and loss? Why would it not be the same for the life form that "created" us in his "image"?

The early Christians were warned about the danger they faced ahead. In the book of Acts of Apostles in Chapter 20 verses 29 & 30 read, "I know that after my going away oppressive wolves will enter in among you and will not treat the flock with tenderness, and from among you yourselves men will rise and speak twisted things to draw the disciples after themselves."

How oppressive and twisted do you have to be to offer "God's people" as a sacrifice to the "god of war"? Would you burn your child alive to some false pagan god? No you would not! That "life form" is a part of you! Yet how many children were burned to death in Europe and Japan as the warring nations poured explosives and incendiaries all over each other! World War Two cost over fifty five million lives sacrificed to the "god of war" with the blessing of the clergy on both sides! The families of fifty five million people had been cut to the heart, the sorrow, the tears, the pain and anguish, the loss of a loved one that they believed would never be seen again! If the families of those lost loved ones were filled with grief, pain and tears, do you not think that this also hurt Jehovah God as he watched people destroy each other and ruin the earth in the process? It had to hurt him, how could it not?

THE MOST WORSHIPED GOD

We learned earlier that Nimrod was not only the ruler of the world in his day but he also became a god to his people, the first "God of the Sun". We learned that his wife Semiramis first set herself up as "mother earth" and also became "goddess of both heaven and moon" after the death of her husband Nimrod. She claimed that her pregnancy was an "immaculate conception", that it was Nimrod returning from his place in the heavens and with the birth of her son, Tammuz (Nimrod incarnate), Semiramis now became "the mother of god", the first Madonna, three thousand years before the birth of Jesus the "Christ" or "Messiah".

This main theme of a "sun god", a "fertility goddess" and a

reincarnate "child god" became the central teaching of almost every religion from the days of the "Tower of Babel" down to our day today!

Where the teaching of this idea of sun god, fertility goddess and their child, is first understood lies with the first world power, Egypt. Re, or Ra, was the "midday sun god" and was represented by a "solar disc". It is interesting that the Catholic Church represents the "body of god" with a disc called "the host"; coincidence? I don't think so! Ra became better known as Horus, whose mother was Isis. Again we have a "goddess" giving birth to the "god of the sun"

The teachings and religions of ancient Egypt are still with us today! The same central beliefs, symbols and deities are worshiped today by the world's most popular religions. The really sad thing is that the devoted masses of these religions have no idea that they are involved with pagan sun worship and idolatry! Sun worship is really worldwide and has very deep roots in history, right back to the very start of civilization. We already learned about Ra or Horus of Egypt and here are some of the other names given to the "God or Goddess of the Sun". Amaterasu, son goddess of Japan, Apollo Greek and Roman sun god, Frver and Sol Norse sun gods, Surva the Hindu sun god, Utu Mesopotamian sun god, Tonatiuh Aztec son god, Inti Inca sun god, Lugh Celtic sun god, Liza West African sun god are just a few of the different names that are given to the same personage, the first one who set himself as the "god of the sun".

SUN WORSHIP TODAY

Most likely you are thinking, "Who worships the sun today?" Certainly they must be a most primitive and pagan people, where would you even look for them? Maybe you would find them in third world countries or in the deepest jungles of the world? Yes, you may find them there, but you really don't have to look that far! Chances are that you, or someone in your family, are religiously worshipping the sun! What do I mean?

While there are people who outright worship the sun, they are happy doing so. They carry out the traditions of their family, of their people and they are content doing this generation after generation. However, that is not the case with most people. In fact the world's two largest religions tell their parishioners that they are the path to the "Most High God" and then they perpetrate a horrible lie upon these poor people.

Fact is if you are either a member of Christendom or a member of Islam, you are a pagan sun worshiper! What is worse you do not even know it! You have been lied to by those who are suppose to know better! The people who have been your "Spiritual Leaders", those who have been your pathway to a "Higher Power" have lied to you! Yes they have lied to us all! When they tell us that they are god's representatives here on earth, or that they are divinely appointed and are blessed by god to rule over us, they are not telling us that god is Lucifer, the "Light Bearer"! The same person called Devil and Deceiver in the Bible is still doing his best to deceive mankind today just the same as he has been doing from the beginning with our first parents, Adam and Eve. Oh yes just another Bible story right?

Let's look at the facts! First, if you have been lied to by the very people who are "leading you to God", you can't ask them anything and expect an honest or correct answer! So what do you need to do? Start doing some investigative work on your own. Look around in your "place of worship" and what do you see? Are there statues and icons of religious personalities? If so ask yourself, "What does "God" have to say?

If you read the Bible book of Exodus chapter 20 you will be reading the Ten Commandments. These are the most important laws given to man by "God"! These are the "BIG TEN" and you really don't want to break these laws because you would be "flying in the face of God", going directly against what he told us he wants us to do, pure disobedience! Let's see what the first two commandments have to say. Exodus 20: verse 3 "You must not have any other gods against my face." Verse 4 "You must not make for yourself a carved image..." "God" is being very direct here he said, "You must not..." so there is no mistake!

After reading what "God" tells us about worshiping other gods and making idols or religious statues, if you look around in your place of worship do you indeed see these things there? Do people not venerate and pray to these religious statues? Are they not breaking this commandment of "God"? Yes they are breaking "God's" commandments, but who tells us that having religious statues and praying to them is ok and it is what "God" wants us to do? Is it not the religious leaders themselves? Do they not read the Bible? Do they not know what "God" wants and does not want? Obviously they don't have any idea what Jehovah God wants or they would not be telling their followers to sin against God!

This is only one area of your investigation. You must look at the things that are used in worship, what do they represent? What was their first use in history, what is their origin? If religious leaders do not represent "God" and indeed are making us sin against "God", then whom do they really represent? You would do well to find the answer to this question!

The three major religions of the world are all interlinked. Judaism, Christianity and Islam all have the same roots. They all believe in one "Supreme God" and in fact it is the same "God" they all believe in. They each have its' own icon or symbol that they are known by. If I showed you the "Star of David", two intersecting blue triangles, you would think of the Nation of Israel and the Jewish people. If I showed you a "Cross", you would think of "Christians" and if the "Cross" had an emaciated dead man nailed to it, you might think Catholic. If I showed you a "Crescent Moon with a Star", no doubt you would think of Islam. What do all of these "signs", these "icons" have in common?

Beside the fact these icons or symbols represent three of the world's largest religions, they are also fertility icons used in ancient pagan Egyptian religion! Why would religions that claim to all represent the "True God" be using sex symbols as identifying signs to represent their brand or style of religion? Which god are they really representing? If the symbols they are using have their origins in pagan religion, how could they be representing the one

"True God"? Maybe they should read the counsel in the Bible at 2 Corinthians chapter 6 verse 14 which reads "...For what fellowship do righteousness and lawlessness have...?" Good question, why do those who claim to be from the "True God" use pagan Egyptian sex symbols to represent him?

What was the chief god of the Egyptians? Was it not the "god of the sun" Re, or Ra? Yes it was. The Egyptians were sun worshipers and it is obvious that the hierarchies of the world's three main religions are sun worshipers too! So what does that make them? Worshipers of none other than Lucifer himself, Satan the "slanderer", the Devil and "deceiver"! They are not worshiping the god they are telling you they are, they are worshiping his enemy! What is worse is that they know it but they, like their father, the "Devil", are deceivers! They have deceived all of their flock and tricked them into worshiping the Devil!

Here is what those icons or symbols truly represent. The intersecting blue triangles of the Nation of Israel symbolized sexual intercourse, not just in Egypt's pagan worship but in other religions too. Intersecting squares are also used to symbolize sexual intercourse. We find these used as decorations in both Churches and Mosques. The Cross is nothing more than an erect male phallus that was used in many cultures as a fertility symbol. The Egyptians had several different styles of crosses, but the one most associated with the ancient Egyptian cultures was the ankh cross and it is both the male and female in sexual union. Islam has just a crescent moon and a star. What is sexual about that? The Headdress of Hathor is a headdress of two cow horns with the sun disc in the middle. Some of Hathor's titles are 'Mistress of Heaven', 'Eye of Re' (the sun god), 'Goddess of Love', 'Motherhood', 'Beer', 'House of Horus', and 'Royal Goddess'. Her headdress symbolized the "sun in the womb" and she is credited with the birth of the sun Re' or Horus. It is said that Isis wore many different headdresses also and therefore took on the different aspects of the gods of those headdresses. So Isis became many different gods, representing the sun, the moon and fertility. Our Islamic friends have a symbol which depicts Isis, the moon goddess, giving birth to Re, or Horus, or as we know him better, Lucifer. Do not be surprised by this my Islamic friends, was not Mohamed's wife Roman Catholic and very rich and powerful? How could you not escape the lies of the Church of Lucifer?

We are going to find these same symbols in the Catholic Church and they are made known during every time communion is given! Look closely at a monstrance, the holder of the "host" or "body of the "Christ". The actual part where the "host" is placed is called the "Luna" and it is shaped like a crescent moon. The monstrance itself looks like the sun with gold rays emanating out all around.

Now follow what is going on here, you have the golden monstrance in the image of the sun, centered in the monstrance is a crescent moon which holds the body of "Christ" the god. What we have here is Nimrod, the first sun god, Semiramis, goddess of the moon, and her sun god child, Nimrod incarnate, Tammuz! So who's body are you getting in the "host"? Jesus? No it is the body of Tammuz. Every time you take communion, your priest should tell you "Eat up sun worshiper, you are making Lucifer a happy god!" This may sound harsh, but at least they would be telling you the truth!

The nation of Israel is a little harder to understand with it's icon of sexual intercourse. You have to go a bit deeper into the secret teachings of the Kabala to see where the worship of Lucifer takes place, but Jesus understood who was controlling the rulers of Israel when he was on the earth. He told the Jewish religious leaders of his day in the Bible book of John in the 8th chapter verse 44 He said, "You are from your father the Devil, and you wish to do the desires of your father..." The symbol of the star is being used as a symbol of Satan himself! Did not Christianity spring from Judaism, and did not Islam spring from Christianity? So should it be a surprise that the same symbols are passed from the "parent" religion to the new offspring religion, especially when there is a direct connection between them?

We were warned about this almost two thousand years ago in the Bible, in 2 Corinthians chapter 11 verse 14 reads, "And no wonder, for Satan himself keeps transforming himself in to an angel of light." The 15th verse reads, "It is therefore nothing great if his ministers also keep transforming themselves into ministers of rightness. But their end shall be according to their works."

It is obvious that "God" knew that this was going to happen and He had the above information recorded for us today. It should be no surprise to anyone that the religions of the world have been corrupted and even the ones that claim to be true are nothing but dens of liars!

The days of religion are numbered! Soon will come a time when the nations of the world will say enough! We have had enough of the wars, murders and lies cast upon us by religion! Impossible you say? No the fate of all religion has already been sealed as it was foretold almost two thousand years ago in the Bible book of Revelation in Chapters 17 and 18. You will learn that the Kings of the earth turn on a great city called Babylon the Great, the Kings destroy her, eat her fleshy parts and burn the remains with fire. Do you think this is impossible? What happened to religion in the former Soviet Union or in any communist country left today? It was all but eradicated with many religious people "purged" from the Soviet society and put to death or sent to concentration camps. Remember, Joseph Stalin was credited with the deaths of more than fifty million people as he "cleaned" the dissidents out of the Soviet Union!

THE AGE OF ENLIGHTENMENT

During the eighteenth century, religion started to lose its grip on society and education was taking its place. Men like Isaac Newton, Voltaire, and Thomas Jefferson were no longer bound to the Bible or the standard accepted doctrine of the Church for answers. Remember it was the Church who up held the belief that the sun revolved the earth and it was Nicholas Copernicus, who by observation and mathematics, discovered that the earth revolved around the sun. When he made his findings known it set the Church in an uproar, and for fear of being excommunicated he recanted his findings and said he was wrong. However, after dying a good Catholic and no longer facing excommunication by the Church, his work was published proving once and for all that the earth did revolve around the sun!

Many followed in Nicholas Copernicus' path and looked to science instead of the Church for the true answers. It was becoming more obvious that the days of the Church burning people at the stake for reading the Bible and the dark ages were over!

The Renaissance in Europe ushered in an age of learning and education. Great minds were questioning the doctrine and superstition of the Church and were studying nature and the world around us using observation and "scientific process". New things were being learned and new things discovered. Volumes of information were being recorded and then taught to the next generation. Places of higher learning, universities were being established and learned men, scientists of the day were leading the way! A new way of thinking was taking hold, an enlightened way, different then what was being taught by the Church or religion in general and so the "Age of Enlightenment" was underway!

THE NEW CLERGY

While it was obvious that the Church was losing its grip during "The Renaissance", the Catholic Church itself started to fractionate into many different sects, but beyond that as the "Age of Enlightenment" took hold it's followers grew into what was to become a new religion of sorts. Most learned men of this new "Age of Enlightenment" became "Deist". A "Deist" believes in "God" or a "Supreme Being", but they do not believe in miracles. They believe that everything has a scientific answer or explanation. In fact Thomas Jefferson had a Bible that he literally cut all the passages out of that had anything to do with "miracles". This Bible can still be seen today at Thomas Jefferson's home, Monticello, in Charlottesville, Virginia.

Yes, a new "clergy" was being formed; it was being made

up of the best minds of the most learned men. In fact many of the "Founding Fathers" of the United States were "Deist" and served as a "clergy" class to further their personal beliefs and ideals. If you doubt this, you have to look no further than the Constitution of the United States of America and the Bill of Rights. These are very important documents because The United States of America was the first country not to be ruled by a monarch, but by "elected officials" qualified to lead or represent their fellow citizens. It would be made up of three "branches" to balance the power of the new government. This "triad" would be made up of the Executive, Legislative and Judicial branches.

The ideas for the United States Government came out of the European "Age of Enlightenment". Learned men were busy questioning everything that was put in place. The old standards were out dated, the Church had no place in science and Monarchies who ruled by the grace of "God" were oppressive and decedent. So everything in the society of that day seemed to have a need to be replaced, or at least overhauled. Very influential people were discussing many new ideas. Corruption was rampant everywhere, so it was easy to see the need to replace the old order with a "New World Order", one that would replace the corrupt powers that were in charge at that time.

Out of the Age of Enlightenment, came the idea for the "Illuminati" or the "Illuminated Ones", the "Enlightened Ones". Another very powerful group, a name that keeps coming up over and over again, the Free Masons, instantly embraced the ideas that were presented by the Illuminati. We will explore this link a bit further in another chapter, but Adam Weishaupt is credited as being the farther of the Illuminati. He saw five major things that needed to be changed for his idea to bring a peace to the world to take place. The catch phrase of the Illuminati and their purpose is to bring a "New World Order", which in Latin would be Novus Ordo Seclorum, or New Order of the Ages. We find this on the back of the United States one-dollar bill, under the pyramid and it is part of the "Great Seal of the United States". So is the United States of America really the idea of European "secrete society"? Regardless of what the official answer is we would have to say yes! Remember to look at the symbols that are being used as a way of identification! When you see the same symbols, regardless of what you are being told, they are an identifying mark. If you saw an upside down star with a goat's head in the middle of it, what would you think? Devil worship was involved, right? So when you see the same symbols being used by different organizations would you not believe that they are related or even one and the same? If you saw Swastikas on different buildings around the world, would you not think, Nazi, Hitler? Yes you would! That symbol has been burned into our minds as ultimate evil! Regardless where you were in the world, if you saw a Swastika, you would have the same thought, why is that so? It is because symbols mean things to the people that use them first and then are recognized by others. If you see a "red cross" would you not think medical emergency or a place where you could get medical help? Sure you would! So we need to look at the symbols different organizations are using and learn what those symbols, icons or statues and monuments really mean.

NEW AGE RELIGION, OLD AGE RELIGION REBORN?

What the "Age of Enlightenment" was to religion, "New Age Religion" is to the "Age of Enlightenment". What I mean by that statement is the teaching of the "Church" was being questioned by scientific process; in fact religion, the Bible and the existence of a "Higher Power" are all brought into question! Science has questioned "God" right out of existence; we are told that we evolved from lower life forms, so really there is no need for a god to even exist. "New Age Religion" now starts to call into question the teachings of "Science", pointing to the metaphysical world and the things Science cannot explain. "God" is not in heaven, "God" is everywhere and in everything!

New Age Religion" breaks away from the teachings of "main stream" religions too, and merge with pagan beliefs, the occult and Wicca. Wicca is most likely one of the oldest cult teachings there are. It has its roots in the specialized knowledge that the “fallen angles”, the “sons of God”, gave to the women they took for wives back before the flood of Noah, while their sons the Nephilim were in the earth. But one thing is for sure, their god is the sun and their goddess is the moon and they worship “mother earth. This is an interesting point. Where have you heard this before? Does it sound like the teachings of Semiramis, wife of Nimrod? Yes, they are her teachings exactly!

So science went too far and New Age Religion had to bring it back a little with spirituality, mysticism and the workings of the occult. The attractive thing about the belief of this New Age Religion is that you can make it what you want. There are no set doctrines, just a central outline of basic beliefs. If you like the spiritual god side, the metaphysical side, or the occult side of New Age Religion, there really is something for you! You get to make “your religion” as you want, isn't that great?

There are a couple of core beliefs in the “New Age” movement you may find interesting. One is to take care of our environment, to keep “Gaia”, “Mother Earth” healthy (Semiramis must live). Another belief is that there is good in all religions and all religions lead to “God”, so a “Universal” religion is what they are working toward and hope for. One religion for all mankind, made up of bits and pieces of all religions. However, the most interesting of the beliefs of the New Age movement is that a “New World Order” is coming, so all mankind will give up their national or tribal alliances and all people will have a concern for the world and all people. This would usher in a worldwide utopia where wars would end along with food shortages, pollution, disease, discrimination and poverty. Wow doesn't this sound good? A “New World Order”? Isn't that like “Novus Ordo Seclorum” which is printed on the second side of the Great Seal of the United States of America and can be found on every U.S. dollar bill? Interesting isn't it? Could the United States of America be behind the “New Age Religion” movement?

It is very unlikely that The United States has anything to do with the New Age religious movement. What is likely though is that the same people, or organizations, which were behind the formation of the United States of America, are also behind the New Age religious movement! Why else would the same goal of a New World Order be part of a central belief of the Illuminati, Free Masons and now a religious movement? Remember a "one world government" and a "one world religion" was what Nimrod and Semiramis were working toward with the building of the "Tower of Babel". Remember too, that they were doing the bidding of or were being directed by the fallen angel Lucifer.

Here we are five thousand years after the "Tower of Babel" and nothing has changed! The world was one language then, and it was being controlled by a central government and had an official "state religion" of sun, moon and earth worship. Today the world is becoming one language with the aid of the internet. The United Nations is trying to bring the world under one government. The New Age religious movement calls for a "New World Order" and a one world religion with sun, moon and the worship of "mother earth" at its core. I ask you again, what has changed in five thousand years?

Just as "God" took an interest in what was happening at the building of the "Tower of Babel", he is taking an interest in what is now going on here on earth! There is no doubt that just as he got involved with the domination of mankind, the Bible indicates that he is soon to get involved with what is happening on earth today! Lucifer will not win and his earthly "seed" or organization will be destroyed completely.

ONE WORLD RELIGION JUST A DREAM?

If you think about it a world with one religion doesn't sound too bad. At least everyone would believe in the same thing and we would have to give up on religious wars. So at the very least the world should become a more peaceful place. Think about it, you could go any place on earth and the people that you meet there would have the same beliefs as you! Wouldn't that be great!

You may ask though, "What about freedom of religion?"

What if that one world religion doesn't teach the things you believe? What then? Yes having a world where everyone believes the same thing would be great, but only if everyone believed what you believed. So how likely is a one world religion to ever take place in our life time? Please we have the three most populist religions Judaism, Catholicism and Islam on the earth that can't get along with each other and it would take an act of "God" to bring these religions together or have them change to another religion.

Yes it would take an act of "God" to unite the world's religions, or an act of Lucifer! Remember the symbols of the religions we are talking about. Are they all not linked to ancient Egypt and used to worship pagan gods? Yes they are! So if they are all linked to the same source, maybe, just maybe they are truly controlled by the same "powers" that are controlling the rest of the world.

The fact is that we are told in the Bible at 1 John 5:19 *"... the whole world is lying in the power of the wicked one."* If the Apostle John realized that two thousand years ago, how much more evidence do we have today that we are living in a wicked world! So if a one world religion should come to be, who then would you expect to be behind it if the whole world truly is lying in the power of the "wicked one"?

THE UN AND ONE WORLD RELIGION.

It seems that almost from the time of its creation, religion has become an issue within the United Nations. In 1947 the United Nations paved the way for the formation of the State of Israel. While you may say that this was a political move to create a country on behalf of a people who had no country to call their own, remember that it was the religious persecution of the Jewish people and the "Holocaust" inflicted by Adolph Hitler and Nazi regime, which caused of the United Nations to create the country of Israel. Now the Jewish People could have their own homeland back and carry on freedom of religion without the fear of religious persecution.

Chapter 8 ~Religion Its Start

Over the years we have seen endless visits of religious dignitaries trying to have an influence over the policies of the United Nations. At the same time there have always been factions within the United Nations that have a distain for religion and using religion's strong involvement in war and world conflicts have tried to pass world laws to limit the power of religion, or to do away with it all together. The big problem is that the United Nations preaches tolerance and acceptance of all religions worldwide and that all people have the right to choose what religion they want to be and worship the god or gods they want to worship. On November 25th 1981, The General Assembly of the United Nations passed the "Declaration on the Elimination of All Forms of Intolerance and of Discrimination Based on Religion or Belief". In short the "Declaration" states that everyone, all governments, peoples and other religions, must tolerate the beliefs of others.

The exception, is in Article 1, point 3 of the "Declaration" which reads; Freedom to manifest one's religion or belief may be subject only to such limitations as are prescribed by law and are necessary to protect public safety, order, health or morals or the fundamental rights and freedoms of others. If your personal religious beliefs are in violation of the "Law of the Land" whatever that may be, then your religion can be subject to being "outlawed". Also if you are part of a religion that can be seen as a menace to public safety, it can be outlawed or banned.

How could a religion be a menace to public safety? Maybe you can ask the survivors of a religiously inspired suicide bomber. The fact is that the three largest religions on the face of the earth are the ones that are the most intolerant of all religions. More blood has been shed in the name of religion, by Jews, Christians and Muslims than any other religions ever! The bloodshed and intolerance has a history that is thousands of years old! The amazing thing is that these three major religions of the world all claim to worship the same god so how could that be? They all do their best to have a control or at least an influence over the politics of the United Nations. They try to ride the United Nations like it was a horse, trying to direct it to the best political outcome that will be to their own benefit.

Can you imagine having three riders on one horse all trying to go in a different direction? How long do you think that the horse is going to tolerate this before it throws its riders and tramples them under hoof? All the United Nations would have to do is pass a declaration that these three religions are not intolerant of each other and they are intolerant of all other religions and therefore are a menace to "public safety" and should be outlawed.

In fact, if you look at the history of these three religions, this is what you find. That the Jewish peoples have been killing those of other beliefs from the time they entered the "Promised Land" over three thousand years ago. Christians have been fighting Muslims from the days of the "Holy Wars" almost a thousand years ago and with the current wars in the Middle East, although politically motivated over oil and terrorism, Christians are still in the Middle East fighting Muslims. Only now Muslims have taken their fight to the rest of the world through terrorism. So what is the United Nations going to do about all this religious blood shed?

PLANS FOR A ONE WORLD RELIGION.

While the United Nations declares tolerance for all religions, there is a lot of concern for the fundamentalism of Judaism, Catholicism and Islam because they are not tolerant of other religions. So what is the United Nations to do? How about support the more tolerant religions making them a positive example of what the United Nations wants religions to become? While the United Nations is busy promoting one religion, why would they not be doing things covertly to undermine the support of the religions that were a problem and didn't fit in with, or go along with the purpose of the United Nations and its charter? Face facts, if you were in a club and a few members kept creating problems for the club and were giving it a bad name, would you not want to throw them out or do things to make these members leave? Sure you would! Do you really think that as time goes on that the United Nations will not get to the point where it views these intolerant religions as a problem? In fact, it will!

In the mean time we have an interesting trend going on in the political and religious world. There are two religions that seem to have the blessing of the United Nations. The first one we discussed earlier is New Age religion with its belief of a "New World Order" and the other which we have not talked about is the Baha'i Faith, whose main teaching is that of the unification of all mankind under one civilization, so that all nations, peoples and religions will become one unified nation. In their own words, "...humanity is one single race and that the day has come for its unification in one global society." I would say that falls in line with the theme and purpose of the United Nations to establish a one world government, wouldn't you?

WILL A ONE WORLD RELIGION EVER COME?

One may think it would be impossible to ever have a one world religion and with all the intolerance in the world, you might be right. However those religions of the world have forgotten one thing, you cannot bring about a religious change through political means. By working with the United Nations in establishing a "One World Religion", they are working against "God"! How so? Remember the start of this whole problem to begin with. Did "God" Jehovah, have the right to rule over life forms that had "free will"? Who was it that raised this question again? It was Lucifer! So how could the "Wicked One" use world politics and world religion to produce something good for mankind? The fact is he can't!

A one world religion will come and one day soon, but it will not come by the hands of man or by the hands of Lucifer. When Jesus was on the earth he taught his followers how to pray by using the model prayer he told them. We call it "The Lord's Prayer". We can find this in the Bible book of Matthew, the sixth chapter. Matthew 6:10 reads, "Let your kingdom come. Let your will take place, as in heaven, also upon the earth." Jesus is teaching his followers to ask for "God's" will to take place in heaven and on earth. What is "God's" will? He wants his family back! He wants peace and happiness for all mankind, but most of all he wants that one on one relationship he once had with the first human man, Adam, with all mankind! Did you ever think about it this way?

By reading the Bible book of Revelation we find out that "God's" will has already taken place in "heaven" or the multi-dimensional world that "God" and the other spirit life forms live in. Revelation chapter 12 verses 7- 9 explains that war broke out in heaven and that "Michael" who is Jesus in his "kingly role" and his angels battled with the "Dragon" and his angels and the Dragon and his angles were thrown out of heaven and where were they thrown? Verse 12 tells us "On this account, be glad you heavens and you who reside in them! Woe for the earth and the sea, because the Devil has come down to you having great anger, knowing he has a short period of time." By examining world events we have no problem realizing that this happened around the year 1914, by the outbreak of World War I.

So after almost two thousand years of praying for "God's" kingdom to come, could it be the time for it to take place? Could the prayers of mankind finally be answered? Yes! But first both the religions and the governments of this world have to be done away with! Why you ask? It is because they are obviously serving the "ruler of this word", Lucifer, or Satan the Devil. He was thrown out of heaven almost one hundred years ago and now his time here on earth is coming to an end!

CHAPTER 9
THE RULERS OF TODAY, FREEMASONS, THE ILLUMINATI?

Almost every place you look today someone somewhere is writing something about the "mysterious" Freemasons and the group that doesn't exist, or at least we are not suppose to know they exist, the Illuminati.

Many years ago a close friend of mine told me he was joining the Freemasons. I was a little confused about this, because he knew nothing about masonry he worked as a quality control expert in the electronics field. I wondered why he would join a club of masons. Did he want to learn brick laying or something? Obviously, I had no clue what the Freemasons were all about. I thought that they were a guild of workers skilled in the trade of masonry. Really as a new initiate to the Freemasons, he could not tell me much more than they were people from all trades and more like a business club for men.

Freemasons today are upstanding leaders in business and the communities in which they live. While many members are your everyday "Joe" much like my friend, wishing to be part of a private club of businessmen whose main goal seems to be the betterment of self and community. Throughout the history of the Freemasons, some very powerful people have been members of this private fraternity. In fact many of our world leaders today are Freemasons and come from a long family line of Freemasons.

There is no doubt that the Freemasons have some lofty ideals but they work toward those ideals like it was a religion! In the United States alone the Freemasons donate over two million U.S. dollars per day to charitable programs in child health, medical facilities, caring for fellow "Masons" who are in their elder years and other programs to better society.

While Freemasons are a fraternity and only open to men

as members, they do not discriminate against race, nationality, or one's personal beliefs or religion. While you must have a "sponsor" to become a member, the only other requirement is that you are a man. The Masons' basic goal is to unite the brotherhood of mankind under "God". So really what bad things can you say about Freemasons?

When you look into the history of the Freemasons, you will find there really is not any legitimate history that goes back more than three hundred years. There are evidences of "Masonry" in the mid sixteen hundreds, but "organized" Freemasonry started on the 24th of June 1717. There are many beliefs that Freemasons were just stonemasons who formed "guilds" or "lodges" throughout the ages. Remember that stone and bricks have been the main building material from the very first cities that were built on the plains of Mesopotamia over five thousand years ago. While slaves cut stones and made bricks, it was the trained mason who constructed the buildings.

The world's first major building project was the Tower of Babel, and because of it being made mostly of bricks in what is now a desert, it has literally been blown away by the sands of time. The next major building project was started with the rise of Egypt as a world power. Stonework of every kind was being completed and, in fact as we all know, the monuments, temples and other buildings still exist today and have a large influence on our world. Because of the fantastic monuments and various buildings of antiquity and their survival down to our day today, we can appreciate the skill and knowledge that it took to erect these stone buildings that have stood throughout the ages.

If you look at the fantastic cathedrals that have been erected throughout Europe, you have to look in wonder about all the stone work that was involved to create these artful buildings, the graceful flying buttresses, the lofty arched ceilings, the carved images in the stone work of saints, deities or nobles, different patterns symbols and designs. Somehow, without the aid of computers and advanced instruments available today, the true masons of history created some fantastic buildings many of which are still with us!

These masons who have worked to create impressive buildings both through time and wherever they were located must have had very specialized knowledge and you can be sure that they were not going to share it with just anyone. It is not really understood how or why it happened but the "Masons" started allowing non-masons, such as people who had no knowledge of building in stone but who were businessmen, those who were politically influential, and royalty. So why would these other men, who were not masons by trade but were among the rich and powerful, want to be part of an organization of tradesmen or builders of the day? That is like the modern equivalent of a "captain of industry" or a government official wanting to join the "Teamster's Union". What would be the purpose of doing that? "Teamster's" are mostly truck driver's who have formed a "union" or "guild" to ensure that they are receiving a good wage for the work that they do and have access to health care and other benefits that the "Union" helps provide for them. So could there have been something else to unite men from the rich and powerful to the lowliest and humble under one "trade union"?

The answer to this may not be as strange as it may seem. Let's take a look of what was being built throughout history. If we start with the Tower of Babel and go forward through history, who would have commissioned the building work and where would the money have come from? In the case of the Tower of Babel, it would have been Nimrod and Semiramis. When Egypt was a world power it was the Pharaohs who commissioned these building projects. The building of Solomon's Temple, a key anchoring point in "Masonic" history, was commissioned by Solomon's father King David, and Solomon himself over saw the building project. With the spectacular cathedrals throughout Europe, it would have been the "Church" who commissioned and paid for the building project. In each case the "Master" mason would have had to get building designs and instructions as well as finances from the people who wanted to have the building done and these "people" would have been the richest most powerful men of their time. No doubt there was a lure the Masons had to entice some of the richest and most influential people of their time to join their guild or brotherhood.

THE TEMPLAR INFLUENCE

The Knight's Templar was one of several "orders" of the time that the Catholic Church commissioned to "rescue back" the "Holy Land" from the hands of Islam and so started two hundred years of "Holy Wars" between people who claimed to worship the same god.

The Templar Order was started by four French noblemen who were brothers, but in time the Knight's Templar became the second most powerful organization in all of Europe only behind the Catholic Church itself. They became rich and powerful and almost above the law of the land at that time.

Much has been written about the Knights Templars but most of it revolves around the "Templar treasure" which all but disappeared the very day that they were outlawed by the "Church". There is much folklore about the "Holy Grail", the alleged secret of a descendant of Jesus Christ, and a "Holy Bloodline". One thing is seldom talked about but which may very well be true. It is widely accepted that the Templar Knights excavated tunnels under the Temple Mount in Jerusalem looking for treasure that was possibly buried by the Jewish rulers when Israel was under siege by the Babylonian world power in 607 BCE. The key prize they were looking for was the "Arch of the Covenant" which contained the Ten Commandments given to Moses by "God".

The "Arch of the Covenant" was the most sacred thing that ever existed in all of Jewish history and much more valuable than all the cups that Jesus ever drank out of! In fact there is nothing more valuable on the face of the earth both historically and for its own pure value. The "Arch of the Covenant" in as much was the start of monotheism and a written contract between Jehovah God and the Nation of Israel. From that "contract with "God", came the worlds three largest religions. So not only is the Arch of the

Covenant the centerpiece of Jewish religion and the Nation of Israel, it has deep symbolic meaning for Christianity and Islam and for the rest of the world. If the Arch of the Covenant was ever found, it would pretty much prove that the Nation of Israel were "God's" chosen people, at least at one time.

The fact is that when the Babylonians sacked Jerusalem in 607 BCE, they did make off with all the gold ornaments and utensils from the Jewish temple. In the Bible book of Daniel in the fifth chapter it is recorded that Belshazzar, the King of Babylon, gave the command to "bring in the vessels of gold and silver that his father Nebuchadnezzar had taken away from the temple that was in Jerusalem." However there has never been any record of the Arch of the Covenant! If the "Arch" was hidden in a cave or tunnel under the temple, why weren't the rest of the holy valuables hidden with it? If the Arch of the Covenant was hidden under the temple mount, why didn't the Babylonian army find it? Why wasn't the Arch returned to the temple after the Jewish people rebuilt it when the Babylonians released them from captivity? When the Roman armies destroyed Jerusalem in the first century, why didn't they find the Arch? Again the Jewish temple was destroyed and the valuables carried off to Rome and the Arch of the Covenant was nowhere to be found.

So are we to understand that after the armies of two world powers sacked and destroyed Jerusalem and took valuables from the Jewish temple after fifteen hundred years of being hidden, that the Knight's Templars succeeded in finding a vast wealth including the Arch of the Covenant right under everyone's nose?

There is one factor that we need to take into consideration here. Was the Knight's Templar all Christians? Remember that the Roman Army under General Titus took about eighty thousand plus captive Jews back to Rome. Now we are about one thousand years past the destruction of the Jewish temple and those Jewish captives that returned to Rome were now part of European society and under the rule of the Roman Catholic Church. While Jews were an object of hatred because "they" killed Jesus Christ, you can be sure that it was the common uneducated Jewish person who was bearing the brunt of the "Christian wrath". When we consider that the world's richest families are Jewish, many of them from Europe, we can only believe that many Jewish families were outwardly Catholic so as to blend in with their peers and be able to own land and prosper while under the rule of the "Church".

When the idea of capturing the "Holy Land" became popular throughout Europe, you would have to imagine that the "Christian" Jewish people would have taken an interest. More so, the thought of getting back to their "home land" even in the guise of being Christian had to have an appeal to most Jewish people in Europe. History was born when the United Nations established the State of Israel in 1947. Jews from all over the world flocked back to Israel so they would again have a land they could call their own. Unfortunately it took the death of six million Jewish people at the hands of a well-financed Nazi mad man to accomplish this!

If you ask any Jewish person in Israel today what they want to see happen to the "Temple Mount" in Jerusalem, they would most likely tell you they would like to see the "Dome of the Rock" removed and Solomon's Temple be rebuilt and take it's place. Now you have to wonder, could the Arch of the Covenant have been found by the Knights Templars and taken back to Europe? Could the Arch of the Covenant be in a secret hiding place controlled by Zionists and a secret society determined to gain world control? It is not a secret that the Jewish people want to have their temple back again and they truly believe that one day they will and that day is not far off.

Think about this, why would a group of "Christian monks" go to war to regain control of the Middle East start digging under the Jewish Temple Mount? They would have known that General Titus already carried off the valuables of the Jewish Temple; Rome built the Arch of Titus, which depicts the valuables of the "Temple", and the Jewish captives being taken back to Rome. So could the Knight's Templars been made up and directed by a secret Jewish faction, Zionist? It could explain their name "Templars" and their first interest was the Jewish Temple. So it is possible that

Chapter 9 ~The Rulers of Today, Freemasons, The Illuminati?

"Christian-Jewish" Nobel Men, European Monarchs who hid their true religious beliefs from the Catholic Church that would surely find them "heretics", controlled the "innermost" hierarchy of the Knight's Templar? Could they have indeed found the Arch of the Covenant and put it into a rebuilt "Solomon's Temple" once they had permanent control of their "homeland"? You cannot rule this out!

Think about this for a moment! What if the Catholic Church learned that the Templars did indeed find the Arch of the Covenant? What would they do? Would they not want that "religious relic" for the Church? Because of the power it would give the "Church" and take away from the Jewish people, yes they would! How far do you think the "powers" of the Catholic Church would have gone to recover the Arch of the Covenant from the Knights Templars? If the Church found out a faction of "Christian Jews" controlled the order of Knights Templar, do you think the Church would accuse the Knight's Templar leaders of being heretics, round up them up and torture them to find out where the Arch of the Covenant was and to punish them for their beliefs? That is exactly what happened! However there is no mention of the Arch of the Covenant directly. The only reference made was that the treasure of Knight's Templar disappeared along with their fleet of ships and most of the order of the Templars.

There is no doubt that the Knight's Templar made themselves very rich and powerful, but you have to remember that in the name of "God" they waged a war not just in a city, but throughout a whole region of Islamic lands and they sacked city after city and pillaged all the valuables. Remember too that trade in "religious relics" and "icons" was very lucrative! Both the "Church" and Monarchy of Europe all wanted a piece of the Holy Land. It was the "in" thing at the time. Having bits and pieces of early Christian history was in vogue and having a more impressive collection of religious relics than your neighbor, not only showed your wealth but also showed your devotion to Christ and the "Church". The Templars also put together what amounted to tour packages for pilgrims traveling to the Holy Land.

In two hundred years, the Knight's Templar basically rebuilt the infrastructure of Europe, established a banking system, built fortifications, expanded trade routes over land and by sea and built hundreds of churches and monasteries, some of them being the most elaborate churches ever in history and in the process they became extremely wealthy and powerful!

THE NEW CLERGY

We do know one thing that the Knight's Templar brought back with them from the Middle East, "specialized knowledge". Gnosticism and teachings of the Cabbala is what the Knights Templars learned. These were "secret teachings" based on the occult, mysticism and "magic" that the Egyptian priest had knowledge of and demonstrated. Some have even said that the "specialized knowledge" was given to man by the fallen angels. Exactly what that knowledge was is unknown, but the Bible can give us some insight as to what the power of that knowledge was able to do. If we read the Bible book of Exodus chapter 7 verses 10-12, the latter part of the tenth verse reads, "...Accordingly Aaron threw his rod down before Pharaoh and his servants and it became a big snake. However, Pharaoh also called for the wise men and the sorcerers and the magic-practicing priests of Egypt themselves proceeded to do the same thing with their magic arts. So they threw down each one his rod, and they became big snakes..." So what kind of knowledge was this?

Now I am not saying that the Knights Templars could turn sticks into snakes, but the Egyptian priests could and it was their knowledge that was being handed down and has been handed down from generation to generation. Remember the Egyptians were very good at documenting things, so it really does not take too much of a stretch of the imagination that incantations to invoke spirit life forms, "the Gods" to do their "bidding" were written down. It is very possible that the most powerful people on earth are using today these incantations today!

Chapter 9 ~The Rulers of Today, Freemasons, The Illuminati?

So who could behind such power like this? There is only one that could be behind it, the "Angel of Light", the god of this system, none other than Lucifer! This was at the core of what was being learned by the Knights Templar; regardless of what religion they actually were, they were now learning the "specialized knowledge" went way beyond "philosophy", or the prescribed teachings of the Catholic Church of that time. The new knowledge that the Knights Templar were learning, along with their new prosperous and successful life, indeed made them a very powerful organization to deal with.

No doubt, the "specialized knowledge" that became the core of the Templar belief system was a closely guarded secret only known by the elite and the most powerful of the order. The new recruit knight that was ready for battle was sent onto the front lines. He would have to prove himself and be of a high enough family bloodline to be accepted into the inner core and become one of the "elite" and be made privileged to this knowledge. The knowledge that the Knights Templar were keeping a secret was the real treasure.

There is a certain truth that is part of every organization on the face of the earth, from the time mankind was set to start building cities, down to this very day! That truth is this; there are always three levels of knowledge! There is the general teaching that is given to the common or uninitiated members and the "masses" of humankind. Then there is the knowledge given to those teaching the masses. Last but most important is the core belief or knowledge of those who teach the teachers. You will never know the "truth" of what that core belief is until you are accepted as part of that inner core. When you become accepted at that level and are given specialized knowledge, you are not going to betray those who made you one of their own. No doubt you took a long time to achieve that level of acceptance to start with, so you would not let that knowledge fall into the hands of the common man if it were a closely guarded secret, would you? No, you would not, because you are now part of the elite!

The Knights Templars must have gotten word that they were going to be banned and arrested for heresy. An organization as powerful as the Knights Templars had become most certainly had spies within the Church and throughout different rival factions, or anyone who may have posed a threat to them. It should be no surprise, that when the command went out on that fateful day to arrest the Templars that not much of anything was found. All of their vast wealth somehow disappeared and many of the Templars went into hiding. Some of the Templar order joined other orders of the day. The Church took the land owned by the Knights Templar and some of it was given to other religious orders that the Church deemed worthy.

So where did the Templars disappear to, and what happened to the specialized knowledge they took with them? Scotland and Switzerland are the short answer, but you have to remember something here, we are not talking about common criminals! These men, the Knights Templar, were the nobility of Europe. Remember it is King Richard I, "the Lion Heart" of England, also fought as a Knights Templar. So you can see these are not just ordinary men we are talking about. No doubt, some of those of the Knights Templar were among the most royal bloodlines of Europe aristocracy. Some of these families can trace their "blood lines" for hundreds of generations and believe that they have the "divine right" to be rulers.

The idea of having the "divine right" to be part of a "ruling class", combined by the specialized knowledge that the Knights Templar brought back from the Middle East, would set up a very elite group of people with a very unique power, to ensure their rule over their subjects.

There is no doubt that the effect the Knight's Templar had on Europe led to the "Renaissances", a time of learning and education and the establishment of culture and fashion, art, the sciences and a massive building work of great stone buildings, castles, palaces and cathedrals. They commissioned buildings that in themselves were works of art! While the Knights Templar are busy commissioning stone forts, churches and monasteries throughout Europe and the Middle East, would it not be skilled masons who would be building these structures for them? Naturally it would be!

The masons at that time were divided into three groups; the lowest masons, who were new to the "craft" and were learning apprentices. Then there are the skilled or learned masons who knew their craft and would be instructing the apprentices. At the top, were the true artisans, the masters of the craft who were skilled in turning stone into buildings of art, but these men were builders not warriors.

As the "Dark Ages" and the Knights Templar disappeared, the Renaissances with all its decadent glory and fantastic building works took their place and a small obscure group started to take shape and somewhat take the place of the Knights Templar. That group of men is known as the Freemasons.

What started as a guild of educated craft men having special knowledge in engineering, fantastic structures in stone, and a claim that their history goes back to the days of the Jewish King Solomon and the building of the Jewish Temple on Mount Mariah. This is the same sight of the Temple Mount in Jerusalem where the Dome of the Rock sits today. You have to ask yourself at this point, why do the Masons and the Templars both have a tie back to King Solomon's Temple? Could both groups have had knowledge of the secret teachings of the Cabbala of the Jews as well as mystical knowledge from ancient Egypt, whose building works still puzzle and confound engineers today and whose religious practices and icons we still find fascinating and part of today's culture?

As the Renaissances progressed and the true knowledge of science and mathematics replaced the superstitions and false dogma of the Church, the Age of Enlightenment was born! Freemasonry was also becoming organized and gaining in popularity with the now educated ruling class and some of the Monarchy of Europe.

Keep in mind that the then ruling class was and is no

different from the "Jet Setters" or the "Rich and Famous" of today. They wanted to be on the cutting edge of everything and own the best of everything. They were being educated by the best minds of their day and studied the new philosophies of the "Age of Enlightenment". However, one thing remained central, the domination of those they ruled over. Why is it that the "ruling class" are always given special knowledge but the everyday people who are doing their best to make a day to day living are kept in the dark and are never enlightened, even down to our day today?

With the acceptance of all people to the mason ranks, it became obvious that the craft of stone working and masonry was no longer the purpose of Freemasons. Really, why would members of royal families who ruled over the people of Europe want to learn how to lay bricks? The answer to that question is easy, they were not interested in bricks at all, it was the domination and control of the common people by any means possible, politics and religion, and now business. That is the goal of Freemasons today, to form business relationships and make the world a better place to live in under their direction and rule.

Think about this, the tallest most beautiful buildings in Europe up to this time were churches. Religion was at the center of people's lives. The Knights Templar was financing the most opulent cathedrals and no expense was spared. What do we see today? The god of business has replaced religion! The tallest most opulent buildings today are nothing more than cathedrals to the god of business. What has changed? Do you remember the goals of the Freemasons were to unite men of the world as brothers and to foster business and commerce? After the Knights Templar returned from the Middle East, "God" was no longer in the picture, if He ever was to begin with.

You must remember that today, the Freemasons are not at the center of the specialized knowledge. They are the teachers and the leaders of the masses. The Freemasons is only an international fraternal organization that accepts all men as members and then educates them to the "craft" of Freemasonry. The question you have to ask is "Who are the ones teaching the Freemasons and what have they taught them?

Depending on the group of Freemasons you would join, there are thirty-two levels in one order and thirty-three levels in the other. Either way there are levels of education of the Freemasons that one progresses through before becoming a "Master Mason" and completing the highest level of education. This process usually takes many years of dedication to the "craft" and whatever "specialized knowledge" you learned along the way, you are not going to divulge it to lesser Masons, let alone someone who is not a Freemason. If you look at some of the people who are thirty-second or thirty-third degree Freemasons, you are going to find out that they are world leaders, captains of industry, and among some of the most powerful men on earth.

So who is instructing the Freemasons? Nobody is instructing them and that is pretty much the truth. The Freemasons already have their instructions, their mission and all the knowledge they need and they are following those instructions and carrying out their mission. Mission? What mission is that? Each Freemason Lodge seems to have a slightly different mission, but the basic one is to foster a fraternal brotherhood worldwide with men from all nations and religious beliefs. That sounds very harmless, until you realize that to unify the world under the teachings of the Freemasons would give you a one-world government! The truth is if you are trying to unite mankind together with one single belief or way of life and you are doing it on a worldwide level, you would really be working toward a one-world government, a "socialistic", or worse a "communistic" government, or even worse than that, a world wide dictatorship! That sounds like the rule of the foretold "Anti-Christ" that everyone is worried about coming. The fact is he is already here!

THOSE BEHIND THE SCENES

The Freemasons are a very visible worldwide organization and always happy to bring new fellow Masons into their ranks and start their "Masonic education". So based on what we know about the three levels of the teaching of specialized knowledge, the Masons are the first line, or the masses that are being taught. So if the Freemasons are the masses that are being taught, where did the Freemasons get their education? Who taught the Freemasons?

We need to go back to the Age of Enlightenment for the answers to who were the educators. Keep in mind here that we are talking about a time in history where science, philosophy and the arts had replaced the accepted erroneous teachings and dogma of the "Church". The men who influenced society during this time ranged from Isaac Newton to François-Marie Arouet better known by the pen name Voltaire, to Wolfgang Amadeus Mozart. These men and men like them were trying to enlighten the world around them by their ideas, discoveries and philosophies. The world around them seemed to be falling apart with the "Church" and monarchies of Europe crushing the common people under their rule and domination.

The idea of seeing equality between all people kept being pushed to the forefront between philosophers during the Age of Enlightenment. More and more the idea of a one world order, where all men would be equal and live free, was not only being discussed it was being planned for. Something was becoming very obvious, the monarchy of Europe had become overly decedent and it seemed the Monarchy of France was leading the way in over indulgency, while the common people of France were literally starving to death. Something really needed to be done about this condition!

On May 1, 1776, the German philosopher Adam Weishaupt formed the "Order of Perfectibilists", which later became known as the Illuminati. Their goal was to abolish all monarchical governments and religions and replace it with a "New World Order". Weishaupt was initiated into the Freemason order and became a member of the lodge of Theodor zum guten Rath", at Munich in 1777. He embraced the Gnostic teachings of the Freemasons and eventually wove his own teachings of a New

World Order in among the teachings of the Masons. It was easy to accept because the present world order of corrupt "Church" officials and the decadent European Monarchy was not working. With the revolt going on in the American Colonies against the English Monarch King George, the hopes of a new government emerging from the chaos of war were high!

In the American Colonies, the Revolution that had started was organized by the most powerful and influential men at the time who were willing to put their lives on the line for the ideals they believed in. These men were great philosophers and statesmen, who wanted to see a new country that would break with the traditions of Europe and not have a monarchy, but would instead of a monarchy, install a government of the "people", a government where all men were equal and had a right to say how they would be led and governed. Most of the leaders of the American Revolution just happened to be Freemasons with strong ties to the Freemasons in Europe, all of which were strong supporters of the Age of Enlightenment and the new philosophies it was adopting and supporting. Now finally with the American Revolution taking place, the form of government that would rule over the American people was being designed by Freemasons in America and in Europe. The start of the New World Order was upon us!

There was never any deep dark conspiracy that was planned against the United States of America or the people in America. The people who were the leaders of the day, the elected officials, had an idea for a new government and the people who elected them wanted to try their ideas and be a free people and be equals to the people who were ruling over them. Maybe if we all became Freemasons, we would not be thinking about a conspiracy but we would be working along with the powers that be, toward that New World Order.

Really, if Freemasons were the ones who were put in charge of the American Government, why would it be a surprise to anyone that the symbols, ideas and architecture of the United

States of America are Masonic in nature? Really, it goes back further than that, the Masonic Symbols are Egyptian in nature. Let us strip away the history that is taught in our places of education and let's look at the facts.

First, we need to go back to Europe and look what was going on there. With the Age of Enlightenment at full speed and some of the most influential minds in history among the ranks of the Freemasons, these men were in the process of shaping the future by using whatever specialized knowledge they had. With the philosophies they had adopted, the centerpiece of which became the New World Order, what better place to carry out this idea than in the "New World"? If there was a deception on the American Colonists, it was put there by the Europeans to begin with. If this new idea for a One World Order would fail, of what loss would it be to the European power brokers? It would only be an inconvenience that time would fix.

America was looked at as a land of great natural resources that could make many merchants and businessmen very wealthy. Business was at the center of the expansion of America and as business expanded and the "Colonies" became an organized political power, the time was right to break away from England and be an independent government of the people. The New World Order of the United States of America was going to have a new "Democratic" form of government. This must have shaken up the Monarchies of Europe pretty good. There would be no King of America and if this idea took hold in Europe, what then? So you can understand, "secret orders" that supported the idea of a one world government or uniting all the brotherhood of mankind had to be just that, "secret orders". Talk of that nature could get you killed by your local monarch. Adam Weishaupt, the "father" of the Illuminati, who were to be select men of the Age of Enlightenment, the most brilliant and powerful, faced that fate when his plan for the Illuminati fell into the wrong hands. Weishaupt was banished from Bavaria, but the Illuminati was already being formed.

The Monarchs of Europe were correct to worry about this New World Order called the United States of America. The idea of democracy was about to take place in France and one of the most decadent kings ever was about to lose his head. With both time and war, almost every monarchy in the world has fallen to democracy and the monarchs, "The Royals", are no more than figure heads for the countries they once ruled over. However, if you look at who the world's most famous Freemasons in history are, you will find that they were some of the Monarchs of Europe and their families, Statesmen, high ranking members of the "Clergy", the Royalty and family members of rich Islamic countries. Some of the men who were and are considered the greatest people in history were all Freemasons. It has to make you ask, who is writing our history?

So, who are the most powerful Freemasons today? All you have to do is turn on the news or look at the world rulers and the power brokers. In the first presidential administration of George H.W. Bush, almost every member of his cabinet was a Freemason. Fact is many of the world leaders today are Freemasons! So now the question, whose interest are they putting first, the interest of the people they represent, or the ideals and the teachings of Free and Accepted Masonry? What do you think?

Yes, it seems that the One World Order of democracy and the idea of equality for all mankind has almost become a total reality. Could all this have taken place just because of a few men that had an idea? Most certainly not! To change the face of the world takes more than just a good idea, it takes money and power and the need to act covertly. This takes a central body of directors, men with an enlightened idea, and the money and power to make a difference.

THE ILLUMINATI CONNECTION

Adam Weishaupt's idea for the Illuminati took hold. At first, it was filled with the greatest thinkers of the Age of Enlightenment, but soon the most powerful, richest families of the world infiltrated their ranks. These families are ones who claim that by their bloodlines they have the right to rule over all of mankind. Some even go so far as to think that their bloodlines are from an angelic source and they have a divine right to rule.

Today these families are among the elite of the elite, they do not act through the Freemasons, they are the ones behind the scenes! Very little is truly known about the members of the Illuminati, but much is written about them so to understand what is true and what is myth is almost an impossibility. To get an understanding of who make up this elite group, you have to understand the mission of the Illuminati that is a "New World Order". So, who would benefit the most by having a one-world government?

Now you have to look at the most powerful men in the world, many of them are already part of the Freemason fraternity and hold high positions in governments or big business around the world. Most likely you have never heard the names of the vast majority of these men, but some of their family names are known world wide, by every day people.

The structure of the Illuminati is supposed to be made up of three hundred men. These men are then reduced to a group of thirteen and the thirteen are broken down to a triad. Yes, it is alleged that the future of the world is in the hands of three men.

Who these three hundred men are really is not important, but no doubt, they are members of the world's richest families. It is said that eighty percent of the world's wealth is controlled by nine families. We will discuss who some of these families are later, but if they are the world's richest families they have to be involved in banking or the largest of industries, or both!

To say the Illuminati are ruling over or directing the Freemasons is not really a true statement. While I am sure many of the Illuminati are Freemasons, maybe all of them are, there is no way to know for sure and it really does not matter any way. The Illuminati are more interested in controlling world events and addressing world issues. Freemasons are only an organization of less than six million men worldwide. They happen to be made up of many world rulers and influential men in government, industry and religion. Yes, many world religious rulers are Freemasons too. Maybe they believe it is better to rule in "Hell" then serve in "Heaven".

That statement may have more truth to it than you may think. While the symbols of Freemasonry only hint to serving Lucifer and while there are volumes of secret knowledge to be learned before you reach the highest levels of Masonry, they are not out right Luciferians. The Illuminati most likely are Luciferians and take pride in the worship of their deity! The main symbol of the Illuminati is the "All Seeing Eye" with in the triangle. Both these are directly related to and taken from the same magic practicing priest in ancient Egypt who could change their sticks into snakes, so what special knowledge do the Illuminati have? Do they know the incantations to summon the gods of Egypt? If they do, are they serving the gods, or are the gods serving them? You wonder why the masses of the earth ask for, cry out for, indeed even pray for peace, but only have war cast upon them, upon us? Maybe we are praying to the wrong god? When you pray, are you praying to Lucifer, the Angel of Light, the god of this world and system we live in, or are you praying to Jehovah, "He who causes to become"? Time to examine the things you have learned and what things you are being taught!

THE SEVENTH WORLD POWER

Between England and the United States, both governments have controlled the world stage either in commerce, or in war, or both. Remember the "Opium War" was to ensure the sale of opium to China. It was "His Majesties" war ships, which literally blasted open the ports of China, so the East India Company could sell opium to the Chinese people. It was reported that over eighty percent of the population of Hong Kong and Shang Hi were addicted to the drug opium.

England took control of one country after another and had "colonies" all over the world. The imperial power of England was indeed worldwide. As England was flexing its world wide muscle, the seed of democracy and a One World Order had sprouted into a country trying to stay organized and focused on the reason for its being.

The Eagle that was The United States of America was still a fledgling and learning how to become a world power based on democracy. However, The United States was starting to lose its way and the southern states were in themselves starting to become little monarchies and those Americans who owned large plantations were now becoming like the land barons of Europe. In fact, many of the very wealthy plantation owners were becoming close social friends of European Nobility and the ideas and life style of the European Monarchs were now becoming the ideas of the pseudo monarchs of the southern states in America. Something had to be done to stop this "cancerous" idea and way of life if there was ever going to be a New World Order!

If you believe the history books that the "War Between the States", better known as the "Civil War" even though there was nothing civil about it, was fought to end slavery, you really need to look more deeply into the subject! The fact is the "Southern States" had developed a way of life that resembled the Monarchies of Europe and that was unacceptable! It was not what the plan was for the United States of America. The plan was for the monarchies to end not to foster new ones in America!

Just as the Monarchs of Europe made their living on the back of the surfs they allowed to work their land, the southern plantation owners were making their fortunes on the back of slaves they forced to work their land. The idea of owning slaves was not objectionable to the founding fathers of America, but developing monarchies was!

Obviously, some action needed to be taken to end the "American Monarchy"! By making slavery an issue, it would force the plantation owners to change their way of life. The plantation owners would now have to free their slaves and pay them for their labor, this would be a great cost to the plantation owners and their profits would plummet. They obviously did not like the idea at all.

Chapter 9 ~The Rulers of Today, Freemasons, The Illuminati?

The political powers of the "South" would rather abandon the plan for a New World Order and keep the way of life they have come to enjoy. This was unacceptable not only to the Northern States, but to the Illuminati who were working for a New World Order and the bankers that were financing and profiting from this plan. So war broke out at the cost of the largest loss of American life ever, over 600,000 American lives were sacrificed to keep the idea of a New World Order alive!

The fact is that this was only going to be a taste of things to come as far as the number of dead that would pile up in the name of this New World Order. It was going to take millions of lives to bring America to the point of being a world power!

By the end of the Second World War, the "American Eagle" had shown its might both as an industrial power and as a world military power. With the explosion of atomic weapons over Japan, it left very little doubt that America was now large and in charge!

SUPER POWER TODAY

President Ronald Reagan can be personally credited with bringing The United States of America to the point of being the worlds greatest and only "Super Power". By both negotiation and out spending the Soviet Union on military weapons, the Soviet Union collapsed from the inside out from economic ruin. There was no way that the world could survive an all out war between the United States of America and the Soviet Union. This was obvious by the number of nuclear weapons that each side had. It has been estimated, that at one time there was nuclear explosive firepower to equal 20,000 tons of TNT for every man woman and child on the face of the earth. The knowledge of that should make you sleep much better at night!

With the destruction of the Soviet Union, many new democratic instantly emerged on the world seen. These countries would need a lot of help to get their economies up and running and would have to rely on the world bankers to help them with loans. How convenient for the World Bankers that they now can control these poor countries from the inside out. By establishing a sound banking system and making loans, these new countries were now deeply in debt and at the beck and call of the bankers. While in the country of Ukraine a few years ago, I was reading a newspaper article about Ukraine defaulting on a loan made to them by European bankers. Ukraine was trying to renegotiate the current loan and borrow more money. The bankers told the Ukraine officials that they would have to take a loan out of 150,000,000 US Dollars and use this money to fight AIDS if they wanted any more money.

Fighting AIDS sounds like a good idea, but here is a country that does not have enough money to run properly and is trying to get money just to keep the country working and not have an economic collapse. The Ukraine could not pay back the money they already borrowed, now they need more and in order to get it they have to take out additional loans that they did not plan for. Yes, it is great that the world horror of AIDS is being addressed, but not to have a choice and be forced into debt even further is only going to hurt the people of Ukraine. Do the bankers care about the people, or about control? Now there should be an obvious answer, it is all about money and control or domination.

With the United States of America winning the "Cold War" over the Soviet Union, it was now the only world power. With the fall of the Soviet Union, the world must have wondered just how powerful the United States was, considering not a shot was fired. What was the power of the military might of the United States? The world would soon find out with the country of Iraq invading the country of Kuwait.

With world leaders in an uproar over the invasion of Kuwait, the United Nations passed a resolution demanding that Iraq remove its army from Kuwaiti borders. The demand fell on deaf Iraqi ears. Possibly the start of World War III was on the minds of world leaders. The Iraqi army was one of the best and well-equipped armies in the world, so there was reason to be concerned. Could this be the start of the Bible's Armageddon?

Chapter 9 ~The Rulers of Today, Freemasons, The Illuminati?

After all, the armies of the world were now gathered together in the Middle East and ready to do battle! No, this was not the case at all, but there is a correlation. The Bible book of Revelation talks about many "Wild Beasts". What we are seeing here is the emergence of the "Two Horned" wild beast that is talked about in Revelation 13:11. This "Two Horned Beast" has two horns like a lamb, but it speaks like a dragon. This "Beast" represents the Anglo-American world power of England and the United States. We will talk more about this and other "beasts" of Revelation in a later chapter.

The United Nations mandated a coalition army, led by the United States of America and followed by Great Britain and many other countries, routed and destroyed the Iraqi Army in less than two months. The Armed Forces of the United States of America had a chance to flex its muscle in war and had plenty of new weapons and the latest technology available to manage warfare. It made no difference which branch of the US Armed Services was engaged in battle, they all acted with deadly precision, destroying every part of the Iraqi Army they were sent after. By the end of Desert Storm, the world knew just how powerful the United States had become!

There is no doubt that the "Founding Fathers" of the United States of America would have been proud with how the US Armed Forces rose to the challenge and how well they performed in Desert Storm! I am sure those who dreamed up a New World Order, too would have been very proud, that what once was an idea that became a country, had now grown in to the worlds only "Super Power", ready to vanquish anyone who stands in the way of the goal of that New World Order!

GOVERNMENT LEADERS, RELIGIOUS LEADERS, BUSINESS LEADERS WORKING TOGETHER

If one day you walked in to your local restaurant and you happened to see the Mayor of the town having dinner with the minister of your church and the owner of the company you worked for, you would most likely wonder what these men were doing together, especially if they all had different religious beliefs. So why are these men of different backgrounds and interests all together? They are all Freemasons and they just finished making their plans for the Mayor's re-election at a private meeting. The Mayor is looking for support and money to run his campaign, he knows he can count on his fellow Masons for help, and they know that the Mayor will also help them promote their interest as he secures his job for one more term.

The truth is this happens every day at every level within Freemasonry from the local government to world governments including the United States. However, those Freemasons who are also part of the Illuminati give their first allegiance to the ideals and goals of the Illuminati! So in fact, you have the "Enlightened Ones" who believe they have a "divine right" to rule over and make decisions for the benefit of humankind and the world.

The problem is that the Illuminati are doing the will of the "god" they worship and that is Lucifer! Yes and they know they are getting their direction from this former "Angel of Light". They know whom it is they are worshiping and you see it in the way world leaders will greet or acknowledge certain other people; they hold their hand and fingers to make a "Devil Horn" sign. See the sign; you will know what is on their minds and that is the total domination of every living thing on this planet! Yes the common everyday person who is doing their best to live by the laws of the land and earn a living, are nothing more than cattle, or worker ants to the Illuminati. Who gets stepped on, or who is led to slaughter really makes no difference to them, as long as they can stay in power and profit from it!

You see in our little dinner scenario above, the mayor is really the President of the United States. The owner of your company is there because they are the largest manufacturer of oil drilling and recovery equipment, and yes, your minister, because you are Islamic and he is from the House of Saud, one of the richest and most powerful families in the world! What do these men all have in common? They are all Freemasons and at least one of them is believed to be part of the Illuminati. When you change the importance of the people at the meeting in our restaurant, you now have world-wide implications!

Meetings by the "power brokers" of the world happen on almost a daily basis. When these meetings draw many world leaders and the meetings are "closed door" or private meetings, you can be assured that the fate of the people of the world is in the balance. You can also be assured that with the decisions that are made by the world leaders at these meetings, if there is a profit to be made someplace, they are going to be the first ones in line to make that profit, even if it is at the cost of many human lives.

The historic list of Freemasons is very long and very impressive. It includes Presidents, Kings and nobility, Heads of State worldwide. Religious leaders, including Popes of the Catholic Church, famous Ministers of the "Religious Right" in America, the founding fathers of Mormon, and leaders of Islam. Many leaders, in the "New Age" religious movement are Freemasons. When you look to the business world, many of the large banking and oil families of the United States and Europe are deeply involved with the "Craft". The founders of some of the world's largest and most successful companies were and are Freemasons.

So you can see the influence that the Freemasons have is expansive and when you combine that with the involvement by the most powerful people in the world being members of the Illuminati as well, you can control almost anything you want! So why do we not have peace? Why is there always a conflict of some kind? There is a very logical reason for this. First, everyone has their own agenda and it is all about money and power. The second reason is that there are many factions and secret groups, all having their own ideals and are vying for power! Herein lies the problem, because they are all Lucifer worshipers and can only reflect his qualities. If what we read in the Bible is true then the qualities that they are reflecting are those of lies and deceit! Think about this, Lucifer had questioned "God's" right to rule over life forms with free will. God gave Lucifer a chance to raise up a "seed", an organization that would worship Lucifer willingly and he has given people of the world every type of religion they can think of, as long as worshiping the "God of Light" or the "Goddess of Life" is part of that worship. However the Illuminati worship Lucifer directly, and they know it and at times they flaunt it!

WHY ARE THERE SO MANY FACTIONS?

When you look at a picture of the earth from space, it is a pretty planet, the most beautiful in our solar system! As you look at it you will notice all the blue water that make up our oceans and then the green and brown land masses that make up the continents. You notice the white snowcaps of the Arctic and Antarctic circles, you will see the continents and think maybe of what countries make up those continents. What happens though when you map out all the countries? You have divided the planet. When one people cross the line of another people, history has proved that war most likely has broken out. We have become so intent on "owning" the dirt under our feet that we feel that we must protect it with our lives! However, why is this?

Let us remember the Prince of Persia; although a "spirit life form" he was directing the actions of the Persian Empire. The Prince of Persia was doing his best to stop the Angel Gabriel from delivering his message to the Profit Daniel, because he was protecting his interest in the Persian Empire, which he "owned". The account in the Bible book of Daniel in the tenth chapter records this account. At the end of the chapter, Gabriel tells Daniel that he is going back to fight with the Prince of Persia and that the Prince of Greece was coming. Remember too that the Bible book of Revelation in the twelfth chapter tells us that the great fiery colored "Dragon", the one called Devil and Satan, yes Lucifer, dragged a third of the stars with him. These stars are fallen angles "spirit life forms" that have sided with Lucifer in the rebellion against Jehovah and now want to dominate the intelligent life forms on the planet earth. That is us, you and me!

Chapter 9 ~The Rulers of Today, Freemasons, The Illuminati?

As the different gods were "invented" to distract the people from worshiping the "True God" Jehovah, these gods were also invented to venerate the "fallen angels" that sided with Lucifer. It would make logical sense that if Lucifer had to develop a "seed" or an organization that seed would start with the angels that sided with him. They were his friends and allies and no doubt they be given prominent positions of ruler ship over the people, the intelligent life forms of the earth. When you look at all the factions that this world has been split into, we can only guess that there must be a very large number of these life forms that sided with Lucifer.

So now, we have negative influences assigned to all parts of our life. Face the facts, if you are an everyday person, not one of the "ruling class" of Luciferians, you are faced with negative things from the time you get up in the morning until the time you go to bed at night. Turn on the radio, if it didn't already wake you up to begin with, and you hear all the rotten things that people did to other people during the night, you hear it is going to rain all day, you have a long drive to get to work and you already know the traffic is going to be terrible. You rush to work to start your day laboring for a corporation that hardly knows you are there and you are working for a manager who can care less, is stealing from the company and abusing his power and is trying to get his brother-in-law a job, maybe your job. You fight your way home at night to sit down and relax, only to find there was a problem with one of your children at school and a stack of bills that need to be paid.

If you are married, the chances are that your wife had almost the same day as you did. If you are married, there is more than a fifty percent chance that your marriage will end in divorce. If you are a single parent, you are dealing with all this on your own and I applaud you and wish you the best in your efforts! At the end of your busy almost crazy day, maybe you get a chance to watch some TV and forget about your own problems for a while. If you are like the average person today, you will watch the most popular programs, which are written by people who get a chance to influence our thinking and do not care anything about us. They are only interested in pleasing top TV executives by carrying out their will and driving up ratings. Now remember who these top TV executives are associated with, no doubt Freemasons at the very least, but I would believe more, the Illuminati! I say the Illuminati, because it is their propaganda that is bombarding us from every angle! So, if you are interested in changing your life, start that change by listening to, or watching positive things. Choose entertainment that will enhance your life in some way. If you do not than you are accepting the influence of those who are doing their best to control us!

Depending on exactly how many one third of the "stars", or angels, that sided with Lucifer there really are, we can guess that most if not all have their assignments and are placed in some area to control us humans, by controlling the thoughts of those who control us. This may sound far-fetched to some, but remember the over all picture, who has the right to rule! Those who are ruling over us are Luciferians, if not outright Satan worshipers. The religious classes that report to them are "sun" worshipers first, but they love the "goddess of heaven" just as much! The religious class teaches everyone that they are worshiping "God", the "Holy Mother Mary", and "Jesus", when in fact they are worshiping Nimrod, Semiramis and Tammuz, her son. This is the sickest of deceptions, because this leaves all the populous of the earth believing that they are worshiping "God", the "Father" of Jesus, when in deed they are really worshiping Lucifer, yes the Devil, just as their instructors do and those who teach their instructors. The difference is that the instructors know that they are Devil worshipers.

Those ruling over us have deceived us! We have been deceived for so long, that now we believe that what we are being taught is the truth. We have been "programmed" to live in the "here and now". Our lives are full with trying to make a living and provide for our families, so who has time to think about what really is the truth. We are too accepting of the things told to us by the rulers of this world. We easily forget that Lucifer is the ruler of this earth, even though we are told that many times in the Bible.

Chapter 9 ~The Rulers of Today, Freemasons, The Illuminati?

We all know that politicians lie to us. It is common knowledge and we just take it for granted. I am sure many Americans remember the phrase "Read my lips! No new taxes!" spoken by one former President, who after winning the election raised taxes. What about, "I did not have sex with that woman!" We all knew that President was lying, in fact, if you look at the video of his public address when he spoke those words, he could not even look the people in their eyes. So, if we know that these people lie to us and do so with impunity, we only have ourselves to blame for giving them power over us. It is time to stop believing the lie and start looking for the truth!

THE NEW GOLDEN RULE, HE WHO CONTROLS THE GOLD MAKES THE RULES!

He who controls the gold makes the rules! That really is not a new rule, but it has been true from the time that people realized that gold was a precious metal. However, that standard is set for every person on the face of the earth today! It does not matter if you are rich or poor, if you live in the richest country on earth or the poorest, the most free and liberated or the most controlled and closed government, everyone wants more gold, or more money! How many times have you heard the phrase, "It is all about the money"? In this world, it is all about the money.

You know that people will steel, rob, kill and murder for money. It is said, "Everyone has a price". In other words, if there is enough money involved, you can get anyone to do anything you want them to do. Therefore, what if you met someone, money was no object to them, and they wanted you do something that compromised a belief of yours, would you?

It is very hard for most people to comprehend large sums of money. That is one reason why there are so many economically distressed people in this world. We are not taught about money, we are only taught about the things we need to know to be part of a very large "working class". That does not change the fact that everything in this world takes money and the more money you have, the more you can take!

Here is another phrase for you to think about, "Follow the money trail". Nothing happens in this world until money changes hands! It does not matter if you are buying your groceries at the market, or if you are plotting to take over a country, it all takes money. Now you know where your money came from and how hard you had to work to earn it, but where does the money come from when one country attacks another country? Where does the money come from to fund terrorism? Where does the money come from to elect the president of a country? Really where does all this money come from?

When a country has to borrow money, as many countries have to do to stop an economic collapse from happening, who lends them the money? A better question for you to think about is who has that much money? In order to stop the collapse of the economy of the United States of America, the United States Government is going to have to borrow almost one trillion dollars. Let me say that a different way. The United States Government is going to borrow almost $1,000,000,000,000.00 USD. Who has that kind of money? Think about this, the United States is not the only country having to borrow very large sums of money to stop economic collapse!

Could you even fathom having to pay back that much money to someone? Well here is a reality check for you. As of this writing the national debt broken down to every man, woman and child living in the United States of America is almost $35,000.00. That means that you, your wife and all of your children, including your newborn that you just got a social security number for, each owe someone $35,000.00. Let us see here, if you are the typical American Family and have 2.3 children, your family owes some one about $150,000.00 plus the accruing interest.

Who are the people that we owe this money to? Who could be so rich and powerful that they have this much money to loan anyway? They are the richest and most powerful banking families in the world. Many of them reside in Europe and they control not only the World Bank but every Federal Bank of every country in the world! They control the money.

Who are these families? Who they are is not as important as what they are doing! First, remember that these people have the same mind set as the Pharaohs of Egypt and they worship the same gods. They are the ones who own the governments of the world. Yes, I said own! Think about it, how many countries in the world are in debt today? The truth is that almost all of them are and they are in debt to the world bankers, more accurately most of them are in debt to the World Bank.

The World Bank says this about it self. "Since inception in 1944, the World Bank has expanded from a single institution to a closely associated group of five development institutions. Our mission evolved from the International Bank for Reconstruction and Development (IBRD) as facilitator of post-war reconstruction and development to the present day mandate of worldwide poverty alleviation in close coordination with our affiliate, the International Development Association, and other members of the World Bank Group, the International Finance Corporation, the Multilateral Guarantee Agency, and the International Centre for the Settlement of Investment Disputes."

While that sounds very noble and even caring to an extent, realize that the initial reason for the World Bank was to rebuild Europe after it was finished being destroyed. I say finished because the formation of the World Bank was in 1944, a year before the end of World War II, and that last year produced the majority of the destruction that came to Europe. With Allied forces pushing the German Army all the way back to Berlin, city after city and town after town were destroyed and reduced to piles of rubble. So, this was all going to have to be rebuilt. What was the cost of this all going to be and who was going to pay for all the reconstruction?

Keep in mind that while the World Bank was looking for ways to profit from the destruction of World War II, someone, "bankers", were still financing the war effort. The United States and Russia were becoming industrial powerhouses and producing war machines at a record pace. Remember too, that for ten years before World War II, Germany was busy building one of the deadliest armies to ever go to war! So where did the money come from? In fact, it came from many people who were sympathetic to the Nazi cause, or people who saw a way to make money financing the Nazis. Either way you look at it, the money had to go through banks some place and the bankers were getting richer every day.

One of the great causes that the World Bank touts today is working with "Third World Countries" and helping them to develop and grow to the point of "world standards". The reality is that these countries that are already suffering under economic depression, poverty and political unrest, are saddled with national debts that they can never repay. But it is not just "Third World Countries" that are under control of the World Bank, which ever countries owe money to the World Bank are under the control of the bankers!

ONE FAMILY DOMINATES THE BANKING INDUSTRY AND THE WORLD!

Of all the banking families of the world, the Rothschild family tops the list among the most influential and powerful. This is what the Rothschild Banking Firm has to say about them. "Rothschild has been at the centre of the world's financial markets for over 200 years. Today, it provides Investment Banking, Corporate Banking, and Private Banking and Trust services to governments, corporations and individuals worldwide.

The Rothschild banks are organized globally, so that clients can obtain the advice and services they require wherever it suits them. Through 40 offices in more than 30 countries, from the Americas through Europe to Australia, clients can access Rothschild ideas and expertise. It ranks amongst the world's largest privately owned banks. It is believed that the Rothschild Empire could control as much as 500 trillion dollars worldwide.

Rothschild is committed to the pursuit of excellence, and for this reason concentrates on sectors and markets in which it can excel, where the bank ranks with the very best. Its influence and reputation flow from the quality of its people and the standing of its clients. This combined with a culture that values pragmatic innovation, integrity and intellectual rigor above all else, has resulted in a reputation for ground breaking ideas that are practical as well as imaginative."

The Rothschild family history and their rise to the top of the banking world are quite interesting. Until now, I have not needed to get personal with any of the secret groups, fraternities, or those who are actively working to a New World Order. Who they are is not as important as what they are doing; they are the messengers and the servants of those who control them. The world leaders are nothing but "puppets" of those who put them in office and then pull their strings!

Yes, that includes the President of the United States of America. Some Presidents have just been more obvious about being a puppet than others. You would think that the president of a country has to be very intelligent to achieve that level of public office. When it becomes apparent that the leader of a country is not very smart, you really have to stop and think, "How did he get there?" When you have a president of the most power country on earth, elected to office and not have the popular vote of the people, and then realize he is not very smart either, now you are insulting not only my intelligence, but the intelligence of everyone!

It will be interesting to see what is in store for the new President of the United States of America! When I realized that a "Man of Color" with a Middle Eastern name was running for the office of President of the United States of America, somehow I instantly knew that I was looking at the next President even two years before the election.

Think about this, every President of the United States of America has tried to bring some kind of peace to the Middle East. The last President of the United States put a sword of war in the Middle East and two of the last seven countries on earth that did not have a Rothschild bank in them now had fierce wars raging against them by a collision of other countries that all do have Rothschild banks in them.

A side note to the Afghan War. It has never been a secret that the CIA was running that war. They are still large and in charge there and I guess they most likely will be for some time to come. Notice the following article;

By **Karen DeYoung**
Washington Post Staff Writer
Saturday, December 2, 2006; Page A01

Opium production in Afghanistan, which provides more than 90 percent of the world's heroin, broke all records in 2006, reaching a historic high despite ongoing U.S.-sponsored eradication efforts, the Bush administration reported yesterday.

In addition to a 26 percent production increase over past year — for a total of 5,644 metric tons — the amount of land under cultivation in opium popples grew by 61 percent. Cultivation in the two main production provinces, Helmand in the southwest and Oruzgan in central Afghanistan, was up by 132 percent.

This is now a 2.6 billion dollar industry in Afghanistan and is about one third of the Gross National Product. Is it any wonder why heroin use has been replacing cocaine use?

I was telling a friend of mine about some findings I came across about the CIA trafficking cocaine into the United States. They were using the money to fund "Black Operations". I had known that he was a US Army Ranger, but he never talked much about it and I never asked. However, his response to me telling him this was shocking to say the least! He gritted his teeth, started pounding the table with his fist, and said, "I know it, I know it, I was involved with that shit and I can't talk about it, I've said too much about it already!" This moved him to an anger that I have never seen in him before then suddenly the anger almost turned to tears and that was the end of our conversation on that subject. I tried to find out more about his involvement at another time and got the same reaction, with almost the same words. I could do nothing else than to believe that my findings were true and I never approached the subject with my friend again.

If the CIA is running the war in Afghanistan, who do you think is buying the opium? Fact is more land is being used to grow opium poppies in Afghanistan than is used to grow coca plants for cocaine in South America. So, who do you have to thank for the new drug epidemic in your town? Is it comforting to know that the Opium Wars are still with us? No, it is not! It is a plague cast upon society today with the blessing of those who would be our rulers! In no way am I saying that the Rothschild family are drug dealers, they are bankers right? Consider the amount of money involved in the world's drug trade. Tell me how do you move that much money around without banks getting involved?

What is much more valuable than the profits made on the drug trade, are that those profits are used to carry out covert operations that quote "never happened" or "never existed" or no one has any knowledge of that kind of thing ever taking place, the fabled "Black Ops."

To have a full understanding of the way our world has been manipulated, you have to research the Rothschild history. After doing so you will conclude that this family is at the center of evil in the world today. There is no lack of information regarding the Rothschild family history and the involvement they have had with world affairs. While some of the information differs slightly, there are plenty of supporting facts as to the influence and domination they have on the world today. Most of this domination is inflicted by a means of cause and effect. First, you create a problem and do so in a covert way so no one knows or understands that you are the one behind it. Then you rush in after the disaster and offer to help fix it. Kind of like the arsonist who wants to be a fireman.

In the case of 911 and the destruction of the World Trade Center and the attack on the Pentagon Building, we have what may appear to be a terrorist attack on the people of the United States of America and the first attack ever on United States soil. The problem is how could this have happened and how are we going to stop it from happening again? The answer was for Americans to give up their freedom so government surveillance can be carried out on the population of America without obstruction. It also started something else that will become much more insidious in the years to come. That is reporting any suspicious activity that your neighbors may be involved in to the authorities. In the former Soviet Union, tens of millions of innocent people, guilty of nothing, were rounded up, executed and buried in mass graves because of their neighbors thinking they were guilty of something, or just not liking them.

With all the information about the Rothschild family available, one does not have to question that the motive of this family is one of world domination, which they seem to have accomplished. From one man, a network of evil is cast over all the earth. Just as a spider web is woven as an almost invisible net to catch and entangle its prey, so the Rothschild family's web has been cast and has now entangled the countries, religious orders and the largest of industries of this world. If it has entangled the largest of the world, then it has entangled us too!

Author Andrew Hitchcock wrote a very comprehensive time line of Rothschild history titled "The Synagogue of Satan". The following information regarding the Rothschild family is partly based on Mr. Hitchcock's research and work.

The Rothschild family started in 1743 in Frankfort, Germany, with the birth of Mayer Amschel Bauer. He was the son of a Jewish moneylender by the name of Moses Amschel Bauer. It is said, that on the front of Moses' shop was a sign with a red hexagram on it much like the blue hexagram on the State Flag of Israel. In case you have to wonder, yes there is a link. Either way it is very curious that a Jew would hang an Egyptian symbol representing the sun god having intercourse with the goddess of heaven and earth. One triangle is pointing down and intersecting another triangle pointing up. Other information puts the Roman two-headed Eagle on the red sign for Moses Bauer's business. Either way, you have to ask why a Jewish man would have these pagan symbols as part of his identification. What was it that Moses Amschel Bauer really believed? Whatever it was, it was not Hebrew as is taught to the masses.

The Red Hexagram is said to be the "Seal of Solomon", a sacred sign of the mystical teachings of the Cabala. The Cabala has it roots back to the teachings of the magic practicing priest of Egypt and the worship of the sun or Lucifer. You can be sure whatever Moses Bauer believed, was taught to his son Mayer! What was it that induced Mayer to change the family name from Bauer to Rothschild? Could it have been his knowledge of Cabala and the mystical power involved with this Seal of Solomon? Yes, obviously the "red shield", this sign of Lucifer, was now the sign of the family Rothschild.

What about the flag of the country of Israel, yes what about the "Star of David"? It does not matter what name you give the "Hexagram" it is still a sign of Satan! Jesus words in the Bible book of John were probably never truer when he said in the eighth chapter in the 44th verse, "You are from your father the Devil, and you wish to do the desirers of your father. That one was a manslayer when he began...when he speaks the lie, he speaks according to his own disposition, because he is a liar and the father of the lie." Jesus was talking to the Jewish leaders of his day, whom were Zionist then and we have their descendants with us today. There is no doubt that the Rothschild family is at the heart of Zionism today and controlling its every move. Nor is there any doubt that the family is deeply involved the worship of Lucifer and it is the Devil himself, who is at the heart of their power.

The "Star of David", or the "Seal of Solomon", which ever you wish to call it, has a much older and sinister meaning. The star being tied to the god Moloch and is called the "Star of Moloch". In Hebrew Moloch means King of Shame, but it is a god's title not his name. The god that seems to have had the largest impact on the Nation of Israel was Baal. The nation of Israel always had a problem with this pagan god and for some reason liked to worship him.

Baal has both "male" and "female" qualities. Baal was a fertility god so large orgies would be held in the start of the year to ensure prosperity and in the end of the year, sacrifices would be offered to Baal, who became the form of the god Moloch.

Moloch or Baal required the live sacrifice of human children. Baby Hebrew children were burned alive in the flames of the fire in the idol's lap. Loud drums beat and music played, helping to drown out the screams of the children as they burned to death.

Ultimately, Moloch, or Molech both are variations of the same word or title, are the same as Baal. The god Baal is tied back to the sun god and in fact is the same god. The sun god is none other than Lucifer, who is called either Satan, or Devil in the Bible, in both Hebrew and Christian scriptures.

The "Star's" connection to King Solomon came from one of his pagan wives. Solomon built a temple to Moloch for her and started to offer up "whole burnt offerings" of Israelite babies to gain the favor of Moloch, or Baal. The word "Holocaust" means "Whole burned offering", it is a positive reference to the sacrifice! There is no connection to King David and the Star of Moloch at all. King David would have put all those in Israel who worshiped Moloch to the sword. David would not have tolerated the competition with the Hebrew God YHWH or Yahweh.

This "Star of David" is and has been used in occult astrology and pagan worship back to before Egypt became a world power. However it can be directly related to Egyptology in the worship of the "star god" Rephan also spelled Remphan. The Romans called him Saturn and celebrated him with the holiday Saturnalia and today we call this holiday Christmas. The reality is that the star god Rephan is the representation of Lucifer! The star of Rephan, or Saturn most likely got its start as a representation of Nimrod as sun god and Nimrod incarnate, Tammuz the illegitimate son of Nimrod's wife Semiramis who was conceived after Nimrod's death. So it is plain to see that this star does not have the approval of the faithful servant of the God Yahweh, or Jehovah, the Israelite King David, nor does it represent Jehovah in any way, but is a clear representation of his enemy Lucifer!

In the Bible book Acts of the Apostles chapter 7 verse 42 & 43 reads "Then God turned away from them and gave them up to serve the sun, moon, and stars as their gods! In the book of the Prophets it is written, 'Was it to me you were bring sacrifices during those forty years in the wilderness, Israel? No your real interest was in your pagan gods- the shrine of Molech, the star god Rephan, and the images you made to worship them, so I will send you away into captivity far away in Babylon.'"

We can see that Lucifer has again confused the issue and maneuvered all three of the world's largest religions to use symbolism and holidays to worship him, not the true God of Israel, Yahweh. So with out even knowing it the people of the world have become Luciferians and do not worship the true God Yahweh, or Jehovah.

During the 1760's, Mayer Amschel Bauer is suppose to have worked for a bank owned by the Oppenheimer family in Hamburg, where he started to "network" and make connections that would be valuable in his life. When Mayer's father dies, he returns to Frankfort to take over the family business. For some reason, possibility in sympathy for different Zionist revolutionary groups at the time, Mayer, inspired by the red hexagram over the door of his father's shop and the power it represented, changed his family name to Rothschild, meaning "Red Shield".

Through the connections that Mayer Amschel, now "Rothschild", made, he was able to start doing business with the royalty of Germany. He soon became their "money lender" and banker. It was very clear that lending to heads of state and governments was much more profitable and the Rothschild banking empire was started!

By the 1770's, the "House of Rothschild" becomes an appointed or certified business by the German Prince William of Hanau. This is an endorsement by the Prince and Rothschild's introduction to the rest of the royalty of Europe to do business. As the decade progresses Mayer starts his family and three of his five sons are born. Mayer Amschel Rothschild's sons would learn the family business as well as his Luciferian beliefs while they were children. The nation of Israel was told to instruct their children from infancy so these boys would be learning the special knowledge of the Cabala and of being money lenders, bankers, from the time they could understand simple concepts.

Remember that in 1776 German philosopher and Professor Adam Weishaupt started the Illuminati. There is a connection between Weishaupt and Rothschild. Some believe that it may have been Mayer Amschel Rothschild who is responsible for the inception of the Illuminati, and it was Weishaupt who was the promoter and "Front Man", with financial backing from Rothschild. Most likely the truth of the connection may never really be known, however there is a close connection between the ideals of Zionism and the ideals of the Illuminati. Their goals seem to be one and the same, world domination. It took no time at all for the Illuminati to infiltrate the order of Freemasons at the highest levels. Rich, educated and powerful people who joined the Illuminati were already Freemasons and rich and powerful Freemasons joined the Illuminati. All of these connections would give Mayer Amschel Rothschild a larger group of powerful people to do business with and have greater control over by lending them money. Remember at this time there was a war between England and the American Colonies and Mayer Amschel Rothschild was doing his best to help finance both sides of the conflict. After all, it takes money to run a war and a lot of it!

By the end of the 1780's the country of France finds itself in a state of political unrest and members of the Illuminati take advantage of this and induce the French Revolution. Again Mayer Amschel Rothschild was there financing the revolution and then influencing the new laws and banking system to his benefit.

In 1791, Mayer Amschel Rothschild established The First Bank of America. The bank was given a twenty-year charter, and at the end of the twenty years in 1811, the United States Congress refused to renew Rothschild's charter. At this time, the House of Rothschild was the largest banking firm in England, headed by Mayer Amschel Rothschild's son Nathan. It is said, Nathan became so indignant when the banks charter was not renewed by Congress he was quoted to say, "Teach those impudent Americans a lesson. Bring them back to colonial status!" Nathan Amschel Rothschild ordered the British government to declare war on America and he financed it. This is what caused the War of 1812. In 1815, the war ended and in 1816, the Rothschilds had another bank in the United States of America and a twenty-year charter to go with it.

While this was going on in America, the Rothschild brothers set up banking houses in France and Vienna, as well as England and Germany. Eventually Italy would join the group of countries with Rothschild banks in them.

Mayer Amschel Rothschild dies but before he does, he gives strict instructions that his sons are to carry out. The main point is to keep the money and the power in the Rothschild family. It was forbidden for anyone in the family to marry outside the family, if they did, they would be cut off from the Rothschild money and power.

Napoleon came to power in France, and backed by Rothschild money, set off conquering Europe. While Jacob Rothschild was financing Napoleon, Nathan Rothschild was financing Wellington. It was a win, win situation for the Rothschild brothers since they would make money and control the outcome of the war. This would become a standard method of operation for the Rothschild family; play both sides against each other to achieve the desired outcome. The actual term is "Theses verses anti-theses equal syntheses". No better example of this exists than the Second World War. The Rothschild Family financially backed the different opposing political ideas of the governments involved on both sides of the issue. Both the Allied and Axis powers of World War II were financed by the Rothschild family, including Adolph Hitler's Nazi party.

Through the banking system the Rothschild family had set

up throughout Europe, they also developed a postal system of couriers that would deliver vital news of important events back to the Rothschild family before they became public knowledge. This led to the first "insider trading" scheme and an event that would put the Rothschild family in charge of most of the world's wealth. To support the war between England and France, the English wrote bonds to help finance the war publicly. The bonds were on the stock exchange, much the same way stocks or commodities are traded today. The Rothschild courier had reported to Nathan in London that Wellington had won the war for England. Nathan quickly instructed his workers on the floor of the stock exchange to sell his war bonds; this started a huge sell off at a frantic pace and the value of these bonds dropped dramatically because other brokers thought that Nathan Rothschild had heard something about the war. Maybe it was bad news and that is why he was selling his holdings. When the bonds hit their low point, the Rothschild stockbrokers quietly started buying back all the bonds they could get their hands on. When Wellington's own courier made it back to England with the news that England had won the war with France, these bonds had increased in value and Nathan Rothschild had made a very substantial profit on his investment.

What Nathan Rothschild did with the information he knew is called "insider trading". It is illegal and it still happens today, but only the ultra-rich can do it and get away with it. If you were the president of a country and you knew well in advance of a problem that was coming, like a war, you could start instructing your agents to make investments in industries that manufactured military goods. This could be done very quietly, even years in advance of the potential problem becoming public knowledge.

Nathan Mayer Rothschild was now the richest man in England and therefore most likely the richest man in the world. This one event gave the Rothschild family control over the British economy and forced England to set up a new Bank of England with Nathan Rothschild in charge of it. Obviously, this is a game that will be played repeatedly throughout economic history down to our day today!

Chapter 9 ~The Rulers of Today, Freemasons, The Illuminati?

In 1822, the Rothschild family has arrived, and they enter the royal ranks of Europe, are legitimized and become "Royals" themselves. The Emporia of Austria makes the Rothschild brothers all barons.

By the 1820's, the Rothschild Family has pretty much gained control of the banking system of Europe. There are many other rich and powerful banking families but none are like the Rothschild's in their domination or cunning. There were only two target countries left, Russia and the United States of America that the Rothschild's did not have a dominant foothold in. The Czar of Russia knew the cunning of the Rothschild's and while he did business with them he refused to let them gain control of Russian banks. Many American politicians also understood the danger of letting an outside power gain control of the American banking system and so did the Rothschild's. Nathan Rothschild also knew if he could control a country's money supply he could control the country.

When Andrew Jackson became President of the United States of America, he made it his goal to put an end to the Rothschild's Second Bank of America and he succeeded! He considered this the one greatest act of his administration. There would not be another bank on American soil controlled by the Rothschild family until 1933. This does not mean that they just gave up. The Rothschild family started to infiltrate other banks in the United States and gain foot holds in business.

When the United States started to become divided into a "Northern" and "Southern" way of life, the Rothschild family was quick to jump in and stir up differences between the States of the North and South. The issue of slavery quickly overshadowed the real issues between the States, such as taxation and representation. Newspapers and other media of the day were quickly swaying public opinion that slavery needed to be abolished. Think about it for a minute, slavery was part of the Americas long before there was a United States. The United States was built in part on slave labor both in the North and in the South. So why does slavery now become such a big issue? Did the people of the United States of America suddenly find a conscience some place and conclude that slavery was wrong?

The real problem between the States was that the new Southern "monarchies" would rather do business with their European counterparts instead of the industrialized Northern States. The Southern Freemasons were obviously not working with their Northern counterparts in building business relationships and holding to the fraternity and ideals intended by the "Founding Fathers" of the United States.

With the Northern States becoming more industrialized, immigrants were coming to the United States in droves and they would enter the country mostly through the ports of Boston and New York. The population of the North was growing faster than that of the South, therefore giving the North a larger say in passing laws in Congress. Taxation of imported goods was increased in an effort to get the South to "Buy American" and do business with the domestic manufacturers in the North. The attack of slavery, how wrong it was and how it must be abolished was pretty much the end.

While less than ten percent of the population had slaves, they were a very rich and influential part of the population. These were the people who the politicians "worked for" and were put into political office by. Therefore, you could understand the political outrage and protest launched by Southern politicians. As we know, the War Between the States, better known as the Civil War, broke out.

In order to finance the War, President Lincoln passed the European "money lenders" who were running the banks in America at the time, printed new American Script, and issued it as legal tender. This must have totally infuriated the Rothschild's because the Czar of Russia declared if either England or France interfered by helping the South it would be considered an act of war against Russia, and he sent his navy to protect the east and west coast of America from their interference.

Had either English or French troops taken up the fight along side the South, there would be no doubt that the War Between the States would have had a very different outcome and the Rothschild's would have taken control of the United States, or at least the Southern States much sooner than they did.

It is very unfortunate for both President Lincoln and the Czar of Russia Alexander II that they crossed the Rothschild family. Lincoln paid with his life quickly when he assassinated in 1865, but it would take a little more than fifteen years later in 1881, before Czar Alexander II would meet up with his assassin and it did not stop there. The Rothschild's would get their chance to take their wrath against Russian Empire yet again.

THE PLOT THICKENS!

It is said that in 1895 Edmond James Mayer de Rothschild took an exploratory trip to Palestine and there after provided the funds to start the first Jewish colonies there. This would be the start of the formation of the State of Israel.

In 1897, the Zionist Congress formed as an international political organization, with the goal of repatriating Jewish peoples to their homeland in Palestine. About 200 people attended this First Zionist Congress from 17 countries. The meeting is to be held in Munich, Germany, but after the local Jewish population learned the purpose of the Zionist meeting, they raised such a protest that the meeting location had to be changed from Munich, Germany, to Basel, Switzerland. Obviously, these German Jewish people were very happy where they were living!

You may wonder why there would be such a protest over the plan to create a country for the Jewish people, especially when it was their original "home land" of Palestine. Well think about it for a minute, these Jewish people were Germans and had lived in Germany all their lives! In fact, they had lived in Germany for well over one thousand years. Germany was their homeland!
What would you do if someone were making plans to relocate you and your family from the country you lived in now to another part

of the world that looked nothing like country where you grew up? Most likely, you would protest and get others to protest this plot too!

Right from the start, the Zionist knew they were going to have a very big problem repatriating Jews to Palestine. If the Jewish population in Munich did not want anything to do with moving to Palestine, why would you think that any Jews around the world, who had established lives and families, would give it all up and willingly relocate themselves to a distant land that they knew very little about?

The Zionist, most of who are wealthy and powerful, obviously have an agenda for the Jewish peoples around the world which is to move them to Palestine, but what is their motive? Why would the "elite" of the Jewish people, the Zionist, take it upon themselves to decide that Jews from around the world needed to move back to their "homeland" when everyone was happy where they lived now? Really, anyone would need a very large incentive to leave his or her home and move to a foreign part of the world and resettle.

It only took 5 years for this incentive of come along, how convenient was that? In 1903, persecution of the Jews again broke out in Russia. Thousands of Jewish people were murdered, their homes destroyed and their belongings stolen! They were a people without a country, or were they? The people who left Russia did not head for Palestine, but mostly moved to the United States. Many Jews, who stayed behind in Russia became Bolsheviks and started plotting the revolution to overthrow the Czar.

Before long history would bear out that whatever the Rothschild family wanted, they were going to have what ever it was, that included their own country and the control of world governments and their affairs.

A NEW WORLD ORDER IS BORN!

If we go back to the year 1814 in September, the Congress of Vienna began and would last until June of 1815. At this time, many European countries were in debt to the Rothschild family. The Rothschild's tried to use this debt to leverage the European countries to form a world government. With many countries around the world under the colonial rule of the governments of Europe and national and personal debts owed to the Rothschild family by the governments and royalty of Europe, this would have given the Rothschild's virtual control of the world.

The big obstacle to this plan was Czar Alexander I of Russia. Russia was not in debt to the Rothschild's nor did Russia have a Rothschild bank controlling its money. Because the Czar of Russia would not go along with this plan of a world government the idea failed and this enraged Nathan Mayer Rothschild so badly, it is said he vowed revenge against the Czar, his family and his descendants and he would see to it that the Czar and his family would be destroyed!

The desire of world domination and rule must have been a Rothschild family plan, not just a desire of an old Ashkenazi Jew. We can say this with confidence because almost one hundred years later the Great War breaks out in Europe. It is almost astounding that the assignation of one person could start a world war, but it did!

The Rothschild's were quick to start financing Germany, England and France so they could destroy each other and much of Europe with war. You could be sure that financing would be there for reconstruction of the war-ravaged countries too! Soon even the United States would be drawn into the war largely do to the influence of Rothschild controlled media and the infiltration of Rothschild controlled "agents" into the government of the United States.

THE UNITED STATES OF AMERICA COMES UNDER CONTROL!

The presidency of Woodrow Wilson was a turning point for the United States. Because of his indiscretions, he put himself and his administration under the control of the Zionists. The claim is that President Wilson was being blackmailed in effect by Samuel Untermyer, who now found a way to get pro-Zionist lawmakers into political office. Untermyer's biggest accomplishment came when President Wilson surprised everyone and got Louis Dembitz Brandies appointed as Supreme Court Justice.

Louis Dembitz Brandies was the head of the Provisional Executive Committee for Zionists Affairs and indeed the head of Zionists in America. Do you really think that Justice Brandies was going to be pro American in his decisions, or pro Zionist? The problem was not with his religious beliefs or that he was Jewish. The problem is that the Zionist had their first allegiance to another country, Israel. It does not matter what government they are part of, or in what country that government is, Zionist are and always will be pro Israel!

As the Rothschild organization grew in the United States, they were now finally getting the control that the family had wanted for so long. To help ensure that no one would dare stand in the Rothschilds way, the Anti Deformation League is formed under the direction of Jacob Schiff. The Anti Deformation League's purpose is to combat anti Semitic, or anti Jewish sentiments. In reality, the ADL promotes Zionist interests and the Zionist really do not care very much for the Jewish people who are not Zionist themselves.

In an interview that I personally had the privilege to see, the host interviewing a Hasidic Jewish man who lived with family lived in Israel, asked the question of how did this Hasidic man view Palestinian aggression in Israel? The response from this Hasidic Jewish man was most unexpected! His response was that the Zionist caused the real problem and that Jewish and Arabic peoples have lived together in peace for hundreds and hundreds of years. I have to believe this man, because a good friend of mine has a Jewish mother and an Iranian father and he told me pretty much the same thing, that it is all politics, the people just want to live in peace!

Interestingly enough, it was during Wilson's administration

the Rothschild family established the Federal Reserve Bank. You have to remember that the Federal Reserve is a private bank and not part of the government of the United States of America. It is good to remember too that the United States of America is in debt to the Federal Reserve by more than ten trillion dollars now. Thank you President Wilson! This debt will no doubt keep the people and the government of the United Stated under their control for some time to come.

With the First World War raging, the nations were being plunged deeper and deeper in debt to the bankers of the world. The United States of America is sucked into the First World War about the same time as the Bolshevik Revolution starts in Russia. Russia is already fighting Germany and Japan, a two front war, and now a war from within the country will bring an end to the Russian Monarchy and death to the Czar and his family. Interestingly enough, the Germans, the Japanese and the Bolsheviks are all funded by Rothschild controlled banks.

With the death of one of the most powerful royal families in the world, a loud message was sent to the rest of the European and world monarchies and leaders. Never cross the Rothschild family or it will be your death!

Russia is now under control of the Rothschild family and a Zionist backed Communist government is started as a "Social Experiment" in opposition to the Democratic Social Experiment that was already underway. Europe is laid to waste once again with its countries now even deeper in debt to the Rothschild bankers. They had to borrow the money to destroy each other's countries and now they are going to have to borrow money to rebuild. Once again, the Rothschild family had a bank in the United States, the Federal Reserve, and Zionists had infiltrated the United States Government at the highest levels. Yes, life was good in the Rothschild Empire!

It was now time to end the war and return peace to the world. In order to restore world peace and never have a world war again, a beast is created out of the sea of world war and that beast is going to be known as the League of Nations. It would be yet again an attempt for a world government, except for one thing. The United States would not join the League of Nations.

Even though President Woodrow Wilson wrote the charter for the League of Nations, he could not persuade congress enough to join the "League". Most Americans viewed the League of Nations as a European Organization and saw no need to get involved! So the "crown jewel" of countries, The United States of America, was not going to be a part of a world government. It was going to take a great depression and another world war to convince the United States to come to its senses, be part of a New World Order and come under the rule of the Zionist and the Rothschild family.

The United States did not have to wait very long before problems induced by the Rothschild banking family would strangle America into submission and plunge the world into depression. In 1929, the money supply is tightened to the point where businesses collapse and the stock market crashes. The American economy was in shambles, the Great Depression had taken grip on the lives of Americans and the Untied States is brought to its knees. Unemployment was over twenty-five percent in some areas and mortgages were being foreclosed on by the tens of thousands. Millions of hard working Americans had no jobs and now no homes!

A NEW ORDER TAKES HOLD!

The year 1933 brings a change to America and the rest of the world. Franklin Delano Roosevelt takes office and becomes the thirty-second President of the United States of America.

Franklin Delano Roosevelt says this in his inauguration address about the cause of the Great Depression.

"Primarily this is because rulers of the exchange of mankind's goods have failed through their own stubbornness and their own incompetence, have admitted their failure, and have abdicated. Practices of the unscrupulous moneychangers stand indicted in the court of public opinion, rejected by the hearts and minds of men. True, they have tried, but their efforts have been cast in the pattern of an outworn tradition. Faced by failure of credit they have proposed only the lending of more money. Stripped of the lure of profit by which to induce our people to follow their false leadership, they have resorted to exhortations; pleading tearfully for restored confidence...The moneychangers have fled from their high seats in the temple of our civilization. We may now restore that temple to the ancient truths. The measure of the restoration lies in the extent to which we apply social values more noble than mere monetary profit."

These were interesting words for President Roosevelt to use, considering that the Roosevelt family owns the oldest bank in America, the Bank of New York. It is also interesting that President Roosevelt also had an office in the same building as the Rothschild's Federal Reserve Bank building in New York City.

It would take massive amounts of money to put Americans back to work and President Roosevelt started the largest socialist program seen in America. Among these socialistic programs, was the establishment of the Tennessee Valley, the "TVA". The TVA was responsible for building over 20 hydroelectric dams in Eastern Tennessee and throughout the Smokey Mountains of North Carolina. It was no real coincidence that Oak Ridge Nuclear Laboratory and the ALCOA aluminum processing plant, the largest aluminum processing plant in the world, would both be located outside of Knoxville, Tennessee. Both of these facilities use enormous amounts of electric power and would play key roles in a war that was soon to come!

The United States of America was on its way to an economic recovery, thanks to some socialistic plans aimed at benefiting the common working family. President Roosevelt's popularity grew by leaps and bounds and still today, he is hailed as one of the greatest presidents America ever had. President Roosevelt was no doubt thankful for the success of his "New Deal" programs. To show Americans that better economic times were coming, the look of the One Dollar bill of the United States was going to change. The Dollar was now going to sport the Egyptian Pyramid of the Freemasons, the all Seeing Eye of the Zionist backed Illuminati and in Latin, the translated words New World Order! Make no mistake where the money was coming from to get the American economy started again.

So, what was happening in Germany? Let us see, in 1933 Germany has a new Chancellor, Adolph Hitler. Germany is in worse condition than the United States, because beside the worldwide depression that has struck, Germany had to honor the Treaty of Versailles and pay for war damages too. Hitler is faced with a more formidable task than Roosevelt was, but he used the same approach and got funding to start many socialist programs and a New World Order was born in Germany. It was called the Third Reich! Before long Hitler used the funds he was getting to build out Germany's military might and secure his power in office.

While there are many coincidences between Hitler's Nazi administration and Roosevelt's Democratic administration, the two men have vastly different backgrounds. While Roosevelt was born to the oldest banking family in the world and was preened and educated to achieve a position of power, Hitler is somewhat of an anomaly.

Hitler has a questionable background at best. The most popular belief is that his father was the bastard child of Baron von Rothschild, because Hitler's mother was a servant in the employ of the Rothschilds at the time of her pregnancy. When it was discovered that she was pregnant, she was dismissed and returned to her hometown. The truth is anyone could have gotten Hitler's grandmother pregnant. However, if it is true that Adolph Hitler's grandfather was a Rothschild, and his grandmother, a young servant girl taken advantage of and then cast away like yesterdays trash, it would explain Hitler's predisposal to hate Jewish people.

When Adolph Hitler came to power, he dismissed all the Jews from government office. This angered President Wilson's dear friend and Zionist, Samuel Untermyer, to call for a worldwide boycott of Germany and German made products. Untermyer became Hitler's number one enemy. While Adolph Hitler was doing his best to get the Germany economy going again, Untermyer was doing his best to force Hitler to reappoint all the Jews to the government positions they previously held.

One could only imagine how Roosevelt would have reacted to someone in another country who was getting the world to boycott America, while he was doing his best to rebuild the American economy. I am sure this could be considered a paramount to war, but Untermyer was a private citizen of the United States of America, so there was not much Hitler could do. However, Samuel Untermyer was also a politically active Zionist. A worldwide Zionist State is the government that had Untermyer's allegiance, not America!

During the 1930's, American companies were doing great business with both Germany and Japan. Ford Motors and Stand Oil both had factories in Germany. Ford's plants made everything from cars to battle tanks and were on the Allies "do not bomb list" during the Second World War. The United States was shipping all kind of goods to help the Axis powers build their military might, including vast sums of money. In fact the father and grandfather of our Presidents Bush, Prescott Bush was arrested and his assets seized under the "Trading with the Enemy Act" for helping the Thyssen family owned Union Banking Corp. funnel funds to Hitler and the Nazi Party. Bush was one of the directors of the bank at the time and he was a partner in the firm Brown Brothers Harriman. Germany even lobbied the United States to join the war on the side of Germany. Really, the United States of America and Nazi Germany were allies and trading partners up to the point that Japan bombed Pearl Harbor.

So how did the problem that Hitler had with the Jewish population get out of hand? One thing is for sure, Hitler was not a world leader. He was an underachiever all his life and the only thing that Adolph Hitler had was the gift of speech. Adolph Hitler was little more than a puppet gone mad! His handlers, the true brains and power behind the Nazi Regime, evidently did not want to be under a Zionist New World Order. Secret pacts were made with the Catholic Church to be the "Official State Religion" of the Third Reich and get their backing and financial support to help launch a worldwide Christian Third Reich. Remember that the Catholic Church dominated life in Europe for almost two thousand years and if Germany would win the Second World War, the Catholic Church would carry out not only the domination of Europe, but the rest of the world as well. The Catholic Church had a stake in Hitler's success for world domination.

If a lesson could be learned from the First World War, it was the hard lesson that the Czar of Russia learned. Remember, Russia had a war on two fronts; they were fighting Germany on the western front and Japan on their eastern front. The war had been raging for three years and Russian resources were already stretched, when the Zionist backed Bolsheviks over threw Russia and turned it into a communist state! Hitler, or at least his handlers, knew this history lesson and were not going to let it happen in Germany.

Samuel Untermyer proved to be successful in his efforts to get the Jewish Community worldwide to boycott Germany. Adolph Hitler and his handlers knew that it would be easy for the Jewish Community within Germany and the surrounding countries to cause a "Bolshevik" type revolution under Untermyer's direction and supported with Rothschild and other Zionist money, just as it had happened in Russia during the First World War.

You can question if Samuel Untermyer had not caused the boycott of Germany. In an effort to get Hitler to reinstate Jewish people to their government posts, would Hitler have reacted to the Jewish people the way he did? Really, there is no way of telling. Hitler gave the Jewish people the same choice that the Zionist Bolsheviks gave the Czar of Russia and his family, no choice at all.

More than likely, Hitler would have done exactly the same thing that he did. Remember that the Third Reich had a pact with the Catholic Church, the Holy Roman Empire. After the success of the Bolshevik Revolution, concentration camps sprang up all across Russia and who were those interned and executed with no choice? Millions of Christians both Catholic and Eastern Orthodox were being put to death and buried in mass graves by their Bolshevik captors.

Hitler had a lot of incentive to carry out the cruelty and the extermination of the Jewish people. As he carried out this horrific travesty on a nation of people, the Catholic Church only looked the other way and continued to support the Nazi cause in the hope of the success of the next thousand-year reign of the Third Reich!

The Second World War was truly a battle for the future rule of the world. Was it going to be a Christian backed one thousand year reign of the Third Reich, or a Zionist backed New World Order? Germany's military might marched through any country they wished and they did. Country after country fell to Hitler and the Nazis. The Christian Third Rich was on the way to world domination. With most of Europe secured by the Nazis, except for Great Britain, Hitler focused on Germany's biggest enemy, Communist Russia.

Russia was an important conquest for Germany, because Russia had a vast amount of natural resources that Germany needed to supply its war machine. It was a gross miscalculation on Germany's ally Japan, to attack the United States and bring the industrial might of the United States to the War. It would have been better if Japan attacked Russia along with Germany and used the resources of Russia to rebuild and increase the size of their armies. The United States was part of the New World Order; there was no doubt which side of this conflict it was going to take. It was just a matter of time before the United States would be dragged into the conflict and Japan was used to do just that.

With over 50,000,000 dead and most of Europe once again reduced to rubble, the fate of this Upstart Christian Third Reich whom hoped to rule the world, was reduced to smoke and ash and its leaders were executed by a world court of the countries who made up the New World Order.

THE SACRIFICE IS MADE, THE FUTURE OF THE "NEW WORLD ORDER' IS SECURE!

As the Allied Forces pushed their way to Berlin, the atrocities of the Third Reich were being uncovered and reported to the public! Concentration camps and death camps are discovered throughout Germany and its occupied lands. What would amount to the murder of more than 6,000,000 people, mostly Jews, would come to be called the Holocaust, a "whole burnt offering". Why, is the word "holocaust" chosen to describe what had happened to these people? Yes, many were burned after being murdered by poison gas. Did the children of Israel pass through the fires of the god Moloch again? Where the innocent of Israel made to pass though the fire of Lucifer as a sacrifice, as a "whole burnt offering" a Holocaust? If this was the case, what would be the blessings that were being looked for? Why the sacrifice of more than six million "children of Israel" made to Lucifer? Why was the sacrifice of more than fifty million gentiles made to the god of war? What was gained by all this death and destruction?

The Wild Beast of the League of Nations, who was to keep the peace of the world, was severely injured by the Second World War. It came back as the United Nations headquartered in New York City. Now it was stronger because the United States was a full fledge member of the United Nations. The strongest most powerful countries were now all part of the United Nations.

The Balfour Declaration of 1917, which was a letter from British Foreign Secretary Arthur James Balfour to Lord Walter Rothschild, was now going to have real meaning. A copy of this document below was transmitted to the Zionist Federation of Great Briton and Ireland;

Chapter 9 ~The Rulers of Today, Freemasons, The Illuminati?

Foreign Office
November 2nd, 1917

Dear Lord Rothschild,

I have much pleasure in conveying to you, on behalf of His Majesty's Government, the following declaration of sympathy with Jewish Zionist aspirations which has been submitted to, and approved by, the Cabinet.

"His Majesty's Government view with favor the establishment in Palestine of a national home for the Jewish people, and will use their best endeavors to facilitate the achievement of this object, it being clearly understood that nothing shall be done which may prejudice the civil and religious rights of existing non-Jewish communities in Palestine, or the rights and political status enjoyed by Jews in any other country."

I should be grateful if you would bring this declaration to the knowledge of the Zionist Federation.

Yours sincerely,
Arthur James Balfour

With the atrocities of what the Nazis did to the German Jews, which became so widely publicized, was a mass out pouring for the "Jewish Plight". There was no "Home Land" for the Jewish Nation as a whole, or was there? The Balfour Declaration to the Zionist in Great Britain paved the way for the creation for the state of Israel and in 1947 the United Nations past resolution 181 approving the creation of the State of Israel. The dream of the Rothschild was finally a reality. The Zionist now had control of the "Holy Land" and the Temple Mount was now back in the hands of the leaders of the Nation of Israel and the Jewish people had a home land and a country they could call their own.

There was a problem however. Even though there was now a Jewish nation and a homeland, not many Jews were heading to Israel. Only in areas where persecution broke out in Jewish communities, were they willing to move to the Middle East. In fact, most Jews who escaped persecution in Germany, Eastern Europe and Russia, emigrated to the United States and not Israel. Only Jews who were living in Arabic countries who came under persecution readily moved to Israel. Even after the Holocaust, it would take oppression and persecution to get Jews to move to Israel. It does not take a genius or a world of research to figure out who was behind the persecution of the innocent Jewish people in different countries in an effort to drive them to populate the land that the Rothschild's built, the State of Israel.

The Rothschild family had designs on Palestine and in 1895, Edmond James de Rothschild provided the funds to start the first colonies in Palestine. It was at the first Zionist Congress in 1897 where the plan was unveiled to relocate the Jewish population to Palestine. It was also at this time that the flag for the Zionist State of Israel was designed. The mystic sign of the Star of Moloch, which was the sign of Amschel Mayer Rothschild's business, was changed from the red "Seal of Solomon" to the blue "Star of David" on the Zionist Flag.

With the wake of destruction and death in their path, the Rothschild family obviously connected with Lucifer, and not the Hebrew God Yahweh. Fact is Jesus said the same thing about the Jewish Zealot leaders of his day. In the Bible book of John chapter 8, verse 44 he says, *"You are from your father the devil, and you wish to do the desires of your father. That one was a manslayer when he started...he is a liar and the father of the lie."* Do the research yourself and see how many deaths can be attributed to this one family and their network of stooges and the governments they control! Is it any doubt that these people are Luciferians and have promoted the worship of Satan either directly or indirectly? What is worse is they have forced this worship of Lucifer on the population of the world, either by promoting false religious teaching or distracting society to the more basic satanic things of the world.

It took a little more than fifty years of political pressure and two World Wars for the Zionist to create the State of Israel, but the Rothschilds got their Luciferian State and put the old family sign on the new State Flag of Israel. However, you still need people to make a country so the main goal was to provide free passage to Israel for any Jew wishing to live there.

What came with the State of Israel was the first Luciferian Government and the first Luciferian led military and intelligence agency. Now a real spy network could be set up around the world and feed the most secret information back to those in control. In 1951, Mossad, the Israeli Intelligence Agency was formed and takes the motto "By Way Of Deception, Thou Shalt Do War". This almost sounds as if it could be the motto of the Rothschilds. The fact is that no friendly country spies on the United States of America as much as Israel does. Mossad has been connected with many covert operations against the United States. They are strongly suspected of being involved in the assignation of John F. Kennedy because of several reasons, but the primary one is that Kennedy was totally against nuclear proliferation and Israel was trying to develop the atomic bomb. Joseph Kennedy convinced the Zionist state in America to back his son John in the 1960 election, and if they did, they would have a president in the White House who would vote favorably toward Israel. This could not have been further from the truth and President Kennedy became an obstacle to Israel that needed to be removed!

It is also believed that Mossad was involved with the destruction of the World Trade Center. Americans lost their freedom the day the World Trade Center fell. Really, we did not lose our freedom but gave it up willingly, so we could be better protected from those who would attack us as a nation. Now we are monitored by super computers capable of doing millions of calculations every minute on every man woman and child on the planet. Why, you may ask? It is so as a nation, we can be monitored more easily and closely. However, it is not just the United States that is being spied on it is the whole world in an effort to bring us all under more control.

THE GREAT DEPRESSION OF THE TWENTY FIRST CENTURY!

In the "Dot-Com" era of the 1990's, new wealth was found for many people not only in the United States but around the world. So much money was being made, that the National Debt of the United States and other countries was being paid down quickly. Without debt, the banks of the world would have no hold over the nations and people who owed them money. This was going to be a disaster for the Rothschild banking network. The debt to the Rothschild owned Federal Reserve Bank was vanishing right before everyone's eyes and the Rothschilds were losing money and power over the United States Government. Something had to be done, but what? When George H. W. Bush was elected president, gasoline sold in the United States for about $1.15 USD per gallon. The world was in relative peace. Remember, it was not the popular vote of the people that put Mr. Bush in the President's Office; it was the system of the Electoral College that made Mr. Bush president of the United States! So, what happened during George H. W. Bush's Presidency? The Dot Com era ended, Terrorists attacked The World Trade Center and Americans give up their freedom. Not one but two wars were started by the United States in effort to stop world terrorism. This does not count the numerous death squads sent to destroy terrorist camps in any country that had them.

The United States goes into a recession after the World Trade Center attack, but somehow the housing market keeps doing well and shows growth year after year, thanks to creative lending laws and low attractive interest rates. It is interesting to learn that this is not just happening in the United States, but it is a worldwide investment of capital into housing.

There is only one problem. With the war dragging on in both

Chapter 9 ~The Rulers of Today, Freemasons, The Illuminati?

Iraq and Afghanistan and with insurgents attacking US troops and US backed local forces, oil speculators on the commodity exchange drive oil prices up to almost $140.00 USD a barrel, which in turn pushes gasoline prices up to over $4.00 USD a gallon in the United States. Even OPCE leaders do not understand what is happening to make world oil prices so high. The reason is manipulation of the oil market. So, who has that much money to control world prices and drive them up to artificially inflated prices?

Why does it always come back to the Rothschild family and their network of Luciferians? It is because we live in the age of the "Golden Rule", remember he who has the gold makes the rules! The Rothschild's control the most gold! By driving the gasoline prices from $1.15 to well over $4.00 per gallon, you just took billions of dollars out of the hands of hard working middle class people around the world. If your budget for gas and oil was for about $100 USD per week to travel to work and heat your house and you now had to pay $400 a week that is an increase of $1200 per month! That is about your average mortgage payment in the United States and you now have a choice to make; you either don't go to work and lose your house or you go to work and lose your house. Either way, if you took advantage of those creative interest rates that banks offered around the world, there is a good chance that you were going to lose your home to bank foreclosure.

As we have seen in 2008, banks were failing all over the world. The worldwide economy was going to grind to a stop just as it had in the great depression of 1929! Something had to be done quickly! Borrow more money! What a great idea!

People of the world should be very incensed over the banking fraud, which we as a people have been thrust in to! In order to stop the collapse of the failing banks in America, the United States Government chose to go to the Rothschild bank, the Federal Reserve, to borrow money to give to banks the Rothschild family or their associates owned. How stupid is this? The world governments are borrowing money from the world's largest banks and giving it to their "branch offices" so the branch offices do not close.

Why do the hard working people of the world have to carry the sickening rich on their backs? Why are the poorest countries only getting poorer and the "middle class" of rich countries are disappearing and becoming homeless and falling into poverty? How did those elected officials who we put into office let this happen to their constituents?

It is good to remember here that the Bush family made their money in oil and banking! Did we pay for George Bush's failure? I really do not think he failed, but he carried out his orders very well. The Bush family made millions if not billions between the rise in oil prices and their bank holdings. Even with all the bank failures taking place, with one trillion dollars in loans from the Federal Reserve, you can accomplish almost anything, including creating a national debt that will never be paid back and plunging the United States deeper under the control of the Federal Reserve Bank. Yes, "George W" did the job he was sent to do. Put America back under the control of the Rothschild family by creating a National Debt never before seen in United States history. One that could burden our children and grandchildren, indeed a debt that could never be paid back! Even worse is that it's going to take even more money to prevent the depression cast on the United States as the new President needs to borrow nearly another trillion dollars from the Federal Reserve. With the stroke of a pen by two presidents in less than a year, the people of the United States will have to pay the additional debt of two trillion dollars to the Rothschild family on top of the trillions we already owe them!

Why would this family want more money? The truth is they do not! They already have all the money and are just printing paper that is backed by nothing of any value. The control of the governments of the world is what the Rothschild family wants. Control of the world and to set up a Zionist New World Order is the primary goal toward which they have been working. From the time of the first Congress of Vienna in 1814, the Rothschild family has been trying to unite the world under one central government they could control. A European Federation was attempted after the

Chapter 9 ~The Rulers of Today, Freemasons, The Illuminati?

Napoleonic war ravaged Europe. The League of Nations was established after the First World War and it failed. After the Second World War, it was the United Nations. Will it take another war to bring the governments into submission of a one-world government? If it does, it will be a war won without a shot fired!

Almost every country in the world is in debt to a bank connected to the Rothschild family. What if you were told you that you would never have to pay income tax again if you voted to join a world government? What if the Federal Reserve said it would wipe out all of the debt of the United States if congress would vote to give total submission and support to the government of the New World Order? What if every country of the world had its national debt forgiven if in return it gave up its national identity and became a state of the New World Order? Impossible you say? Think about how much you had to pay in income tax, property tax, taxes on food and clothing, taxes on imported goods, and sales tax. Just add up all the taxes you pay and take them away.

Just think, if the bank that holds your mortgage called you up one day and said we are going to forgive the mortgage on your house so you no longer have to make any payments. In return, you have to join a political party, the New World Order, and submit and give your allegiance to support it.

The advantage of a one world government would be an almost certain end to war, reduction or elimination of taxes, more even distribution of wealth, and world issues could be addressed quickly and put to rest. Language barriers would fall and international problems would be reduced, if not a thing of the past. Food shortage, health issues and poverty can be dealt with quickly. The end of inflation, recession and depression could be here. You could have the greatest minds of the world working to solve the problems we face as a civilization, such as Global Warming, pollution, energy shortages, food shortage AIDS, and cancer. The natural and political barriers that separated mankind before would be done away with and the world could be united and work together to bring a lasting peace and security to all of mankind!

Yes, if we live in the "Age of the Golden Rule" and he who has the gold makes the rules, then the governments of the world are powerless because they are all in debt! Soon the world's richest banking family will foreclose on the debt of the world to bring it into the submission of its domination and the New World Order will become a reality. The government for the New World Order is already in place, supported by Freemasons, the Illuminati and the Zionist juggernaut. They will divide and rule over all! Do you need proof of this? Just look on the back of your one dollar bill and read the inscription written in Latin around the Masonic pyramid and the all seeing eye of the Illuminati and realize that this dollar was borrowed from the Rothschild-owned Federal Reserve bank and you'll see that the New World Order is already with us!

Remember that the pyramid or upward pointed triangle is the "Ultimate Feminine", so who is the "Ultimate Masculine" that makes up the star of the Israeli flag? The hexagon star of the connecting triangles must be the complete union between Lucifer and his earthly bride.

CHAPTER 10
THE PROTOCOL OF THE LEARNED ELDERS OF ZION

The "Protocol of the Learned Elders of Zion" is supposed to be the minutes to secret meetings of Zionist leaders, with the objective to found a "New World Order", under a "One World Government". It was published over a hundred years ago in Russia and people who were connected to "The Protocol" somehow were murdered or died under mysterious circumstances.

You have to take into consideration too, that in the early days of communist Russia, if you were found with a copy of "The Protocols" you would be shot on sight! Remember that early communism in Russia was placed there by the Zionist backed Bolshevik Revolution. If "The Protocols" were "fiction", or a scheme to make the Zionist look bad, why would there be an automatic death penalty to own this information?

The only logical conclusion is that there is something to the legitimacy of "The Protocols of the Learned Elders of Zion". This book was published over a hundred years ago. Who really cares anymore? True many people do not care and most people have never heard of "The Protocols" and those who have heard of them claim they are just a work of fiction and that they have no real value.

When doing the research for this subject, I came across information that stated that "The Protocols" were plagiarized from a novel and turned into a work of fiction to be used against Zionist interest. I am not sure how you plagiarize something and turn it into a work of fiction. If you took a factual event that someone wrote about, an idea that someone had, and then wrote a story about those facts, I think you would have another novel.

For a book or document to warrant such criticism as has been lobbied against "The Protocols", and for an entire country to not just ban this book, but make its ownership a matter of immediate execution, warrants us to take a closer look at what it says. To think that people may have actually been executed for having this book, makes one think back to the people whom the Church burned at the stake for reading the Bible.

THE PROTOCOLS REACH AMERICA

"The Protocols" was first published in Saint Petersburg, Russia in 1903. It was published in the United States on October 27 and 28. Excerpts from the English translation appeared as the "Red Bible" in the Philadelphia Public Ledger.

After it was translated into English in 1920 and sold one million copies. The American Industrialist Henry Ford took a great interest in what "The Protocol" had to say and sponsored 500,000 copies of the books printing. Mr. Ford had "The Protocols" published in the Dearborn Independent in a series from 1920 to 1922. In an interview published in the New York World, February 17 1921, Henry Ford made the following statement.

"The only statement I care to make about the Protocols is that they fit in with what is going on. They are sixteen years old, and they have fitted the world situation up to this time. They fit it now."

Mr. Ford was going to pay for his support of "the Protocols" and his public awareness campaign. The following is an excerpt from the American Jewish Historical Society.

CHAPTER 85
HENRY FORD INVENTS A JEWISH CONSPIRACY

Henry Ford, the industrial genius who perfected the mass production of motorcars before World War I and thereby revolutionized the way we live, was a reclusive man who brooked no opposition or criticism. Ford's determination to prevent unionism at his plants produced strikes and violence, mostly initiated by Ford's own strikebreakers. He opposed various symbols of social and cultural change around him, including Hollywood movies, out-of-home childcare, government regulation of business, Eastern European immigration and new fashions in dress and music. In 1927, Ford's anti-Semitism brought him, for one of the few times in his life, to humiliation.

In an age that celebrated industrial heroes, Ford was a true giant. In 1922, he considered running for the presidency. Public opinion polls reflected his widespread support. Despite his desire to occupy the most visible position in the nation, historian Keith Sward described Ford as "inaccessible as the Grand Lama" and an anti-democrat. One of the few individuals Ford trusted was his personal secretary, Ernest Liebold, whom historian Leo Ribuffo calls "an ambitious martinet" who took advantage of Ford's dislike of paperwork and refusal to read his mail to control access to the great man. Ford would later blame Liebold for his Jewish woes.

In the period from 1910 to 1918, Ford grew increasingly anti-immigrant, anti-labor, anti-liquor and anti-Semitic. In 1919, he purchased a newspaper, the *Dearborn Independent.* He installed an editor and hired a journalist, William J. Cameron, to listen to his ideas and write a weekly column in his name.

Strangely, Ford came to believe in a Jewish world conspiracy. He blamed Jewish financiers for fomenting World War I so that they could profit from supplying both sides. He suspected Jewish automobile dealers of conspiring to undermine Ford Company sales policies. Ford vented his beliefs about Jewish power public in the pages of the *Dearborn Independent.* For a year, the editor resisted running Ford's anti-Jewish articles and finally resigned rather than publish them. Cameron, Ford's personal columnist, took over the editorship and, in May 1920, published the first of a series of articles titled "The International Jew: The World's Problem."

For the next 18 months, Cameron ran the "International Jew" as a series and later collected the articles and published them as a book. Liebold hired former military intelligence investigators to assist Cameron in gathering so-called "evidence" that "proved" Jewish control of world finance, Jewish organization of radical political movements and Jewish manipulation of diplomacy to cause wars in which Christians died to enrich Jews. The investigators unearthed evidence that president Woodrow Wilson took secret orders over the phone from Justice Brandeis and that a Jewish member of the Federal Reserve Board personally thwarted Ford's plan to purchase nitrate mines from the Federal government.

A few months after the series began, Ford's operatives introduced him to a Russian émigré, Paquita de Shishmareff. She showed Ford a copy of the *Protocols of the Elders of Zion*, a document forged by the Russian czar's secret service at the turn of the century that purportedly recorded a series of lectures by European Jewish leaders that outlined a conspiracy by Jewish communists and bankers to overthrow European governments. Ford passed a copy of the *Protocols* to Cameron and the *Independent* turned its attention to bringing this "blueprint" for world destruction to the public.

As historian Ribuffo puts it, "Whether or not an Elder of Zion actually gave these lectures" described in the *Protocols,* "it was clear [to Ford] that Jews used these ideas to 'corrupt Public Opinion,' [that Jews] controlled finance, sponsored revolution, and were 'everywhere' exercising power." The *Independent* charged that the Jewish-inspired national debt was enslaving Americans and that German Jewish financier Paul Warburg had emigrated to America "for the express purpose of changing our financial system" by creating the Federal Reserve. As an "international nation" of people who cooperated with each other, Jews had an unfair advantage in business over Christians, who relied on individualism to get ahead. The paper even described American Jewish aid for European Jewish victims of pogroms as part of the conspiracy.

For seven years, the *Independent* continued to publish anti-Semitic articles until the target of one series, California farm cooperative organizer Aaron Sapiro, sued Ford for libel. Sapiro was the third Jew to sue Ford and the first to get to trial. Ford refused to testify and apparently staged an automobile accident so he could hide in a hospital. The judge finally declared a mistrial but Ford decided to settle with Sapiro out of court. During the trial, Jewish leaders had called for a boycott of Ford motorcars and slumping sales might have played a role in Ford's decision to put the case behind him.

Leaders of the American Jewish Committee and B'nai Brith Anti-Defamation League negotiated an agreement whereby Ford publicly announced that "articles reflecting on the Jews" would never again appear in the *Independent.* Ford claimed that he was "mortified" to learn the *Protocols* were forged, described himself as "fully aware of the virtues of the Jewish people" and offered them his "future friendship and good will." He claimed to have been too busy to read the pieces and implicitly blamed Liebold and Cameron for printing them. Louis Marshall, chair of the American Jewish Committee, described Ford's statement as "humiliating."

Ford closed the *Independent* in December 1927. He later claimed that his signature on the agreement with Marshall was forged, and that Jewish bankers had caused World War II. Ford died in 1947, apparently unrepentant.

It was very apparent to Henry Ford that saving his business was more important than his personal beliefs, so he did what he had to do to save his business and put the issue he had created with the "Jewish leaders" behind him. By the closing words in the above excerpt, it is obvious that the "Jewish leaders" wanted to teach Henry Ford a lesson he would not forget and to show the solidarity of the Jewish community.

The problem was Mr. Ford most likely thought of all Jewish people as the "same" and a threat to the world and was labeled as anti-Semitic. If Mr. Ford had understood it was the Rothschild family and their controlled banking system and not "Jewish bankers" that were responsible for world wars and the control of countries and their political systems, maybe he would have chosen his words more wisely. Instead, he grouped all Jewish people together as the same.

The problem that Mr. Ford understood quite well was the take over of the world by Zionist and Zionist interests. While Zionist may claim to be of Jewish or Hebrew faith, the Zionists and Luciferians first being Jewish maybe, practicing the true Hebrew faith and keeping the laws of Yahweh, this is furthest from what they want to do! Remember these people either are, or they are being directed by Luciferians, yes devil worshipers at the highest and most pure level!

When you look at world events in the last hundred years, the plight of Jewish people has been horrific! They have faced persecution almost world wide, having had to relocate from country to country to escape religious and social persecution. It took the Holocaust, the "whole burnt offering" to Lucifer, to give the Jewish people their own country.

It would be logical to think that if you were going to give land to a people to start a country that you would give them land that was home to their ancestors. This is what happened in the case of the State of Israel. You would also think that these people would flock to a country they could call their own, as this has not been the case with the State of Israel. Most of the inhabitants of the State of Israel were forced to move to the Luciferian, Zionist house that Rothschild built!

When you look at who is being controlled in this world, by either government or religion, no people are probably controlled more than the Jewish Nation. As a people, they are scattered across the globe, but they react as one group and rally to whatever cause they are asked to by those who lead or control them. You really need to ask how anti-Semitic, the Zionists themselves are, or can be. It seems obvious when you look at events closely, that the common Jewish person is nothing more than cannon fodder for their Luciferian leaders to accomplish their goals.

THE FUTURE IS WRITTEN IN HISTORY.

What are the goals of the Luciferians? We are going to

examine the goals of the "Learned Elders of Zion" and compare them to what has already happened in the past hundred years. If "The Protocols" are a fake, a plagiarized forgery, then there should be very little resemblance between "The Protocol" and the reality of history. Really, what are the chances of writing something to discredit, or bring persecution against a group of people and have it be a prophecy of the future?

In reality, we should and would expect no similarity between what was written over one hundred years ago in "The Protocols" and what history has recorded. That would be a reasonable expectation. Why then did Henry Ford say, "They are sixteen years old, and they have fitted the world situation up to this time. They fit it now." Mr. Ford recognized a pattern between what was written in the protocols and what was happening in the world at that time.

What we are going to do is examine the goals of the Learned Elders of Zion and what was written in "The Protocol and what has happened in reality over the last one hundred years and see if we can find any matches or coincidences between the two.

The Protocols are broken down into twenty-four parts, or chapters. Each chapter deals with a different segment of infiltration to gain world control. It is obvious that many of the plans outlined in "The Protocol" would take many years and a lot of money and in some cases many, many lives both Jewish and non-Jew to accomplish the desired outcome of the Elders of Zion.

The following are excerpts form The Protocol of the Learned Elders. The main purpose of the reprinting of the following excerpts are to allow you, the reader, to decide for yourself if the plan of the Learned Elders of Zion is real or not and if they have had any effect on the Twentieth Century. If they did have an effect on the Twentieth Century, will they also affect us here in the Twenty First Century, if so will they also affect our future? Also, remember that Mr. Henry Ford saw a trend occurring in the sixteen years that "The Protocols" had been published in book form.

What tools would these "Learned Elders" use to gain

control of the governments of the world? Was there really a plan for world conquest and a "New World Order", a world with only one government? Do "The Protocols" reveal that plan? Let us examine them and see!

PROTOCOL I
THE BASIC DOCTRINE

3. It must be noted that men with bad instincts are more in number than the good, and therefore the best results in governing them are attained by violence and terrorization, and not by academic discussions.

6. Political freedom is an idea but not a fact. This idea one must know how to apply whenever it appears necessary with this bait of an idea to attract the masses of the people to one's party for the purpose of crushing another who is in authority. This task is rendered easier if the opponent has himself been infected with the idea of freedom, SO-CALLED LIBERALISM, and, for the sake of an idea, is willing to yield some of his power. It is precisely here that the triumph of our theory appears; the slackened reins of government are immediately, by the law of life, caught up and gathered together by a new hand, because the blind might of the nation cannot for one single day exist without guidance, and the new authority merely fits into the place of the old already weakened by liberalism.

GOLD

7. In our day the power which has replaced that of the rulers who were liberal is the power of Gold...

8. Whether a State exhausts itself in its own convulsions, whether its internal discord brings it under the power of external foes - in any case it can be accounted irretrievably lost: IT IS IN OUR POWER. The despotism of Capital, which is entirely in our

hands, reaches out to it a straw that the State, willy-nilly, must take hold of: if not - it goes to the bottom.

11. The political has nothing in common with the moral. The ruler who is governed by the moral is not a skilled politician, and is therefore unstable on his throne. He who wishes to rule must have recourse both to cunning and to make-believe. Great national qualities, like frankness and honesty, are vices in politics, for they bring down rulers from their thrones more effectively and more certainly than the most powerful enemy. Such qualities must be the attributes of the kingdoms of the GOYIM, but we must in no way be guided by them.

RIGHT IS MIGHT

12. Our right lies in force. The word "right" is an abstract thought and proved by nothing. The word means no more than: Give me what I want in order that thereby I may have a proof that I am stronger than you.

16. Out of the temporary evil we are now compelled to commit will emerge the good of an unshakable rule, which will restore the regular course of the machinery of the national life, brought to naught by liberalism. The result justifies the means. Let us, however, in our plans, direct our attention not so much to what is good and moral as to what is necessary and useful.

17. Before us is a plan in which is laid down strategically the line from which we cannot deviate without running the risk of seeing the labor of many centuries brought to naught.

19. Only one trained from childhood for independent rule can have understanding of the words that can be made up of the political alphabet.

WE ARE DESPOTS

21. It is only with a despotic ruler that plans can be elaborated extensively and clearly in such a way as to distribute the whole properly among the several parts of the machinery of the State: from this the conclusion is inevitable that a satisfactory form of government for any country is one that concentrates in the hands of one responsible person. Without an absolute despotism there can be no existence for civilization which is carried on not by the masses but by their guide, whosoever that person may be. The mob is savage, and displays its savagery at every opportunity. The moment the mob seizes freedom in its hands it quickly turns to anarchy, which in itself is the highest degree of savagery.

22. Behold the alcoholic animals, bemused with drink, the right to an immoderate use of which comes along with freedom. It is not for us and ours to walk that road. The peoples of the GOYIM are bemused with alcoholic liquors; their youth has grown stupid on classicism and from early immorality, into which it has been inducted by our special agents - by tutors, lackeys, governesses in the houses of the wealthy, by clerks and others, by our women in the places of dissipation frequented by the GOYIM. In the number of these last I count also the so-called "society ladies," voluntary followers of the others in corruption and luxury.

23. Our countersign is - Force and Make-believe. Only force conquers in political affairs, especially if it be concealed in the talents essential to statesmen. Violence must be the principle, and cunning and make-believe the rule for governments which do not want to lay down their crowns at the feet of agents of some new power...

24. Our State, marching along the path of peaceful conquest, has the right to replace the horrors of war by less noticeable and more satisfactory sentences of death, necessary to maintain the terror which tends to produce blind submission...

Chapter 10 ~ The Protocol of the Learned Elders of ZION

WE SHALL END LIBERTY

25. Far back in ancient times we were the first to cry among the masses of the people the words "Liberty, Equality, Fraternity," words many times repeated since these days by stupid poll-parrots who, from all sides around, flew down upon these baits and with them carried away the well-being of the world, true freedom of the individual, formerly so well guarded against the pressure of the mob...

26. In all corners of the earth the words "Liberty, Equality, Fraternity," brought to our ranks, thanks to our blind agents, whole legions who bore our banners with enthusiasm. And all the time these words were canker-worms at work boring into the well-being of the GOYIM, putting an end everywhere to peace, quiet, solidarity and destroying all the foundations of the GOY States. As you will see later, this helped us to our triumph: it gave us the possibility, among other things, of getting into our hands the master card - the destruction of the privileges, or in other words of the very existence of the aristocracy of the GOYIM, that class which was the only defense peoples and countries had against us. On the ruins of the natural and genealogical aristocracy of the GOYIM we have set up the aristocracy of our educated class headed by the aristocracy of money. The qualifications for this aristocracy we have established in wealth, which is dependent upon us, and in knowledge, for which our learned elders provide the motive force.

28. The abstraction of freedom has enabled us to persuade the mob in all countries that their government is nothing but the steward of the people who are the owners of the country, and that the steward may be replaced like a worn-out glove.

29. It is this possibility of replacing the representatives of the people which has placed at our disposal, and, as it were, given us the power of appointment.

PROTOCOL No. 2

1. It is indispensable for our purpose that wars, so far as possible, should not result in territorial gains: war will thus be brought on to the economic ground, where the nations will not fail to perceive in the assistance we give the strength of our predominance, and this state of things will put both sides at the mercy of our international AGENTUR; which possesses millions of eyes ever on the watch and unhampered by any limitations whatsoever. Our international rights will then wipe out national rights, in the proper sense of right, and will rule the nations precisely as the civil law of States rules the relations of their subjects among themselves.

DESTRUCTIVE EDUCATION

3. Do not suppose for a moment that these statements are empty words: think carefully of the successes we arranged for Darwinism (Evolution), Marxism (Communism), and Nietzsche-ism (Socialism). To us Jews, at any rate, it should be plain to see what a disintegrating importance these directives have had upon the minds of the GOYIM.

5. In the hands of the States of to-day there is a great force that creates the movement of thought in the people, and that is the Press. The part played by the Press is to keep pointing our requirements supposed to be indispensable, to give voice to the complaints of the people, to express and to create discontent. It is in the Press that the triumph of freedom of speech finds its incarnation. But the GOYIM States have not known how to make use of this force; and it has fallen into our hands. Through the Press we have gained the power to influence while remaining ourselves in the shade; thanks to the Press we have got the GOLD in our hands, notwithstanding that we have had to gather it out of the oceans of blood and tears. But it has paid us, though we have sacrificed many of our people. Each victim on our side is worth in

the sight of God a thousand GOYIM.

PROTOCOL No. 3

3. In order to incite seekers after power to a misuse of power we have set all forces in opposition one to another, breaking up their liberal tendencies towards independence. To this end we have stirred up every form of enterprise, we have armed all parties, we have set up authority as a target for every ambition. Of States we have made gladiatorial arenas where a lot of confused issues contend ... A little more, and disorders and bankruptcy will be universal ...

POVERTY OUR WEAPON

5. All people are chained down to heavy toil by poverty more firmly than ever. They were chained by slavery and serfdom; from these, one way and another, they might free themselves. These could be settled with, but from want they will never get away. We have included in the constitution such rights as to the masses appear fictitious and not actual rights. All these so-called "Peoples Rights" can exist only in idea, an idea which can never be realized in practical life. What is it to the proletariat laborer, bowed double over his heavy toil, crushed by his lot in life, if talkers get the right to babble, if journalists get the right to scribble any nonsense side by side with good stuff, once the proletariat has no other profit out of the constitution save only those pitiful crumbs which we fling them from our table in return for their voting in favor of what we dictate, in favor of the men we place in power, the servants of our AGENTUR ... Republican rights for a poor man are no more than a bitter piece of irony, for the necessity he is under of toiling almost all day gives him no present use of them, but the other hand robs him of all guarantee of regular and certain earnings by making him dependent on strikes by his comrades or lockouts by his masters.

WE SUPPORT COMMUNISM

6. The people, under our guidance, have annihilated the aristocracy, who were their one and only defense and foster-mother for the sake of their own advantage which is inseparably bound up with the well-being of the people. Nowadays, with the destruction of the aristocracy, the people have fallen into the grips of merciless money-grinding scoundrels who have laid a pitiless and cruel yoke upon the necks of the workers.

7. We appear on the scene as alleged saviours of the worker from this oppression when we propose to him to enter the ranks of our fighting forces - Socialists, Anarchists, Communists - to whom we always give support in accordance with an alleged brotherly rule (of the solidarity of all humanity) of our SOCIAL MASONRY. The aristocracy, which enjoyed by law the labor of the workers, was interested in seeing that the workers were well fed, healthy, and strong. We are interested in just the opposite - in the diminution the KILLING OUT OF THE GOYIM. Our power is in the chronic shortness of food and physical weakness of the worker because by all that this implies he is made the slave of our will, and he will not find in his own authorities either strength or energy to set against our will. Hunger creates the right of capital to rule the worker more surely than it was given to the aristocracy by the legal authority of kings.

8. By want and the envy and hatred which it engenders we shall move the mobs and with their hands we shall wipe out all those who hinder us on our way.

9. WHEN THE HOUR STRIKES FOR OUR SOVEREIGN LORD OF ALL THE WORLD TO BE CROWNED IT IS THESE SAME HANDS WHICH WILL SWEEP AWAY EVERYTHING THAT MIGHT BE A HINDRANCE THERETO

Chapter 10 ~ The Protocol of the Learned Elders of ZION

10. The GOYIM have lost the habit of thinking unless prompted by the suggestions of our specialists. Therefore they do not see the urgent necessity of what we, when our kingdom comes, shall adopt at once, namely this, that IT IS ESSENTIAL TO TEACH IN NATIONAL SCHOOLS ONE SIMPLE, TRUE PIECE OF KNOWLEDGE, THE BASIS OF ALL KNOWLEDGE - THE KNOWLEDGE OF THE STRUCTURE OF HUMAN LIFE, OF SOCIAL EXISTENCE, WHICH REQUIRES DIVISION OF LABOR, AND, CONSEQUENTLY, THE DIVISION OF MEN INTO CLASSES AND CONDITIONS. It is essential for all to know that OWING TO DIFFERENCE IN THE OBJECTS OF HUMAN ACTIVITY THERE CANNOT BE ANY EQUALITY...

11. THIS HATRED WILL BE STILL FURTHER MAGNIFIED BY THE EFFECTS of an ECONOMIC CRISES, which will stop dealing on the exchanges and bring industry to a standstill. We shall create by all the secret subterranean methods open to us and with the aid of gold, which is all in our hands, A UNIVERSAL ECONOMIC CRISES WHEREBY WE SHALL THROW UPON THE STREETS WHOLE MOBS OF WORKERS SIMULTANEOUSLY IN ALL THE COUNTRIES...

12. "OURS" THEY WILL NOT TOUCH, BECAUSE THE MOMENT OF ATTACK WILL BE KNOWN TO US AND WE SHALL TAKE MEASURES TO PROTECT OUR OWN.

15. Ever since that time we have been leading the peoples from one disenchantment to another, so that in the end they should turn also from us in favor of that KING-DESPOT OF THE BLOOD OF ZION, WHOM WE ARE PREPARING FOR THE WORLD.

16. At the present day we are, as an international force, invincible, because if attacked by some we are supported by other States. It is the bottomless rascality of the GOYIM peoples, who crawl on their bellies to force, but are merciless towards weakness, unsparing to faults and indulgent to crimes, unwilling to bear the contradictions of a free social system but patient unto martyrdom

under the violence of a bold despotism - it is those qualities which are aiding us to independence.

18. It is explained by the fact that these dictators whisper to the peoples through their agents that through these abuses they are inflicting injury on the States with the highest purpose - to secure the welfare of the peoples, the international brotherhood of them all, their solidarity and equality of rights. Naturally they do not tell the peoples that this unification must be accomplished only under our sovereign rule.

20. The word "freedom" brings out the communities of men to fight against every kind of force, against every kind of authority even against God and the laws of nature. For this reason we, when we come into our kingdom, shall have to erase this word from the lexicon of life as implying a principle of brute force which turns mobs into bloodthirsty beasts.

21. These beasts, it is true, fall asleep again every time when they have drunk their fill of blood, and at such time can easily be riveted into their chains. But if they be not given blood they will not sleep and continue to struggle.

PROTOCOL No. 4

1. Every republic passes through several stages. The first of these is comprised in the early days of mad raging by the blind mob, tossed hither and thither, right and left: the second is demagogy from which is born anarchy, and that leads inevitably to despotism - not any longer legal and overt, and therefore responsible despotism, but to unseen and secretly hidden, yet nevertheless sensibly felt despotism in the hands of some secret organization or other, whose acts are the more unscrupulous inasmuch as it works behind a screen, behind the backs of all sorts of agents, the changing of whom not only does not injuriously affect but actually aids the secret force by saving it, thanks to continual changes,

from the necessity of expanding its resources on the rewarding of long services.

2. Who and what is in a position to overthrow an invisible force? And this is precisely what our force is. GENTILE masonry blindly serves as a screen for us and our objects, but the plan of action of our force, even its very abiding-place, remains for the whole people an unknown mystery.

WE SHALL DESTROY GOD

3. But even freedom might be harmless and have its place in the State economy without injury to the well-being of the peoples if it rested upon the foundation of faith in God, upon the brotherhood of humanity, unconnected with the conception of equality, which is negatived by the very laws of creation, for they have established subordination. With such a faith as this a people might be governed by a wardship of parishes, and would walk contentedly and humbly under the guiding hand of its spiritual pastor submitting to the dispositions of God upon earth. This is the reason why IT IS INDISPENSABLE FOR US TO UNDERMINE ALL FAITH, TO TEAR OUT OF THE MIND OF THE "GOYIM" THE VERY PRINCIPLE OF GOD-HEAD AND THE SPIRIT, AND TO PUT IN ITS PLACE ARITHMETICAL CALCULATIONS AND MATERIAL NEEDS.

4. In order to give the GOYIM no time to think and take note, their minds must be diverted towards industry and trade. Thus, all the nations will be swallowed up in the pursuit of gain and in the race for it will not take note of their common foe. But again, in order that freedom may once for all disintegrate and ruin the communities of the GOYIM, we must put industry on a speculative basis: the result of this will be that what is withdrawn from the land by industry will slip through the hands and pass into speculation, that is, to our classes.

5. The intensified struggle for superiority and shocks delivered to economic life will create, nay, have already created, disenchanted, cold and heartless communities. Such communities will foster a strong aversion towards the higher political and towards religion. Their only guide is gain, that is Gold, which they will erect into a veritable cult, for the sake of those material delights which it can give. Then will the hour strike when, not for the sake of attaining the good, not even to win wealth, but solely out of hatred towards the privileged, the lower classes of the GOYIM will follow our lead against our rivals for power, the intellectuals of the GOYIM.

PROTOCOL No. 5

1. ...What form of rule is to be given to these communities if not that despotism which I shall describe to you later? We shall create an intensified centralization of government in order to grip in our hands all the forces of the community. We shall regulate mechanically all the actions of the political life of our subjects by new laws. These laws will withdraw one by one all the indulgences and liberties which have been permitted by the GOYIM, and our kingdom will be distinguished by a despotism of such magnificent proportions as to be at any moment and in every place in a position to wipe out any GOYIM who oppose us by deed or word.

3. In the times when the peoples looked upon kings on their thrones as on a pure manifestation of the will of God, they submitted without a murmur to the despotic power of kings: but from the day when we insinuated into their minds the conception of their own rights they began to regard the occupants of thrones as mere ordinary mortals. The holy unction of the Lord's Anointed has fallen from the heads of kings in the eyes of the people, and when we also robbed them of their faith in God the might of power was flung upon the streets into the place of public proprietorship and was seized by us.

Chapter 10 ~ The Protocol of the Learned Elders of ZION

MASSES LED BY LIES

4. Moreover, the art of directing masses and individuals by means of cleverly manipulated theory and verbiage, by regulations of life in common and all sorts of other quirks, in all which the GOYIM understand nothing, belongs likewise to the specialists of our administrative brain. Reared on analysis, observation, on delicacies of fine calculation, in this species of skill we have no rivals, any more than we have either in the drawing up of plans of political actions and solidarity. In this respect the Jesuits alone might have compared with us, but we have contrived to discredit them in the eyes of the unthinking mob as an overt organization, while we ourselves all the while have kept our secret organization in the shade. However, it is probably all the same to the world who is its sovereign lord, whether the head of Catholicism or our despot of the blood of Zion! But to us, the Chosen People, it is very far from being a matter of indifference.

5. FOR A TIME PERHAPS WE MIGHT BE SUCCESSFULLY DEALT WITH BY A COALITION OF THE “GOYIM” OF ALL THE WORLD: but from this danger we are secured by the discord existing among them whose roots are so deeply seated that they can never now be plucked up. We have set one against another the personal and national reckonings of the GOYIM, religious and race hatreds, which we have fostered into a huge growth in the course of the past twenty centuries. This is the reason why there is not one State which would anywhere receive support if it were to raise its arm, for every one of them must bear in mind that any agreement against us would be unprofitable to itself. We are too strong - there is no evading our power. THE NATIONS CANNOT COME TO EVEN AN INCONSIDERABLE PRIVATE AGREEMENT WITHOUT OUR SECRETLY HAVING A HAND IN IT.

6. PER ME REGES REGNANT. “It is through me that Kings reign.” And it was said by the prophets that we were chosen by God

Himself to rule over the whole earth. God has endowed us with genius that we may be equal to our task. Were genius in the opposite camp it would still struggle against us, but even so, a newcomer is no match for the old-established settler: the struggle would be merciless between us, such a fight as the world has never seen. Aye, and the genius on their side would have arrived too late. All the wheels of the machinery of all States go by the force of the engine, which is in our hands, and that engine of the machinery of States is - Gold. The science of political economy invented by our learned elders has for long past been giving royal prestige to capital.

MONOPOLY CAPITAL

7. Capital, if it is to co-operate untrammeled, must be free to establish a monopoly of industry and trade: this is already being put in execution by an unseen hand in all quarters of the world. This freedom will give political force to those engaged in industry, and that will help to oppress the people. Nowadays it is more important to disarm the peoples than to lead them into war: more important to use for our advantage the passions which have burst into flames than to quench their fire: more important to eradicate them. THE PRINCIPLE OBJECT OF OUR DIRECTORATE CONSISTS IN THIS: TO DEBILITATE THE PUBLIC MIND BY CRITICISM; TO LEAD IT AWAY FROM SERIOUS REFLECTIONS CALCULATED TO AROUSE RESISTANCE; TO DISTRACT THE FORCES OF THE MIND TOWARDS A SHAM FIGHT OF EMPTY ELOQUENCE.

10. IN ORDER TO PUT PUBLIC OPINION INTO OUR HANDS WE MUST BRING IT INTO A STATE OF BEWILDERMENT BY GIVING EXPRESSION FROM ALL SIDES TO SO MANY CONTRADICTORY OPINIONS AND FOR SUCH LENGTH OF TIME AS WILL SUFFICE TO MAKE THE "GOYIM" LOSE THEIR HEADS IN THE LABYRINTH AND COME TO SEE THAT THE BEST THING IS TO HAVE NO OPINION OF ANY KIND IN MATTERS POLITICAL, which it is not given to the public to understand, because they are understood only by him

who guides the public. This is the first secret.

11. The second secret requisite for the success of our government is comprised in the following: To multiply to such an extent national failings, habits, passions, conditions of civil life, that it will be impossible for anyone to know where he is in the resulting chaos, so that the people in consequence will fail to understand one another. This measure will also serve us in another way, namely, to sow discord in all parties, to dislocate all collective forces which are still unwilling to submit to us, and to discourage any kind of personal initiative which might in any degree hinder our affair... We must so direct the education of the GOYIM communities that whenever they come upon a matter requiring initiative they may drop their hands in despairing impotence. The strain which results from freedom of actions saps the forces when it meets with the freedom of another. From this collision arise grave moral shocks, disenchantments, failures. BY ALL THESE MEANS WE SHALL SO WEAR DOWN THE "GOYIM" THAT THEY WILL BE COMPELLED TO OFFER US INTERNATIONAL POWER OF A NATURE THAT BY ITS POSITION WILL ENABLE US WITHOUT ANY VIOLENCE GRADUALLY TO ABSORB ALL THE STATE FORCES OF THE WORLD AND TO FORM A SUPER-GOVERNMENT. In place of the rulers of to-day we shall set up a bogey which will be called the Super-Government Administration. Its hands will reach out in all directions like nippers and its organization will be of such colossal dimensions that it cannot fail to subdue all the nations of the world.

PROTOCOL No. 6

1. We shall soon begin to establish huge monopolies, reservoirs of colossal riches, upon which even large fortunes of the GOYIM will depend to such an extent that they will go to the bottom together with the credit of the States on the day after the political smash ...

4. The aristocracy of the GOYIM as a political force, is dead - We need not take it into account; but as landed proprietors they can still be harmful to us from the fact that they are self-sufficing in the resources upon which they live. It is essential therefore for us at whatever cost to deprive them of their land. This object will be best attained by increasing the burdens upon landed property - in loading lands with debts. These measures will check land-holding and keep it in a state of humble and unconditional submission.

WE SHALL ENSLAVE GENTILES

6. At the same time we must intensively patronize trade and industry, but, first and foremost, speculation, the part played by which is to provide a counterpoise to industry: the absence of speculative industry will multiply capital in private hands and will serve to restore agriculture by freeing the land from indebtedness to the land banks. What we want is that industry should drain off from the land both labor and capital and by means of speculation transfer into our hands all the money of the world, and thereby throw all the GOYIM into the ranks of the proletariat. Then the GOYIM will bow down before us, if for no other reason but to get the right to exist.

7. To complete the ruin of the industry of the GOYIM we shall bring to the assistance of speculation the luxury which we have developed among the GOYIM, that greedy demand for luxury which is swallowing up everything. WE SHALL RAISE THE RATE OF WAGES WHICH, HOWEVER, WILL NOT BRING ANY ADVANTAGE TO THE WORKERS, FOR, AT THE SAME TIME, WE SHALL PRODUCE A RISE IN PRICES OF THE FIRST NECESSARIES OF LIFE, ALLEGING THAT IT ARISES FROM THE DECLINE OF AGRICULTURE AND CATTLE-BREEDING: WE SHALL FURTHER UNDERMINE ARTFULLY AND DEEPLY SOURCES OF PRODUCTION, BY ACCUSTOMING THE WORKERS TO ANARCHY AND TO DRUNKENNESS AND SIDE BY SIDE THEREWITH TAKING ALL MEASURE TO EXTIRPATE FROM THE

FACE OF THE EARTH ALL THE EDUCATED FORCES OF THE "GOYIM."

PROTOCOL No. 7

1. The intensification of armaments, the increase of police forces - are all essential for the completion of the aforementioned plans. What we have to get at is that there should be in all the States of the world, besides ourselves, only the masses of the proletariat, a few millionaires devoted to our interests, police and soldiers.

2. Throughout all Europe, and by means of relations with Europe, in other continents also, we must create ferments, discords and hostility. Therein we gain a double advantage. In the first place we keep in check all countries, for they will know that we have the power whenever we like to create disorders or to restore order. All these countries are accustomed to see in us an indispensable force of coercion. In the second place, by our intrigues we shall tangle up all the threads which we have stretched into the cabinets of all States by means of the political, by economic treaties, or loan obligations. In order to succeed in this we must use great cunning and penetration during negotiations and agreements, but, as regards what is called the "official language," we shall keep to the opposite tactics and assume the mask of honesty and complacency. In this way the peoples and governments of the GOYIM, whom we have taught to look only at the outside whatever we present to their notice, will still continue to accept us as the benefactors and saviours of the human race.

UNIVERSAL WAR

3. We must be in a position to respond to every act of opposition by war with the neighbors of that country which dares to oppose us: but if these neighbors should also venture to stand collectively together against us, then we must offer resistance by a universal war.

5. We must compel the governments of the GOYIM to take action in the direction favored by our widely conceived plan, already approaching the desired consummation, by what we shall represent as public opinion, secretly promoted by us through the means of that so-called "Great Power" - THE PRESS, WHICH, WITH A FEW EXCEPTIONS THAT MAY BE DISREGARDED, IS ALREADY ENTIRELY IN OUR HANDS.

6. In a word, to sum up our system of keeping the governments of the goyim in Europe in check, we shall show our strength to one of them by terrorist attempts and to all, if we allow the possibility of a general rising against us, we shall respond with the guns of America or China or Japan.

PROTOCOL No. 8

1. We must arm ourselves with all the weapons which our opponents might employ against us. We must search out in the very finest shades of expression and the knotty points of the lexicon of law justification for those cases where we shall have to pronounce judgments that might appear abnormally audacious and unjust, for it is important that these resolutions should be set forth in expressions that shall seem to be the most exalted moral principles cast into legal form. Our directorate must surround itself with all these forces of civilization among which it will have to work. It will surround itself with publicists, practical jurists, administrators, diplomats and, finally, with persons prepared by a special super- educational training IN OUR SPECIAL SCHOOLS. These persons will have consonance of all the secrets of the social structure, they will know all the languages that can be made up by political alphabets and words; they will be made acquainted with the whole underside of human nature, with all its sensitive chords on which they will have to play. These chords are the cast of mind of the GOYIM, their tendencies, short- comings, vices and qualities, the particularities of classes and conditions. Needless to say that the talented assistants of authority, of whom

I speak, will be taken not from among the GOYIM, who are accustomed to perform their administrative work without giving themselves the trouble to think what its aim is, and never consider what it is needed for. The administrators of the GOYIM sign papers without reading them, and they serve either for mercenary reasons or from ambition.

2. We shall surround our government with a whole world of economists. That is the reason why economic sciences form the principal subject of the teaching given to the Jews. Around us again will be a whole constellation of bankers, industrialists, capitalists and - THE MAIN THING - MILLIONAIRES, BECAUSE IN SUBSTANCE EVERYTHING WILL BE SETTLED BY THE QUESTION OF FIGURES.

3. For a time, until there will no longer be any risk in entrusting responsible posts in our State to our brother-Jews, we shall put them in the hands of persons whose past and reputation are such that between them and the people lies an abyss, persons who, in case of disobedience to our instructions, must face criminal charges or disappear - this in order to make them defend our interests to their last gasp.

PROTOCOL No. 9

1. In applying our principles let attention be paid to the character of the people in whose country you live and act; a general, identical application of them, until such time as the people shall have been re-educated to our pattern, cannot have success. But by approaching their application cautiously you will see that not a decade will pass before the most stubborn character will change and we shall add a new people to the ranks of those already subdued by us.

2. The words of the liberal, which are in effect the words of our Masonic watchword, namely, "Liberty, Equality, Fraternity," will,

when we come into our kingdom, be changed by us into words no longer of a watchword, but only an expression of idealism, namely, into "The right of liberty, the duty of equality, the ideal of brotherhood." That is how we shall put it, - and so we shall catch the bull by the horns ... DE FACTO we have already wiped out every kind of rule except our own, although DE JURE there still remain a good many of them. Nowadays, if any States raise a protest against us it is only PRO FORMA at our discretion and by our direction, for THEIR ANTI-SEMITISM IS INDISPENSABLE TO US FOR THE MANAGEMENT OF OUR LESSER BRETHREN. I will not enter into further explanations, for this matter has formed the subject of repeated discussions amongst us.

JEWISH SUPER-STATE

3. For us there are not checks to limit the range of our activity. Our Super-Government subsists in extra-legal conditions which are described in the accepted terminology by the energetic and forcible word - Dictatorship. I am in a position to tell you with a clear conscience that at the proper time we, the law-givers, shall execute judgment and sentence, we shall slay and we shall spare, we, as head of all our troops, are mounted on the steed of the leader. We rule by force of will, because in our hands are the fragments of a once powerful party, now vanquished by us. AND THE WEAPONS IN OUR HANDS ARE LIMITLESS AMBITIONS, BURNING GREEDINESS, MERCILESS VENGEANCE, HATREDS AND MALICE.

4. IT IS FROM US THAT THE ALL-ENGULFING TERROR PROCEEDS. WE HAVE IN OUR SERVICE PERSONS OF ALL OPINIONS, OF ALL DOCTRINES, RESTORATING MONARCHISTS, DEMAGOGUES, SOCIALISTS, COMMUNISTS, AND UTOPIAN DREAMERS OF EVERY KIND. We have harnessed them all to the task: EACH ONE OF THEM ON HIS OWN ACCOUNT IS BORING AWAY AT THE LAST REMNANTS OF AUTHORITY, IS STRIVING TO OVERTHROW ALL ESTABLISHED FORM OF ORDER. By these acts all States are in torture; they

exhort to tranquility, are ready to sacrifice everything for peace: BUT WE WILL NOT GIVE THEM PEACE UNTIL THEY OPENLY ACKNOWLEDGE OUR INTERNATIONAL SUPER- GOVERNMENT, AND WITH SUBMISSIVENESS.

5. The people have raised a howl about the necessity of settling the question of Socialism by way of an international agreement. DIVISION INTO FRACTIONAL PARTIES HAS GIVEN THEM INTO OUR HANDS, FOR, IN ORDER TO CARRY ON A CONTESTED STRUGGLE ONE MUST HAVE MONEY, AND THE MONEY IS ALL IN OUR HANDS.

9. In order to annihilate the institutions of the GOYIM before it is time we have touched them with craft and delicacy, and have taken hold of the ends of the springs which move their mechanism. These springs lay in a strict but just sense of order; we have replaced them by the chaotic license of liberalism.We have got our hands into the administration of the law, into the conduct of elections, into the press, into liberty of the person, BUT PRINCIPALLY INTO EDUCATION AND TRAINING AS BEING THE CORNERSTONES OF A FREE EXISTENCE.

CHRISTIAN YOUTH DESTROYED

10. WE HAVE FOOLED, BEMUSED AND CORRUPTED THE YOUTH OF THE "GOYIM" BY REARING THEM IN PRINCIPLES AND THEORIES WHICH ARE KNOWN TO US TO BE FALSE ALTHOUGH IT IS THAT THEY HAVE BEEN INCULCATED.

11. Above the existing laws without substantially altering them, and by merely twisting them into contradictions of interpretations, we have erected something grandiose in the way of results. These results found expression in the fact that the INTERPRETATIONS MASKED THE LAW: afterwards they entirely hid them from the eyes of the governments owing to the impossibility of making anything out of the tangled web of legislation.

12. This is the origin of the theory of course of arbitration.

13. You may say that the GOYIM will rise upon us, arms in hand, if they guess what is going on before the time comes; but in the West we have against this a manoeuvre of such appalling terror that the very stoutest hearts quail - the undergrounds, metropolitans, those subterranean corridors which, before the time comes, will be driven under all the capitals and from whence those capitals will be blown into the air with all their organizations and archives.

PROTOCOL No. 10

1. To-day I begin with a repetition of what I said before, and I BEG YOU TO BEAR IN MIND THAT GOVERNMENTS AND PEOPLE ARE CONTENT IN THE POLITICAL WITH OUTSIDE APPEARANCES. And how, indeed, are the GOYIM to perceive the underlying meaning of things when their representatives give the best of their energies to enjoying themselves? For our policy it is of the greatest importance to take cognizance of this detail; it will be of assistance to us when we come to consider the division of authority of property, of the dwelling, of taxation (the idea of concealed taxes), of the reflex force of the laws.

OUR GOAL - WORLD POWER

3. We count upon attracting all nations to the task of erecting the new fundamental structure, the project for which has been drawn up by us. This is why, before everything, it is indispensable for us to arm ourselves and to store up in ourselves that absolutely reckless audacity and irresistible might of the spirit which in the person of our active workers will break down all hindrances on our way.

4. WHEN WE HAVE ACCOMPLISHED OUR COUP D'ETAT WE SHALL SAY THEN TO THE VARIOUS PEOPLES: "EVERYTHING HAS GONE TERRIBLY BADLY, ALL HAVE BEEN WORN OUT WITH SUFFERING.

Chapter 10 ~ The Protocol of the Learned Elders of ZION

WE ARE DESTROYING THE CAUSES OF YOUR TORMENT - NATIONALITIES, FRONTIERS, DIFFERENCES OF COINAGES. YOU ARE AT LIBERTY, OF COURSE, TO PRONOUNCE SENTENCE UPON US, BUT CAN IT POSSIBLY BE A JUST ONE IF IT IS CONFIRMED BY YOU BEFORE YOU MAKE ANY TRIAL OF WHAT WE ARE OFFERING YOU." ... THEN WILL THE MOB EXALT US AND BEAR US UP IN THEIR HANDS IN A UNANIMOUS TRIUMPH OF HOPES AND EXPECTATIONS. VOTING, WHICH WE HAVE MADE THE INSTRUMENT WHICH WILL SET US ON THE THRONE OF THE WORLD BY TEACHING EVEN THE VERY SMALLEST UNITS OF MEMBERS OF THE HUMAN RACE TO VOTE BY MEANS OF MEETINGS AND AGREEMENTS BY GROUPS, WILL THEN HAVE SERVED ITS PURPOSES AND WILL PLAY ITS PART THEN FOR THE LAST TIME BY A UNANIMITY OF DESIRE TO MAKE CLOSE ACQUAINTANCE WITH US BEFORE CONDEMNING US.

5. TO SECURE THIS WE MUST HAVE EVERYBODY VOTE WITHOUT DISTINCTION OF CLASSES AND QUALIFICATIONS, in order to establish an absolute majority, which cannot be got from the educated propertied classes. In this way, by inculcating in all a sense of self-importance, we shall destroy among the GOYIM the importance of the family and its educational value and remove the possibility of individual minds splitting off, for the mob, handled by us, will not let them come to the front nor even give them a hearing; it is accustomed to listen to us only who pay it for obedience and attention. In this way we shall create a blind, mighty force which will never be in a position to move in any direction without the guidance of our agents set at its head by us as leaders of the mob. The people will submit to this regime because it will know that upon these leaders will depend its earnings, gratifications and the receipt of all kinds of benefits.

POISON OF LIBERALISM

10. Liberalism produced Constitutional States, which took the place of what was the only safeguard of the GOYIM, namely,

Despotism; and A CONSTITUTION, AS YOU WELL KNOW, IS NOTHING ELSE BUT A SCHOOL OF DISCORDS, misunderstandings, quarrels, disagreements, fruitless party agitations, party whims - in a word, a school of everything that serves to destroy the personality of State activity. THE TRIBUNE OF THE "TALKERIES" HAS, NO LESS EFFECTIVELY THAN THE PRESS, CONDEMNED THE RULERS TO INACTIVITY AND IMPOTENCE, and thereby rendered them useless and superfluous, for which reason indeed they have been in many countries deposed. THEN IT WAS THAT THE ERA OF REPUBLICS BECOME POSSIBLE OF REALIZATION; AND THEN IT WAS THAT WE REPLACED THE RULER BY A CARICATURE OF A GOVERNMENT - BY A PRESIDENT, TAKEN FROM THE MOB, FROM THE MIDST OF OUR PUPPET CREATURES, OR SLAVES. This was the foundation of the mine which we have laid under the GOY people, I should rather say, under the GOY peoples.

WE NAME PRESIDENTS

11. In the near future we shall establish the responsibility of presidents.

12. By that time we shall be in a position to disregard forms in carrying through matters for which our impersonal puppet will be responsible. What do we care if the ranks of those striving for power should be thinned, if there should arise a deadlock from the impossibility of finding presidents, a deadlock which will finally disorganize the country?

13. In order that our scheme may produce this result we shall arrange elections in favor of such presidents as have in their past some dark, undiscovered stain, some "Panama" or other - then they will be trustworthy agents for the accomplishment of our plans out of fear of revelations and from the natural desire of everyone who has attained power, namely, the retention of the privileges, advantages and honor connected with the office of president. The chamber of deputies

will provide cover for, will protect, will elect presidents, but we shall take from it the right to propose new, or make changes in existing laws, for this right will be given by us to the responsible president, a puppet in our hands. Naturally, the authority of the presidents will then become a target for every possible form of attack, but we shall provide him with a means of self-defense in the right of an appeal to the people, for the decision of the people over the heads of their representatives, that is to say, an appeal to that same blind slave of ours - the majority of the mob. Independently of this we shall invest the president with the right of declaring a state of war. We shall justify this last right on the ground that the president as chief of the whole army of the country must have it at his disposal, in case of need for the defense of the new republican constitution, the right to defend which will belong to him as the responsible representative of this constitution.

16. The president will, at our discretion, interpret the sense of such of the existing laws as admit of various interpretation; he will further annul them when we indicate to him the necessity to do so, besides this, he will have the right to propose temporary laws, and even new departures in the government constitutional working, the pretext both for the one and the other being the requirements for the supreme welfare of the State.

WE SHALL DESTROY

17. By such measure we shall obtain the power of destroying little by little, step by step, all that at the outset when we enter on our rights, we are compelled to introduce into the constitutions of States to prepare for the transition to an imperceptible abolition of every kind of constitution, and then the time is come to turn every form of government into OUR DESPOTISM.

19. But you yourselves perfectly well know that TO PRODUCE THE POSSIBILITY OF THE EXPRESSION OF SUCH WISHES BY ALL THE

NATIONS IT IS INDISPENSABLE TO TROUBLE IN ALL COUNTRIES THE PEOPLE'S RELATIONS WITH THEIR GOVERNMENTS SO AS TO UTTERLY EXHAUST HUMANITY WITH DISSENSION, HATRED, STRUGGLE, ENVY AND EVEN BY THE USE OF TORTURE, BY STARVATION, BY THE INOCULATION OF DISEASES, BY WANT, SO THAT THE "GOYIM" SEE NO OTHER ISSUE THAN TO TAKE REFUGE IN OUR COMPLETE SOVEREIGNTY IN MONEY AND IN ALL ELSE.

20. But if we give the nations of the world a breathing space the moment we long for is hardly likely ever to arrive.

PROTOCOL No. 11

3. Having established approximately the MODUS AGENDI we will occupy ourselves with details of those combinations by which we have still to complete the revolution in the course of the machinery of State in the direction already indicated. By these combinations I mean the freedom of the Press, the right of association, freedom of conscience, the voting principle, and many another that must disappear for ever from the memory of man, or undergo a radical alteration the day after the promulgation of the new constitution... What we want is that from the first moment of its promulgation, while the peoples of the world are still stunned by the accomplished fact of the revolution, still in a condition of terror and uncertainty, they should recognize once for all that we are so strong, so inexpugnable, so super-abundantly filled with power, that in no case shall we take any account of them, and so far from paying any attention to their opinions or wishes, we are ready and able to crush with irresistible power all expression or manifestation thereof at every moment and in every place, that we have seized at once everything we wanted and shall in no case divide our power with them ... Then in fear and trembling they will close their eyes to everything, and be content to await what will be the end of it all.

Chapter 10 ~ The Protocol of the Learned Elders of ZION

WE ARE WOLVES

4. The GOYIM are a flock of sheep, and we are their wolves. And you know what happens when the wolves get hold of the flock? ....

5. There is another reason also why they will close their eyes: for we shall keep promising them to give back all the liberties we have taken away as soon as we have quelled the enemies of peace and tamed all parties ....

7. For what purpose then have we invented this whole policy and insinuated it into the minds of the GOY without giving them any chance to examine its underlying meaning? For what, indeed, if not in order to obtain in a roundabout way what is for our scattered tribe unattainable by the direct road? It is this which has served as the basis for our organization of SECRET MASONRY WHICH IS NOT KNOWN TO, AND AIMS WHICH ARE NOT EVEN SO MUCH AS SUSPECTED BY, THESE "GOY" CATTLE, ATTRACTED BY US INTO THE "SHOW" ARMY OF MASONIC LODGES IN ORDER TO THROW DUST IN THE EYES OF THEIR FELLOWS.

8. God has granted to us, His Chosen People, the gift of the dispersion, and in this which appears in all eyes to be our weakness, has come forth all our strength, which has now brought us to the threshold of sovereignty over all the world.

PROTOCOL No. 12

1. The word "freedom," which can be interpreted in various ways, is defined by us as follows -

2. Freedom is the right to do what which the law allows. This interpretation of the word will at the proper time be of service to us, because all freedom will thus be in our hands, since the laws

will abolish or create only that which is desirable for us according to the aforesaid program.

3. We shall deal with the press in the following way: what is the part played by the press to-day? It serves to excite and inflame those passions which are needed for our purpose or else it serves selfish ends of parties. It is often vapid, unjust, mendacious, and the majority of the public have not the slightest idea what ends the press really serves. We shall saddle and bridle it with a tight curb: we shall do the same also with all productions of the printing press, for where would be the sense of getting rid of the attacks of the press if we remain targets for pamphlets and books? The produce of publicity, which nowadays is a source of heavy expense owing to the necessity of censoring it, will be turned by us into a very lucrative source of income to our State: we shall lay on it a special stamp tax and require deposits of caution-money before permitting the establishment of any organ of the press or of printing offices; these will then have to guarantee our government against any kind of attack on the part of the press. For any attempt to attack us, if such still be possible, we shall inflict fines without mercy. Such measures as stamp tax, deposit of caution-money and fines secured by these deposits, will bring in a huge income to the government. It is true that party organs might not spare money for the sake of publicity, but these we shall shut up at the second attack upon us. No one shall with impunity lay a finger on the aureole of our government infallibility. The pretext for stopping any publication will be the alleged plea that it is agitating the public mind without occasion or justification. I BEG YOU TO NOTE THAT AMONG THOSE MAKING ATTACKS UPON US WILL ALSO BE ORGANS ESTABLISHED BY US, BUT THEY WILL ATTACK EXCLUSIVELY POINTS THAT WE HAVE PRE- DETERMINED TO ALTER.

WE CONTROL THE PRESS

4. NOT A SINGLE ANNOUNCEMENT WILL REACH THE PUBLIC

WITHOUT OUR CONTROL. Even now this is already being attained by us inasmuch as all news items are received by a few agencies, in whose offices they are focused from all parts of the world. These agencies will then be already entirely ours and will give publicity only to what we dictate to them.

5. If already now we have contrived to possess ourselves of the minds of the GOY communities to such an extent the they all come near looking upon the events of the world through the colored glasses of those spectacles we are setting astride their noses; if already now there is not a single State where there exist for us any barriers to admittance into what GOY stupidity calls State secrets: what will our positions be then, when we shall be acknowledged supreme lords of the world in the person of our king of all the world ....

FREE PRESS DESTROYED

7. We turn to the periodical press. We shall impose on it, as on all printed matter, stamp taxes per sheet and deposits of caution-money, and books of less than 30 sheets will pay double. We shall reckon them as pamphlets in order, on the one hand, to reduce the number of magazines, which are the worst form of printed poison, and, on the other, in order that this measure may force writers into such lengthy productions that they will be little read, especially as they will be costly. At the same time what we shall publish ourselves to influence mental development in the direction laid down for our profit will be cheap and will be read voraciously. The tax will bring vapid literary ambitions within bounds and the liability to penalties will make literary men dependent upon us. And if there should be any found who are desirous of writing against us, they will not find any person eager to print their productions. Before accepting any production for publication in print, the publisher or printer will have to apply to the authorities for permission to do so. Thus we shall know

beforehand of all tricks preparing against us and shall nullify them by getting ahead with explanations on the subject treated of.

8. Literature and journalism are two of the most important educative forces, and therefore our government will become proprietor of the majority of the journals. This will neutralize the injurious influence of the privately-owned press and will put us in possession of a tremendous influence upon the public mind .... If we give permits for ten journals, we shall ourselves found thirty, and so on in the same proportion. This, however, must in no wise be suspected by the public. For which reason all journals published by us will be of the most opposite, in appearance, tendencies and opinions, thereby creating confidence in us and bringing over to us quite unsuspicious opponents, who will thus fall into our trap and be rendered harmless.

12. All our newspapers will be of all possible complexions — aristocratic, republican, revolutionary, even anarchical - for so long, of course, as the constitution exists.... Like the Indian idol "Vishnu" they will have a hundred hands, and every one of them will have a finger on any one of the public opinions as required. When a pulse quickens these hands will lead opinion in the direction of our aims, for an excited patient loses all power of judgment and easily yields to suggestion. Those fools who will think they are repeating the opinion of a newspaper of their own camp will be repeating our opinion or any opinion that seems desirable for us. In the vain belief that they are following the organ of their party they will, in fact, follow the flag which we hang out for them.

ONLY LIES PRINTED

15. Methods of organization like these, imperceptible to the public eye but absolutely sure, are the best calculated to succeed in bringing the attention and the confidence of the public to the side of our government. Thanks to such methods we shall be in a position as from time to time may be required, to excite or to

tranquillize the public mind on political questions, to persuade or to confuse, printing now truth, now lies, facts or their contradictions, according as they may be well or ill received, always very cautiously feeling our ground before stepping upon it .... WE SHALL HAVE A SURE TRIUMPH OVER OUR OPPONENTS SINCE THEY WILL NOT HAVE AT THEIR DISPOSITION ORGANS OF THE PRESS IN WHICH THEY CAN GIVE FULL AND FINAL EXPRESSION TO THEIR VIEWS owing to the aforesaid methods of dealing with the press. We shall not even need to refute them except very superficially.

19. WHEN WE ARE IN THE PERIOD OF THE NEW REGIME TRANSITIONAL TO THAT OF OUR ASSUMPTION OF FULL SOVEREIGNTY WE MUST NOT ADMIT ANY REVELATION BY THE PRESS OF ANY FORM OF PUBLIC DISHONESTY; IT IS NECESSARY THAT THE NEW REGIME SHOULD BE THOUGHT TO HAVE SO PERFECTLY CONTENDED EVERYBODY THAT EVEN CRIMINALITY HAS DISAPPEARED ... Cases of the manifestation of criminality should remain known only to their victims and to chance witnesses - no more.

PROTOCOL No. 13

1. The need for daily bread forces the GOYIM to keep silence and be our humble servants. Agents taken on to our press from among the GOYIM will at our orders discuss anything which it is inconvenient for us to issue directly in official documents, and we meanwhile, quietly amid the din of the discussion so raised, shall simply take and carry through such measures as we wish and then offer them to the public as an accomplished fact.

WE DECEIVE WORKERS

3. In order to distract people who may be too troublesome from discussions of questions of the political we are now putting

forward what we allege to be new questions of the political, namely, questions of industry. In this sphere let them discuss themselves silly!... WE FURTHER DISTRACT THEM WITH AMUSEMENTS, GAMES, PASTIMES, PASSIONS, PEOPLE'S PALACES .... SOON WE SHALL BEGIN THROUGH THE PRESS TO PROPOSE COMPETITIONS IN ART, IN SPORT IN ALL KINDS: these interests will finally distract their minds from questions in which we should find ourselves compelled to oppose them...

6. Who will ever suspect then that ALL THESE PEOPLES WERE STAGE-MANAGED BY US ACCORDING TO A POLITICAL PLAN WHICH NO ONE HAS SO MUCH AS GUESSED AT IN THE COURSE OF MANY CENTURIES?

PROTOCOL No. 14

1. When we come into our kingdom it will be undesirable for us that there should exist any other religion than ours of the One God with whom our destiny is bound up by our position as the Chosen People and through whom our same destiny is united with the destinies of the world. We must therefore sweep away all other forms of belief... The errors of the GOYIM governments will be depicted by us in the most vivid hues. We shall implant such an abhorrence of them that the peoples will prefer tranquility in a state of serfdom to those rights of vaunted freedom which have tortured humanity and exhausted the very sources of human existence, sources which have been exploited by a mob of rascally adventurers who know not what they do .... USELESS CHANGES OF FORMS OF GOVERNMENT TO WHICH WE INSTIGATED THE "GOYIM" WHEN WE WERE UNDERMINING THEIR STATE STRUCTURES, WILL HAVE SO WEARIED THE PEOPLES BY THAT TIME THAT THEY WILL PREFER TO SUFFER ANYTHING UNDER US RATHER THAN RUN THE RISK OF ENDURING AGAIN ALL THE AGITATIONS AND MISERIES THEY HAVE GONE THROUGH.

Chapter 10 ~ The Protocol of the Learned Elders of ZION

WE SHALL FORBID CHRIST

2. At the same time we shall not omit to emphasize the historical mistakes of the GOY governments which have tormented humanity for so many centuries by their lack of understanding of everything that constitutes the true good of humanity in their chase after fantastic schemes of social blessings, and have never noticed that these schemes kept on producing a worse and never a better state of the universal relations which are the basis of human life ...

5. IN COUNTRIES KNOWN AS PROGRESSIVE AND ENLIGHTENED WE HAVE CREATED A SENSELESS, FILTHY, ABOMINABLE LITERATURE. For some time after our entrance to power we shall continue to encourage its existence in order to provide a telling relief by contrast to the speeches, party program, which will be distributed from exalted quarters of ours .... Our wise men, trained to become leaders of the GOYIM, will compose speeches, projects, memoirs, articles, which will be used by us to influence the minds of the GOYIM, directing them towards such understanding and forms of knowledge as have been determined by us.

PROTOCOL No. 15

1. When we at last definitely come into our kingdom by the aid of COUPS D'ETAT prepared everywhere for one and the same day, after definitely acknowledged *(and not a little time will pass before that comes about, perhaps even a whole century)* we shall make it our task to see that against us such things as plots shall no longer exist. With this purpose we shall slay without mercy all who take arms *(in hand, like Waco? Randy Weaver? Port Arthur? Oklahoma?)* to oppose our coming into our kingdom. Every kind of new institution of anything like a secret society will also be punished with death; those of them which are now in existence,

are known to us, serve us and have served us, we shall disband and send into exile to continents far removed from Europe. IN THIS WAY WE SHALL PROCEED WITH THOSE *"GOY"* MASONS WHO KNOW TOO MUCH;

2. Resolutions of our government will be final, without appeal.

3. In the GOY societies, in which we have planted and deeply rooted discord and Protestantism, the only possible way of restoring order is to employ merciless measures that prove the direct force of authority: no regard must be paid to the victims who fall, they suffer for the well-being of the future... only by such a majestic inflexibility of might as shall carry on its face the emblems of inviolability from mystical causes - from the choice of God. SUCH WAS, UNTIL RECENT TIMES, THE RUSSIAN AUTOCRACY, THE ONE AND ONLY SERIOUS FOE WE HAD IN THE WORLD, WITHOUT COUNTING THE PAPACY.

SECRET SOCIETIES

4. Meantime, however, until we come into our kingdom, we shall act in the contrary way: we shall create and multiply free masonic lodges in all the countries of the world, absorb into them all who may become or who are prominent in public activity, for these lodges we shall find our principal intelligence office and means of influence. All these lodges we shall bring under one central administration, known to us alone and to all others absolutely unknown, which will be composed of our learned elders. The lodges will have their representatives who will serve to screen the above-mentioned administration of MASONRY and from whom will issue the watchword and program. In these lodges we shall tie together the knot which binds together all revolutionary and liberal elements. Their composition will be made up of all strata of society. The most secret political plots will be known to us and fall under our guiding hands on the very day of their conception. AMONG THE MEMBERS OF THESE LODGES WILL BE ALMOST ALL

Chapter 10 ~ The Protocol of the Learned Elders of ZION

THE AGENTS OF INTERNATIONAL AND NATIONAL POLICE since their service is for us irreplaceable in the respect that the police is in a position not only to use its own particular measures with the insubordinate, but also to screen our activities and provide pretexts for discontents, ET CETERA.

5. The class of people who most willingly enter into secret societies are those who live by their wits, careerists, and in general people, mostly light-minded, with whom we shall have no difficulty in dealing and in using to wind up the mechanism of the machine devised by us. If this world grows agitated the meaning of that will be that we have had to stir up in order to break up its too great solidarity. BUT IF THERE SHOULD ARISE IN ITS MIDST A PLOT, THEN AT THE HEAD OF THAT PLOT WILL BE NO OTHER THAN ONE OF OUR MOST TRUSTED SERVANTS. It is natural that we and no other should lead MASONIC activities, for we know whither we are leading, we know the final goal of every form of activity whereas the GOYIM have knowledge of nothing, not even of the immediate effect of action; they put before themselves, usually, the momentary reckoning of the satisfaction of their self-opinion in the accomplishment of their thought without even remarking that the very conception never belonged to their initiative but to our instigation of their thought ...

GENTILES ARE STUPID

6. The GOYIM enter the lodges out of curiosity or in the hope by their means to get a nibble at the public pie, and some of them in order to obtain a hearing before the public for their impracticable and groundless fantasies: they thirst for the emotion of success and applause, of which we are remarkably generous. And the reason why we give them this success is to make use of the high conceit of themselves to which it gives birth, for that insensibly disposes them to assimilate our suggestions without being on their guard against them... You cannot imagine to what extent the

wisest of the GOYIM can be brought to a state of unconscious naivete in the presence of this condition of high conceit of themselves, and at the same time how easy it is to take the heart out of them by the slightest ill-success, though it be nothing more than the stoppage of the applause they had, and to reduce them to a slavish submission for the sake of winning a renewal of success .... BY SO MUCH AS OURS DISREGARD SUCCESS IF ONLY THEY CAN CARRY THROUGH THEIR PLANS, BY SO MUCH THE *"GOYIM"* ARE WILLING TO SACRIFICE ANY PLANS ONLY TO HAVE SUCCESS...

7. If we have been able to bring them to such a pitch of stupid blindness is it not a proof, and an amazingly clear proof, of the degree to which the mind of the GOYIM is undeveloped in comparison with our mind? This it is, mainly, which guarantees our success.

GENTILES ARE CATTLE

8. And how far-seeing were our learned elders in ancient times when they said that to attain a serious end it behooves not to stop at any means or to count the victims sacrificed for the sake of that end .... We have not counted the victims of the seed of the GOY cattle, though we have sacrificed many of our own, but for that we have now already given them such a position on the earth as they could not even have dreamed of. The comparatively small numbers of the victims from the number of ours have preserved our nationality from destruction.

9. Death is the inevitable end for all. It is better to bring that end nearer to those who hinder our affairs than to ourselves, to the founders of this affair. WE EXECUTE MASONS IN SUCH WISE THAT NONE SAVE THE BROTHERHOOD CAN EVER HAVE A SUSPICION OF IT, NOT EVEN THE VICTIMS THEMSELVES OF OUR DEATH SENTENCE, THEY ALL DIE WHEN REQUIRED AS IF FROM A NORMAL KIND OF ILLNESS ..... Knowing this, even the brotherhood

in its turn dare not protest. By such methods we have plucked out of the midst of MASONRY the very root of protest against our disposition. While preaching liberalism to the GOY we at the same time keep our own people and our agents in a state of unquestioning submission.

10. Under our influence the execution of the laws of the GOYIM has been reduced to a minimum. The prestige of the law has been exploded by the liberal interpretations introduced into this sphere. In the most important and fundamental affairs and questions, JUDGES DECIDE AS WE DICTATE TO THEM, see matters in the light wherewith we enfold them for the administration of the GOYIM, of course, through persons who are our tools though we do not appear to have anything in common with them - by newspaper opinion or by other means.... Even senators and the higher administration accept our counsels...

11. In this difference in capacity for thought between the GOYIM and ourselves may be clearly discerned the seal of our position as the Chosen People and of our higher quality of humanness, in contradistinction to the brute mind of the GOYIM. Their eyes are open, but see nothing before them and do not invent *(unless perhaps, material things).* From this it is plain that nature herself has destined us to guide and rule the world.

WE DEMAND SUBMISSION

12. When comes the time of our overt rule, the time to manifest its blessing, we shall remake all legislatures, all our laws will be brief, plain, stable, without any kind of interpretations, so that anyone will be in a position to know them perfectly. The main feature which will run right through them is submission to orders, and this principle will be carried to a grandiose height...

13. Concealment of guilt, connivance between those in the service

of the administration - all this kind of evil will disappear after the very first examples of severe punishment. The aureole of our power demands suitable, that is, cruel, punishments for the slightest infringement, for the sake of gain, of its supreme prestige... FOR EXAMPLES OUR JUDGES WILL KNOW THAT WHENEVER THEY FEEL DISPOSED TO PLUME THEMSELVES ON FOOLISH CLEMENCY THEY ARE VIOLATING THE LAW OF JUSTICE WHICH IS INSTITUTED FOR THE EXEMPLARY EDIFICATION OF MEN BY PENALTIES FOR LAPSES AND NOT FOR DISPLAY OF THE SPIRITUAL QUALITIES OF THE JUDGES...

17. We shall root out liberalism from all the important strategic posts of our government on which depends the training of subordinates for our State structure. Such posts will fall exclusively to those who have been trained by us for administrative rule. To the possible objection that the retirement of old servants will cost the Treasury heavily, I reply, firstly, they will be provided with some private service in place of what they lose, and, secondly, I have to remark that all the money in the world will be concentrated in our hands, consequently it is not our government that has to fear expense.

WE SHALL BE CRUEL

18. Our absolutism will in all things be logically consecutive and therefore in each one of its decrees our supreme will must be respected and unquestionably fulfilled: it will ignore all murmurs, all discontents of every kind and will destroy to the root every kind of manifestation of them in act by punishment of an exemplary character.

19. We shall abolish the right of appeal, which will be transferred exclusively to our disposal - to the cognizance of him who rules, for we must not allow the conception among the people of a thought that there could be such a thing as a decision that is not right of judges set up by us...

21. As you see, I found our despotism on right and duty: the right to compel the execution of duty is the direct obligation of a government which is a father for its subjects. It has the right of the strong that it may use it for the benefit of directing humanity towards that order which is defined by nature, namely, submission. Everything in the world is in a state of submission, if not to man, then to circumstances or its own inner character, in all cases, to what is stronger. And so shall we be this something stronger for the sake of good.

22. We are obliged without hesitation to sacrifice individuals, who commit a breach of established order, for in the exemplary punishment of evil lies a great educational problem.

23. When the King of Israel sets upon his sacred head the crown offered him by Europe he will become patriarch of the world. The indispensable victims offered by him in consequence of their suitability will never reach the number of victims offered in the course of centuries by the mania of magnificence, the emulation between the GOY governments.

24. Our King will be in constant communion with the peoples, making to them from the tribune speeches which fame will in that same hour distribute over all the world.

PROTOCOL No. 16

1. In order to effect the destruction of all collective forces except ours we shall emasculate the first stage of collectivism - the UNIVERSITIES, by re-educating them in a new direction. THEIR OFFICIALS AND PROFESSORS WILL BE PREPARED FOR THEIR BUSINESS BY DETAILED SECRET PROGRAMS OF ACTION FROM WHICH THEY WILL NOT WITH IMMUNITY DIVERGE, NOT BY ONE IOTA. THEY WILL BE APPOINTED WITH ESPECIAL PRECAUTION, AND WILL BE SO PLACED AS TO BE WHOLLY DEPENDENT UPON

THE GOVERNMENT.

WE SHALL CHANGE HISTORY

4. Classicism as also any form of study of ancient history, in which there are more bad than good examples, we shall replace with the study of the program of the future. We shall erase from the memory of men all facts of previous centuries which are undesirable to us, and leave only those which depict all the errors of the government of the GOYIM

7. We shall abolish every kind of freedom of instruction. Learners of all ages have the right to assemble together with their parents in the educational establishments as it were in a club: during these assemblies, on holidays, teachers will read what will pass as free lectures on questions of human relations, of the laws of examples, of the philosophy of new theories not yet declared to the world. These theories will be raised by us to the stage of a dogma of faith as a traditional stage towards our faith...

8... The system of bridling thought is already at work in the so-called system of teaching by OBJECT LESSONS, the purpose of which is to turn the GOYIM into unthinking submissive brutes waiting for things to be presented before their eyes in order to form an idea of them .... In France, one of our best agents, Bourgeois, has already made public a new program of teaching by object lessons.

PROTOCOL No. 17

1. The practice of advocacy produces men cold, cruel, persistent, unprincipled, who in all cases take up an impersonal, purely legal standpoint. They have the inveterate habit to refer everything to its value for the defense and not to the public welfare of its results. They do not usually decline to undertake any defense whatever, they strive for an acquittal at all costs, caviling over every petty

crux of jurisprudence and thereby they demoralize justice. For this reason we shall set this profession into narrow frames which will keep it inside this sphere of executive public service. Advocates, equally with judges, will be deprived of the right of communication with litigants; they will receive business only from the court and will study it by notes of report and documents, defending their clients after they have been interrogated in court on facts that have appeared... This will also, by the way, remove the present practice of corrupt bargain between advocation to agree only to let that side win which pays most .....

WE SHALL DESTROY THE CLERGY

2. WE HAVE LONG PAST TAKEN CARE TO DISCREDIT THE PRIESTHOOD OF THE *"GOYIM,"* and thereby to ruin their mission on earth which in these days might still be a great hindrance to us. Day by day its influence on the peoples of the world is falling lower. FREEDOM OF CONSCIENCE HAS BEEN DECLARED EVERYWHERE, SO THAT NOW ONLY YEARS DIVIDE US FROM THE MOMENT OF THE COMPLETE WRECKING OF THAT CHRISTIAN RELIGION: as to other religions we shall have still less difficulty in dealing with them, but it would be premature to speak of this now. We shall set clericalism and clericals into such narrow frames as to make their influence move in retrogressive proportion to its former progress.

3. When the time comes finally to destroy the papal court the finger of an invisible hand will point the nations towards this court. When, however, the nations fling themselves upon it, we shall come forward in the guise of its defenders as if to save excessive bloodshed. By this diversion we shall penetrate to its very bowels and be sure we shall never come out again until we have gnawed through the entire strength of this place.

4. THE KING OF THE JEWS WILL BE THE REAL POPE OF THE

UNIVERSE, THE PATRIARCH OF THE INTERNATIONAL CHURCH.

5. But, IN THE MEANTIME, while we are re-educating youth in new traditional religions and afterwards in ours, WE SHALL NOT OVERTLY LAY A FINGER ON EXISTING CHURCHES, BUT WE SHALL FIGHT AGAINST THEM BY CRITICISM CALCULATED TO PRODUCE SCHISM . . .

6. In general, then, our contemporary press will continue to CONVICT State affairs, religions, incapacities of the GOYIM, always using the most unprincipled expressions in order by every means to lower their prestige in the manner which can only be practiced by the genius of our gifted tribe...

9. JUST AS NOWADAYS OUR BRETHREN, ARE OBLIGED AT THEIR OWN RISK TO DENOUNCE TO THE KAHAL APOSTATES OF THEIR OWN FAMILY or members who have been noticed doing anything in opposition to the KAHAL, SO IN OUR KINGDOM OVER ALL THE WORLD IT WILL BE OBLIGATORY FOR ALL OUR SUBJECTS TO OBSERVE THE DUTY OF SERVICE TO THE STATE IN THIS DIRECTION.

PROTOCOL No. 18

1. When it becomes necessary for us to strengthen the strict measures of secret defense (the most fatal poison for the prestige of authority) we shall arrange a simulation of disorders or some manifestation of discontents finding expression through the co-operation of good speakers. Round these speakers will assemble all who are sympathetic to his utterances. This will give us the pretext for domiciliary prerequisitions and surveillance on the part of our servants from among the number of the GOYIM police ..

2. As the majority of conspirators act out of love for the game, for the sake of talking, so, until they commit some overt act we shall not lay a finger on them but only introduce into their midst

observation elements .... It must be remembered that the prestige of authority is lessened if it frequently discovers conspiracies against itself: this implies a presumption of consciousness of weakness, or, what is still worse, of injustice. You are aware that we have broken the prestige of the GOY kings by frequent attempts upon their lives through our agents, blind sheep of our flock, who are easily moved by a few liberal phrases to crimes provided only they be painted in political colors. WE HAVE COMPELLED THE RULERS TO ACKNOWLEDGE THEIR WEAKNESS IN ADVERTISING OVERT MEASURES OF SECRET DEFENSE AND THEREBY WE SHALL BRING THE PROMISE OF AUTHORITY TO DESTRUCTION.

GOVERNMENT BY FEAR

5. According to strictly enforced outward appearances our ruler will employ his power only for the advantage of the nation and in no wise for his own or dynastic profits. Therefore, with the observance of this decorum, his authority will be respected and guarded by the subjects themselves, it will receive an apotheosis in the admission that with it is bound up the well-being of every citizen of the State, for upon it will depend all order in the common life of the pack ....

7. Our ruler will always be among the people and be surrounded by a mob of apparently curious men and women, who will occupy the front ranks about him, to all appearance by chance, and will restrain the ranks of the rest out of respect as it will appear for good order. This will sow an example of restraint also in others... The aureole of power requires for his existence that the people may be able to say: *"If the king knew of this,"* or: *"the king will hear it."*

PROTOCOL No. 19

1. If we do not permit any independent dabbling in the political we

shall on the other hand encourage every kind of report or petition with proposals for the government to examine into all kinds of projects for the amelioration of the condition of the people; this will reveal to us the defects or else the fantasies of our subjects, to which we shall respond either by accomplishing them or by a wise rebuttment to prove the shortsightedness of one who judges wrongly.

4. We have done our best, and I hope we have succeeded to obtain that the GOYIM should not arrive at this means of contending with sedition. It was for this reason that through the Press and in speeches, indirectly - in cleverly compiled school-books on history, we have advertised the martyrdom alleged to have been accredited by sedition-mongers for the idea of the commonwealth. This advertisement has increased the contingent of liberals and has brought thousands of GOYIM into the ranks of our livestock cattle.

PROTOCOL No. 20

1. To-day we shall touch upon the financial program, which I put off to the end of my report as being the most difficult, the crowning and the decisive point of our plans. Before entering upon it I will remind you that I have already spoken before by way of a hint when I said that the sum total of our actions is settled by the question of figures.

3. Our rule, in which the king will enjoy the legal fiction that everything in his State belongs to him *(which may easily be translated into fact),* will be enabled to resort to the lawful confiscation of all sums of every kind for the regulation of their circulation in the State. From this follows that taxation will best be covered by a progressive tax on property. In this manner the dues will be paid without straitening or ruining anybody in the form of a percentage of the amount of property. The rich must be aware that it is their duty to place a part of their superfluities at the disposal

of the State since the State guarantees them security of possession of the rest of their property and the right of honest gains, I say honest, for the control over property will do away with robbery on a legal basis.

WE SHALL DESTROY CAPITAL

5. The tax upon the poor man is a seed of revolution and works to the detriment of the State which in hunting after the trifling is missing the big. Quite apart from this, a tax on capitalists diminishes the growth of wealth in private hands in which we have in these days concentrated it as a counterpoise to the government strength of the GOYIM - their State finances.

6. A tax increasing in a percentage ratio to capital will give much larger revenue than the present individual or property tax, which is useful to us now for the sole reason that it excites trouble and discontent among the GOYIM

7. The force upon which our king will rest consists in the equilibrium and the guarantee of peace, for the sake of which things it is indispensable that the capitalists should yield up a portion of their incomes for the sake of the secure working of the machinery of the State. State needs must be paid by those who will not feel the burden and have enough to take from.

12. Purchase, receipt of money or inheritance will be subject to the payment of a stamp progressive tax. Any transfer of property, whether money or other, without evidence of payment of this tax which will be strictly registered by names, will render the former holder liable to pay interest on the tax from the moment of transfer of these sums up to the discovery of his evasion of declaration of the transfer. Transfer documents must be presented weekly at the local treasury office with notifications of the name, surname and permanent place of residence of the former and the new holder

of the property. This transfer with register of names must begin from a definite sum which exceeds the ordinary expenses of buying and selling necessaries, and these will be subject to payment only by a stamp impost of a definite percentage of the unit.

12. Purchase, receipt of money or inheritance will be subject to the payment of a stamp progressive tax. Any transfer of property, whether money or other, without evidence of payment of this tax which will be strictly registered by names, will render the former holder liable to pay interest on the tax from the moment of transfer of these sums up to the discovery of his evasion of declaration of the transfer. Transfer documents must be presented weekly at the local treasury office with notifications of the name, surname and permanent place of residence of the former and the new holder of the property. This transfer with register of names must begin from a definite sum which exceeds the ordinary expenses of buying and selling necessaries, and these will be subject to payment only by a stamp impost of a definite percentage of the unit.

22. YOU ARE AWARE THAT THE GOLD STANDARD HAS BEEN THE RUIN OF THE STATES WHICH ADOPTED IT, FOR IT HAS NOT BEEN ABLE TO SATISFY THE DEMANDS FOR MONEY, THE MORE SO THAT WE HAVE REMOVED GOLD FROM CIRCULATION AS FAR AS POSSIBLE.

GENTILE STATES BANKRUPT

23. With us the standard that must be introduced is the cost of working-man power, whether it be reckoned in paper or in wood. We shall make the issue of money in accordance with the normal requirements of each subject, adding to the quantity with every birth and subtracting with every death.

27. The reforms projected by us in the financial institutions and

principles of the GOYIM will be clothed by us in such forms as will alarm nobody. We shall point out the necessity of reforms in consequence of the disorderly darkness into which the GOYIM by their irregularities have plunged the finances. The first irregularity, as we shall point out, consists in their beginning with drawing up a single budget which year after year grows owing to the following cause: this budget is dragged out to half the year, then they demand a budget to put things right, and this they expend in three months, after which they ask for a supplementary budget, and all this ends with a liquidation budget. But, as the budget of the following year is drawn up in accordance with the sum of the total addition, the annual departure from the normal reaches as much as 50 per cent in a year, and so the annual budget is trebled in ten years. Thanks to such methods, allowed by the carelessness of the GOY States, their treasuries are empty. The period of loans supervenes, and that has swallowed up remainders and brought all the GOY States to bankruptcy.

TYRANNY OF USURY

30. What also indeed is, in substance, a loan, especially a foreign loan? A loan is - an issue of government bills of exchange containing a percentage obligation commensurate to the sum of the loan capital. If the loan bears a charge of 5 per cent, then in twenty years the State vainly pays away in interest a sum equal to the loan borrowed, in forty years it is paying a double sum, in sixty - treble, and all the while the debt remains an unpaid debt.

31. From this calculation it is obvious that with any form of taxation per head the State is baling out the last coppers of the poor taxpayers in order to settle accounts with wealthy foreigners, from whom it has borrowed money instead of collecting these coppers for its own needs without the additional interest.

34. Stagnation of money will not be allowed by us and therefore

there will be no State interest-bearing paper, except a one per-cent series, so that there will be no payment of interest to leeches that suck all the strength out of the State. The right to issue interest-bearing paper will be given exclusively to industrial companies who find no difficulty in paying interest out of profits, whereas the State does not make interest on borrowed money like these companies, for the State borrows to spend and not to use in operations.

38. Our accounts, which we shall present when the time comes, in the light of centuries of experience gained by experiments made by us on the GOY States, will be distinguished by clearness and definiteness and will show at a glance to all men the advantage of our innovations. They will put an end to those abuses to which we owe our mastery over the GOYIM, but which cannot be allowed in our kingdom.

PROTOCOL No. 21

1. To what I reported to you at the last meeting I shall now add a detailed explanation of internal loans. Of foreign loans I shall say nothing more, because they have fed us with the national moneys of the GOYIM, but for our State there will be no foreigners, that is, nothing external.

2. We have taken advantage of the venality of administrators and slackness of rulers to get our moneys twice, thrice and more times over, by lending to the GOY governments moneys which were not at all needed by the States. Could anyone do the like in regard to us? .... Therefore, I shall only deal with the details of internal loans.

4. But when the comedy is played out there emerges the fact that a debit and an exceedingly burdensome debit has been created. For the payment of interest it becomes necessary to have recourse to new loans, which do not swallow up but only add to the capital debt. And when this credit is exhausted it becomes necessary by

new taxes to cover, not the loan, BUT ONLY THE INTEREST ON IT. These taxes are a debit employed to cover a debit.

6. Nowadays, with external loans, these tricks cannot be played by the GOYIM for they know that we shall demand all our moneys back.

7. In this way in acknowledged bankruptcy will best prove to the various countries the absence of any means between the interests of the peoples and of those who rule them.

11. We shall replace the money markets by grandiose government credit institutions, the object of which will be to fix the price of industrial values in accordance with government views. These institutions will be in a position to fling upon the market five hundred millions of industrial paper in one day, or to buy up for the same amount. In this way all industrial undertakings will come into dependence upon us. You may imagine for yourselves what immense power we shall thereby secure for ourselves ....

PROTOCOL No. 22

1 In all that has so far been reported by me to you, I have endeavored to depict with care the secret of what is coming, of what is past, and of what is going on now, rushing into the flood of the great events coming already in the near future, the secret of our relations to the GOYIM and of financial operations

2. IN OUR HANDS IS THE GREATEST POWER OF OUR DAY - GOLD: IN TWO DAYS WE CAN PROCURE FROM OUR STOREHOUSES ANY QUANTITY WE MAY PLEASE.

4. ...Our authority will be the crown of order, and in that is included the whole happiness of man. The aureole of this authority will inspire a mystical bowing of the knee before it and a reverent fear

before it of all the peoples. True force makes no terms with any right, not even with that of God: none dare come near to it so as to take so much as a span from it away.

PROTOCOL No. 23

1. That the peoples may become accustomed to obedience it is necessary to inculcate lessons of humility and therefore to reduce the production of articles of luxury. By this we shall improve morals which have been debased by emulation in the sphere of luxury.

2. Subjects, I repeat once more, give blind obedience only to the strong hand which is absolutely independent of them, for in it they feel the sword of defense and support against social scourges .... What do they want with an angelic spirit in a king? What they have to see in him is the personification of force and power.

3. The supreme lord who will replace all now existing rulers, dragging in their existence among societies demoralized by us, societies that have denied even the authority of God, from whose midst breeds out on all sides the fire of anarchy, must first of all proceed to quench this all-devouring flame. Therefore he will be obliged to kill off those existing societies, though he should drench them with his own blood, that he may resurrect them again in the form of regularly organized troops fighting consciously with every kind of infection that may cover the body of the State with sores.

PROTOCOL No. 24

1. I pass now to the method of confirming the dynastic roots of King David to the last strata of the earth.

2. This confirmation will first and foremost be included in that which to this day has rested the force of conservatism by our learned elders of the conduct of the affairs of the world, in the directing of the education of thought of all humanity.

Chapter 10 ~ The Protocol of the Learned Elders of ZION

3. Certain members of the seed of David will prepare the kings and their heirs, selecting not by right of heritage but by eminent capacities, inducting them into the most secret mysteries of the political, into schemes of government, but providing always that none may come to knowledge of the secrets. The object of this mode of action is that all may know that government cannot be entrusted to those who have not been inducted into the secret places of its art ....

6. Only those who are unconditionally capable for firm, even if it be to cruelty, direct rule will receive the reins of rule from our learned elders.

7. In case of falling sick with weakness of will or other form of incapacity. kings must by law hand over the reins of rule to new and capable hands.

8. The king's plan of action for the current moment, and all the more so for the future, will be unknown, even to those who are called his closest counselors.

KING OF THE JEWS

9. Only the king and the three who stood sponsor for him will know what is coming.

10. In the person of the king who with unbending will is master of himself and of humanity all will discern as it were fate with its mysterious ways. None will know what the king wishes to attain by his dispositions, and therefore none will dare to stand across an unknown path.

13. This terror was indispensable for us till the time comes for both these forces separately to fall under our influence.

14. The king of the Jews must not be at the mercy of his passions, and especially of sensuality: on no side of his character must he give brute instincts power over his mind. Sensuality worse than all else disorganizes the capacities of the mind and clearness of views, distracting the thoughts to the worst and most brutal side of human activity.

15. The prop of humanity in the person of the supreme lord of all the world of the holy seed of David must sacrifice to his people all personal inclinations.

16. Our supreme lord must be of an exemplary irreproachability.

CHAPTER 11
COMMENTARY ON THE PROTOCOL

PROTOCOL I
THE BASIC DOCTRINE

The use of violence and terrorization is a prime tool of the Zionist. What would you call the destruction of the World Trade Center on 9-11-2001? What would you call suicide bombers all over the world, but especially in the Middle East?

In "Democratic" countries, we are told that we have liberty and freedom and then we elect lawmakers to pass as many laws rules and regulations as they can think of. We let them tax us to death and after the terrorist attack on American soil we now give our government permission to spy on us as private citizens. Do we really have "Liberty and Freedom", the cry of our county's founding fathers?

GOLD

We have already talked about the fact that we live in an age where "He who has the gold makes the rules". It is obvious that some people would sell their own mother if the price were right! We have seen "plundering" at every level in business, from the lowest clerk to the richest CEO. However, when you look at the rulers of countries the problem gets worse!

Before George H.W. Bush became president, gasoline sold for about $1.15 in the United States and by the end of his second term, we were paying more than $4.00 for a gallon. How much money did the Bush family make on the war in Iraq? With large holdings in both oil production and banking, there is no doubt that they made hundreds of millions, if not billions, of dollars on a war looking for "weapons of mass destruction" that did not exist! It would have been better if the Congress of the United States had just given the money spent on the war in Iraq to the "war mongers" and no lives had to be lost! The problem with that thinking is that the rest of the oil and banking families would not have made any money. Instead, by having a war in the Middle East and putting oil production at risk, it was very easy to control the price of oil and the price of gold. So, those who had the "gold" made more "gold" off the backs of the common working people around the world!

Here is a fact. Executive Order 6102, signed into law on April 5, 1933, by President Franklin D. Roosevelt forbids the hoarding of gold. All gold coin, bullion and gold certificates had to be turned into the Federal Reserve Bank of New York. The gold is exchanged at a rate of $20.67 USD per troy ounce of gold. A year later, the US Government set the price of gold at $35.00 USD per troy ounce. You could own no more than $100.00 USD in gold coin as a private individual in the United States. Gold was no longer allowed to be used as "legal tender" nor could it be used to satisfy contractual agreements.

The Rothschild family owned and controlled Federal Reserve Bank of New York added about 500 tons of gold to their holdings at a cost of about $335,000,000,000.00 USD. However, the exchange was at $20.67 per troy ounce and a year later, the price of gold was worth $35.00 per troy ounce. This devalued the US Dollar by forty percent and gave the Rothschild family a seventy-five percent profit on their investment, or over $251,000,000,000.00.

Why would President Franklin D. Roosevelt sell out the American people this way? Why would he strip Americans of their wealth and start the United States on a road to enslavement to the Federal Reserve Bank and the Zionist Rothschild banking family?

WE ARE DESPOTS

When we think of despotic rulers of the Twentieth Century, maybe Adolph Hitler is the first to come to mind or Saddam Hussein or maybe you think of the "Killing Fields" of Cambodia. Really, the first despotic ruler ship of the Twentieth Century started in 1917 with the establishment of Communism in Russia. The Bolsheviks set up a system of extermination that put millions to death, mostly all Christians. By the end of the despotic reign of Joseph Stalin, over 60,000,000 Russians, classified as dissidents and enemies of the State, died in concentration camps! Whenever a despotic ruler comes to power, millions of innocent people lose their lives and yet that is the Zionist purpose, to establish a despotic worldwide government, led by their "King" whom they chose as their leader and leader of the world.

WE SHALL END LIBERTY

We have seen almost all of the aristocracies of the world diminished or replaced by the words of Liberty. Almost all governments in the world are under democratic rule. This new aristocracy is one that is led by money and not the values of freedom and liberty. We, as citizens of those countries, vote our liberty away in the hopes of being protected by our government, as in the case of the Patriot Act, passed by the US Congress after the attack on the World Trade Center in 2001. The more terrorism is used against the people and governments of the world, the more we will give up our liberty and personal rights!

PROTOCOL II
ECONOMIC WARS

The wars of the Twentieth Century did very little to reshape the political globe, but what it did do is cause countries to go into debt to fight the wars they found themselves in. Think about how in the First World War the peace treaties set up between the countries of Europe that led to war. All that was needed was the right spark to get every country to start fighting against one another and by the time the war was over, all the governments were in debt because of the war effort. The "Great Depression" of 1929 followed all this! To help end the depression, money was borrowed for social programs around the world causing more debt! Countries were then led to World War II, causing more debt. The cycle repeats itself until the world is plunged into a worldwide recession, a depression really, and the governments are forced to borrow more money to hold off total world economic collapse.

From the 1980's we were told to "Think Globally" in business, the whole world is a marketplace! Now we are seeing "Global" economic breakdown and no country is spared! Whom do we now look to for help? It is the world bankers, the Rothschild family.

DESTRUCTIVE EDUCATION

The teaching and promotion of evolution has replaced "Creationism" in Schools around the world. As we know here in the United States, only evolution is legally taught in schools, so what happened to God? Evolution does away with the need for God, which is the first step to end religion.

History is also twisted and the truth of what happened in history has been obscured or changed to the point where the real importance of our history has been lost. Case in point is the War of 1812. Yes, the United States was once again at war with England, but why did it happen? What started the war? The history books never say that the real reason was the Congress of the United States did not want a Rothschild bank on American soil and this was payback! 1815 saw the end to the war and 1816 saw the reestablishment of a Rothschild bank in the United States.

Today more and more the history taught in the Bible is being questioned at every point. For thousands of years the history of the Bible was never questioned and today it has been reduced to a book of strange stories that no one really believes. Goodbye religion!

Chapter 11 ~ Commentary on the School

PROTOCOL III
METHODS OF CONQUEST

By using the adage of "divide and conquer", the people of the world are reduced to the point of being powerless. We face so many issues in our lives, but the one we face the most is our very existence and how we are going to get through the problems we face every day on a personal level. Our elected officials are more involved with battling each other then addressing the real issues facing people and their families today! The general public around the world has been beaten down in every part of our lives.

POVERTY OUR WEAPON

At the turn of the Twentieth Century, the US Dollar was backed by gold and silver and the dollar was a strong currency around the world. Today our money is backed by air and the belief it is worth the paper it is written on. The truth is that most money used in the world today has no value what so ever! In 1900, the price of gold was $21 US dollars per ounce. In 2008, gold sold for over $1000 per ounce. If the US dollar were backed by gold as it once was, we would have the strongest currency in the world. So, whose idea was it to stop backing the US Dollar with gold and silver and make our money worthless?

WE SUPPORT COMMUNISM

The Zionist backed Bolsheviks put Communism into action and the aristocracy of Russia did not just end, it was destroyed when the Czar and his family were murdered in cold blood! This was a lesson to the rest of the royalty of Europe that was heard loud and clear. Their days of power were numbered. We too should take a lesson here.

When communism took over Russia, the "Goyim", the "Gentiles" who had any established position in society, were rounded up and murdered or used as slave labor. Those Gentiles who survived the purging, would be reduced to working long hours for very little money and had to stand in long lines to get only the fewest necessities to stay alive. Yes when the New World Order comes about, we can expect the same treatment!

JEWS WILL BE SAFE

It would only make sense that if the Zionist are ruling over the world and causing the problems that are reducing governments to their knees, they would want to protect the Jewish population. You may ask what happened during World War II with six million Jews murdered by Adolph Hitler's Third Reich. The world has had to acknowledge the death of these people and rightly so! I ask you, why do we not mourn the murder and death of sixty million Gentiles at the hands of the Zionist backed Communist in Russia? Why is there no world monument to these fallen innocent victims of conquest and murder? It is because we are expendable! Yes, the Gentiles of the world are expendable, but the Jews are precious in the Zionist eyes.

At one time, there were Jewish ghettos in cities all over the world. Now they have been replaced by ghettos of dark skinned peoples, except in South Africa where there are now ghettos of whites from what was once a middle class of people in that country. The Jewish ghettos of the world are gone and Jewish people in every country are good productive members of a growing "upper middle class" in the world. As a group of people, the Jews, as a whole, have become successful in all walks of life, from teachers to politicians, from doctors to lawyers, the world of entertainment and the arts and in science.

PROTOCOL IV
MATERIALISM REPLACES RELIGION

We see that the Learned Elders want to remain secret and they are making full use of the "Masons" and secret organizations to carry out their goals. No doubt, the most secret of all organizations is the Illuminati. Now one must ask, are the Learned Elders of Zion the Illuminati?

WE SHALL DESTROY GOD

By using materialism along with the devaluation of our money or inflation, gone are the days where one worked from 9 to 5. You may work 9 to 5 on your first job, but then you go to your second job and put in another 4 or 5 hours of work before your day ends. In today's world, you have to work about 12 to 14 hours a day if you are going to become successful. What time does that leave for your family? Are you ready to get up on Sunday morning and go to Church, or do you just want to roll over and sleep for a couple hours more? Besides, after working all week you need some time for yourself and you know God will understand.

Really, do you want to go to Church anyway? Look at all the problems the Church is having today. If there is a God, why would the Churches be losing membership and closing their doors?

There is no doubt in the last hundred years that religion has lost its importance in people's lives. Science, industry, material gain and entertainment have replaced God in the hearts of most people today!

PROTOCOL V
DESPOTISM AND MODERN PROGRESS

The people in the world today are sold a bunch of lies about how we are free and liberated from the monarchs and their rule and how much better a self-rule democratic government will be for us. Then we elect politicians to office to pass laws that take those liberties and freedoms away.

People use to have a respect for the monarchs that ruled over them. Today we call our politicians a pack of liars and thieves, but we still support the system that gives them power.

MASSES LED BY LIES

The Learned Elders of Zion claim to have been sowing the seeds of lies for two thousand years among society, causing divisions between races and classes of people. Their agents have entered every part of society and at every level and so the governments are helpless to do anything to get away from their control.

Everything is justified in their minds because of misapplied Hebrew Scripture of the Bible. In the Bible book of Zechariah chapter 8 verse 23, the prophet writes. "...it will be in those days that ten men out of all the languages of the nations will take hold, yes, they will actually take hold of the skirt of a man who is a Jew, saying: "We will go with you people, for we have heard that God is with you people." With the mass of lies perpetrated by the Learned Elders and their agents, leading to the hardship and death of hundreds of millions of people, which god are they representing? It obviously again must be Lucifer, the father of the lie!

MONOPOLY CAPITAL

The monopoly talked about here is the monopoly of government. If you wanted a successful political carrier, you had best start by getting a political law degree from Harvard. You are going to have to learn how the political world works in the United States. Should you want to understand world politics, you are most likely going to have to become a Rhoads Scholar and study internationally to become proficient at knowing how to manipulate the law to your advantage. All this time you have to remember that you are studying a system that the Learned Elders of Zion invented. However, there is one great obstacle that you are going to have to overcome. That is money! Without money, you really cannot change much unless you have a great political agenda and an unheard of support system to get your word out to the public. Really, at this point, you are just another cog in a political machine, run on a worldwide level by the Learned Elders of Zion and their agenda for a one-world government, led by a despotic ruler. We have seen the fore runners of this "World Government" with the League of Nations and the United Nations. Remember, these are just the fore runners for what is yet to come!

PROTOCOL VI
TAKE-OVER TECHNIQUE

The amassing of wealth to the point where both nations and the people living in those nations are in debt to the Learned Elders of Zion has always been their goal. First, the nations of Europe fell during the Nineteenth Century to the banks of the Rothschild's. They controlled the economies of England, France and Germany. With the First World War, the economies of these countries were plunged deeper into debt, the monarchy of Russia was destroyed and the country turned into a Communist State, the first but not the last of its kind.

We saw Americans forced to give up their gold and virtually give it to the Rothschild's and the United States Dollar was destined to become worthless. We have gone from owing these people nothing, to now owing them over eleven trillion dollars and climbing! Who is controlling whom? Our country along with almost every other country has already taken over and controlled the world bankers. If we do not submit to their wishes, they will destroy our already failing economy!

WE SHALL ENSLAVE GENTILES

Have you ever called your boss a "slave driver"? Now you know why! We are slaves to this system and we have been led like sheep to our own slaughter! Our gold is gone and our money does not buy anything. Families have been duped into taking on mortgages they cannot afford and lose everything they have "slaved" for years to achieve.

Our national economy is in serious trouble, as are the economies of almost all governments around the world and there is nothing we can do to fix the problem except throw money, borrowed money, at it. Fact is that before long our Gross National Product will be outstripped by the debt we owe the Federal Reserve Bank of New York. The more money we borrow from them the faster this will happen. As a nation, the United States will collapse when we reach the point where we cannot produce as much as we owe the Federal Reserve. For all intents and purposes, the Federal Reserve Bank of New York will own the United States and the business within its borders and we the people! The saying "It is better to rule in Hell than to serve in Heaven", seems to be the Zionist motto, however we the Gentiles or Goyim are going to be serving in Hell on earth if the Zionist have their way!

PROTOCOL VII
WORLD-WIDE WARS

By the manipulation of political affairs, the Learned Elders have placed rulers in power that will do their bidding. They have chosen the rich of the Gentiles to bring the changes they wanted. By treaties and agreements between countries, they can control which country will go to war against another. When combined with terrorism and arms deals, it is easy to cause a war between countries. Remember, it was the murder of German Arch Duke Ferdinand, which started the First World War. He was a Duke, not the president, or the King and this started a world war?

What was the result of the First World War? The League of Nations, the forerunner of the United Nations and the start of a "New World Order" was formed. The nations of the world were gathered together and united and it took the force of world war to do it, but that was the objective of the Zionist from the before the Protocol was written!

Germany was in economic ruin after the First World War. Political leaders rose up and rebelled against the restrictions forced upon it. The Third Reich, with the Catholic Church's support, gave a deathblow to Zionist, the League of Nations, and their planned New World Order. For this rebellion, Germany is crushed by the Allied Nations, divided up and forced into Zionist submission never to stand in opposition to our Zionist rulers again!

PROTOCOL VIII
PROVISIONAL GOVERNMENT

By using all tools, or weapons at their disposal, the Learned Elders provided special education to those whom they chose and got them into political power by one way or another. A good example of this was the leverage used on President Woodrow Wilson. To save his own political future and himself from public humiliation, he sold out the United States and appointed the most influential Zionist in the United States as Justice on the Supreme Court. He also allowed the Federal Reserve Bank of New York, the Rothschild's bank, to start to do business in the United States and this time the Rothschild's bank would be here to stay!

Thirty third degree Freemason Franklin D. Roosevelt, obviously working with the Rothschild family strips Americans of their gold and gives it to the Rothschild's, again I ask why? No doubt a deal was made. Remember, the Roosevelt Family owned the oldest bank in the United States and war was coming. No doubt, there was going to be a lot of "insider trading" and investments made in factories that would be needed to produce war supplies for the Second World War. In order for all this to happen, Roosevelt announced a "New Deal". You were going to get to have a job again and go back to work...as slaves. The "New Deal" that Roosevelt made was not for the benefit of the people of the United States, it was to their detriment.

These are only two examples of how we the people lost and lost big! We have been sold out by the Freemasons to their handlers the Illuminated Zionists. Why would they do this? It was done for wealth and a position as the ruling class in the Zionist New World Order government.

Remember too, that Presidents George H. and George W. Bush took the world to war to destroy a Hitler type leader Saddam Hussein. Saddam hated the Jews and wanted to destroy the State of Israel. Again, the Freemasons came to the rescue in an effort to please their rulers, attacked the Iraqis without mercy and came to the protection of Israel and the world.

PROTOCOL IX
RE-EDUCATION

There is no doubt to the fact that the Learned Elders will use everything they can at their disposal to accomplish their goals. The wealthiest Freemasons are elevated to a "ruling class" and carry out the message of "Liberty, Equality, Fraternity," throughout the earth.

While still elevated in importance above the Goyim, the general Jewish population is still kept in check, or under control by the Learned Elders, by their using anti-Semitism as a tool against their lesser Jewish brothers.

JEWISH SUPER-STATE

In order to achieve a "Jewish Super State", every kind of evil is used by the Learned Elders. They have successfully divided the populations of countries into mobs led by blinded leaders. Every kind of government or idea of government has been established here on earth. By funding the ideas of different political parties, you can control the way people act or think. By placing your own people in the political process, you then control the minds and ideas of the people in that political party. Find two opposite groups, get them to fight or battle each other then all you have to do is control the winner. After a conflict, you can then promote your own people to help rebuild what is left and look like a hero coming to the rescue.

In the rebuilding of a country after a war, or protecting a country from terrorist attack, people in general will accept anything you give them as long as they think they are better off then before. Laws are given or changed to prevent or help prevent future perceived problems. By having your people there to change the laws or pass new laws, you control the future of the country. The process is easier than you think.

What limits us in our thinking ability of what is possible is largely our lack of money. However, if you remove money as a factor and let your imagination run wild, you can think of all kind of things to do, from bringing world peace to ending world hunger and sickness. Think if you had the power to really make a difference in this world. You could travel the planet and make it the way you wanted it to be.

The Learned Elders of Zion look at the world and the people who live in it that way. They control almost all of the wealth, so money is not an issue. Hence, they can place their operatives in key positions of every government in the world to control the laws that are given to rule over the people.

CHRISTIAN YOUTH DESTROYED

The education system is changed and what is being taught to new students is what you want them to learn. If you do not like a part of history, change it until you have a result you want. We have gone from learning history to learning social studies, so we can better understand the people of the world around us and not what really happened in our country's past. By teaching lies in an education system and establishing a governmental system with ambiguously written laws, you can confuse the general population of any country.

Yes, by controlling a person's income, you can control their ability to act or react to problems that arise and their every day life. By controlling the monetary system of a country, you are going to be able to control the country. That is the basic operating procedure of the Learned Elders of Zion.

PROTOCOL X
PREPARING FOR POWER

Whenever there is an election, the people will rally around

the candidate who has the greatest appeal. This candidate usually has the largest election campaign fund and makes the most promises. Central to those promises are always the claim of lower taxes. So then, why do taxes always get raised after the election? Taxes are a way to force people into servitude. Most Americans have to work for five to six months just to pay taxes! What could you do with five months of extra income? Again, here is a plan by the Learned Elders that most people just accept. You pay the government before you even get your paycheck. Our money is already devalued to the point of worthlessness and then we have to give as much as forty to fifty percent away just for the privilege to earn that money to start with. What kind of system is this? Why do we accept this as a way of life? What is wrong with us? Then our government declares a war and we are ready to lay down our lives and the lives of our children, why? Oh yes an idea, an idea that our government is all knowing and powerful and we want to keep our way of life. I have to ask, why do we want this? Why do we support these stupid ideas that are heaped upon us?

OUR GOAL - WORLD POWER

By secretly creating a world problem, the Learned Elders of Zion hope to come to the rescue to fix the problem that they caused in the first place. The world is facing an economic disaster, countries are in financial ruin and are on the verge of failure and we all seem powerless to fix the problem. If countries start to collapse, it would be very easy for an outside force to come in and take over. By destroying a country from the inside economically, where do you put the blame? With the economic meltdown in the United States, people are blaming government for not having better laws to control the banks. There is no doubt that the United States will have new laws to limit what the banks are allowed to do in conducting business. You can be sure too that these laws will be ambiguous enough to allow some other kind of corruption to take place at the cost of the general population, it happens every time there is a major problem.

Chapter 11 ~ Commentary on the School

We, as a people, a nation and a civilization are being played! We will be manipulated to the point where we cannot take the present system of things anymore. We are told our vote counts and that every one should have a part in the "decision making process" of elections. We are told to get involved, so we can be blamed for our own mistakes and can be shown the need for a "savior" to get us out of the problems that our elected officials created for us.

As the years pass by, the problems of government only get bigger. It makes no difference who is elected, the problems just grow and now they have gotten to the point where they are almost totally out of control. Even the best president can only slightly affect the country he is president of, unless he declares war, then the effect is dramatic! The problems we face today are worldwide and a worldwide solution is going to be proposed by the Learned Elders. If a nation or country does not accept their solution, they will destroy it economically. We are going to be faced with the choice of submit or be destroyed!

POISON OF LIBERALISM

When the Protocol of the Learned Elders of Zion was written, you have to keep in mind that most governments of the world were monarchies. The idea of liberty was planted into the colonist in the Americas and into the peasants of France and then through the rest of the governments where monarchies ruled. Mobs were formed to protest the rule of the monarchies, leaders were raised to direct the mob protest and before long, the mob gets its way.

This same "mob mentality" has been used over and over in many protests around the world either to change an important issue, such as racial discrimination, as was the case in the United States in the 1960s, or the African tribes of Hutus and Tootsies, where mobs hacked hundreds of thousands to death. Mob mentality has been and still is a great tool of the Learned Elders. Look at any so-called hot spot around the world and you will find a mob at the center of the problem. Find out who is inciting and funding the mob and then you find the real cause of the problem.

WE NAME PRESIDENTS

Most of the Presidents of the United States before Woodrow Wilson were free of influence from outside the country. From the time of Woodrow Wilson on, it was obvious that the office of President was a target of Zionist influence. That influence governs the President of almost every country on the earth today! One president that refused to be influenced by the Zionist was President Kennedy and he never finished his first term. It was the Jewish vote in America, which made John F. Kennedy president. When President Kennedy proved to take actions that went contrary to Zionist goals, he needed to be removed as president! Lyndon B. Johnson now became the President of the United States and Zionist goals were realized and one of the most important was for the State of Israel to become a nuclear-armed country.

This also sent a clear message to the rest of the world. Just as with the Czar of Russia and his family, all world leaders were in power by the good graces of the Zionist and if you did not follow instructions you and your family would die! So it was with the Kennedy family who are Americans and Catholic. It is obvious that Senator Edward "Ted" Kennedy got the Zionist message loud and clear. He became one of the most liberal leaders in the United States Government and his support of Israel and Zionist ambitions are obvious. His voting record in congress reflects his understanding of what happens to politicians who cross the Learned Elders of Zion!

WE SHALL DESTROY

When President Kennedy was assassinated, it was said that "Camelot was lost" and America had lost its innocence. Words more true were never spoken! If you look at the Presidencies of the United States, from the time of Harry Truman until today, every president has been pro-Israel and influenced by a Zionist agenda. The presidents that did not work hand in hand with the Zionist did not stay in office and were replaced by those who would. This is not only true in the United States, but all over the world.

It took two wars to topple anti-Jew anti-Zionist, Saddam Hussein and see his death. The result of his removal from power, gave Iraq a Rothschild controlled Central Bank and its first Masonic hall in fifty years. Let the re-education begin!

PROTOCOL XI
THE TOTALITARIAN STATE

The Constitution of the United States of America guaranties us certain “unalienable rights”. Laws are put into place to give us liberty and freedom and to protect these values. However, more and more laws are proposed and passed to take those rights away from us and in fact, we now only have the idea of freedom and liberty. We are actually sitting in a trap and do not know it, because we are distracted by the problems of every day life. By causing a major problem such as a horrific terrorist attack against an already weakened economy, we could find ourselves under martial law and the Constitution of the United States becomes worthless and a memory. Even the most powerful country in the world cannot stop what the Learned Elders have in store for us.

WE ARE WOLVES

The Goyim of the world are looked at as a flock of sheep by the Elders of Zion, who picture themselves as wolves. Just as sheep flee and scatter when being chased by wolves, so do we when we come under attack. The problem is that sheep need a leader and if that leader is already a wolf, then the sheep are doomed.

The Zionist have used the Freemasons as their “wolves in sheep’s clothing”. We look to these people as leaders in our communities, states and countries, we think they are fellow sheep and all the while we are being led to the slaughter by the Zionist who believe they have the "God" given right to do so!

PROTOCOL XII
CONTROL OF THE PRESS

The people in the United States of America have as one of our "freedoms" and "rights" is freedom of speech and freedom of the press, or printed word. During the "Cold War" with the former Soviet Union, Americans saw many examples in the Russian newspaper Pravda of stories that we in America knew, or believed were cover-ups or distortions of the facts. All the time we believed that the news agencies of the United States were telling us the truth. For the most part this was true.

Then we learned that the word "spin" had new meaning. To "spin" a story, or a newsworthy event, is to tell it the way you want the public to know and understand it. It is kind of like going to a restaurant and being served terrible tasting food and complaining to the waiter about it and he proceeds to tell you how hard the chef worked on the presentation and how beautiful the food looked. Sure, it looks great you just cannot swallow it!

So we understand that any government is going to tell the best story possible about any thing, any problem, any event, anything newsworthy at all and we will think it's positive and great about what a disaster is taking place!

WE CONTROL THE PRESS

We understand that the government is always going to "spin" or "candy coat" everything they want us to know. You can be sure that the "Press" is going to cover the event and each news agency is going to try to be the first with news breaking stories. How often though, do the news agencies try to make a story about nothing!

Sensationalism has become a by-word in the world of news. We have all seen the innocent convicted before the case goes to trial by the news media. If the media likes you, they can make you into a god, but if they hate you, even "God" himself would not stand a chance against the media! In the April 8, 1966 edition of Time magazine, the cover article was "Is God Dead?" Newspapers went one-step further and just made the statement "God is dead" and the 1960's became the decade that God died.

FREE PRESS DESTROYED

The Learned Elders came to understand a long time ago that by controlling the news media you could sway public opinion for or against anything. Most people do not realize that public opinion was swayed against slavery in the north before the Civil War in the United States. Slavery was never the real issue and northern people had slaves too, though they were called servants, not slaves. The Press had such a huge impact that slavery finally became a major issue and the only reason given in the history books for the Civil War. Very few people understood that it was the effort by the Rothschild banking family to split the United States into two countries that so many anti-slavery articles were being published. By splitting the United States into two countries, it would be less of a threat to Zionist interest and be more easily controlled.

The attack on the USS Liberty on June 8, 1967 is a good example of how the press is controlled. After nine hours of surveillance, the Israeli Navy had attacked the USS Liberty knowing it was a US ship in international waters. Why did the attack happen? The Liberty was an intelligence ship, keeping track on what was going on during the Six Day War. Obviously, Israel did not want the United States to know what was happening and destroyed the Liberty killing thirty-four and wounding one hundred seventy three. Israel said it was a case of mistaken identity and that was the story reported around the world.

It is plain to see that if you control the Press you can control public opinion around the world. You can rally any group of people to any cause. You can raise up a mob and destabilize a country all by what is publicized in the news media. Investigate for yourself and see who owns the media companies around the world, see if those companies do not reflect the ideals of their owners. What could you accomplish if you used the news media to control public opinion and you controlled the money supply?

ONLY LIES PRINTED

Rising actors in Hollywood would tell reporters, “I do not care what you say about me, just spell my name right!”. They were interested in the publicity more than the truth. Most of the time you are never going to get the truth in news articles when a story is reported, because somehow the facts and truth always come later as a better understanding of the event, or the real facts never come out at all. If the Learned Elders have their way, we will only need one news media company, a communist style Pravda.

PROTOCOL XIII
DISTRACTIONS

Our lives are filled with all kinds of distractions. Nobody can get up in the morning, do a days work, go home and enjoy time with their family and have a good nights sleep without some kind of problem or issue arising and keeping our minds occupied. All day long, we are bombarded with issues; the economy, rising health care costs, politics, and environmental issues such as global warming and pollution. To distract ourselves from these issues we look for some pleasant distraction, something that will take our minds off the issues of daily life, like sports, recreation, or entertainment.

WE DECEIVE WORKERS

At the turn of the Twentieth Century, sports and sport teams were almost unheard of outside of some local or regional team sports such as soccer in Europe and baseball in America. Here is what the Learned Elders said, “*WE FURTHER DISTRACT THEM WITH AMUSEMENTS, GAMES, PASTIMES, PASSIONS, PEOPLE’S*

PALACES .... SOON WE SHALL BEGIN THROUGH THE PRESS TO PROPOSE COMPETITIONS IN ART, IN SPORT IN ALL KINDS" Can anyone calculate the amount of money that we as a nation have spent on sports and entertainment in the past hundred years? One hundred years ago sports was not an industry. In 2005, it is estimated that 200 billion dollars was spent just on sports merchandise alone. What about the money spent on stadiums, players, owners, ticket sales for events, TV production, advertising and promotion and related support industries? We spend trillions of dollars on something that has no real meaning in the day-to-day issues of life!

Movies were not even in existence at the time of the writing of the Protocol, now it is a part of a multi billion-dollar entertainment industry, mostly controlled by Jewish people. Do you really have to wonder how that happened? Again, we spend hundreds of billions of dollars to be distracted from the real issues that face us today!

PROTOCOL XIV
ASSAULT ON RELIGION

We spoke about the 1960's as the decade that "God" died, but who killed him? Christianity has been under outright attack from the time the Bolsheviks overthrew the Russian Government. The theory of Evolution has become the standard explanation of how life formed on earth and it is the only explanation taught in our schools. The teaching of evolution does away with the importance or need of having a Supreme Being all together. With all the negative news stories about the scandals of the Catholic Church and pedophile priests, is it any wonder that people have little or no regard for religion?

WE SHALL FORBID CHRIST

The general attitude of Christianity today is that it has no real use. It is responsible for numerous wars and the death of millions throughout history. Professors, statesmen and politicians, the news media and philosophers, have all had their turn at explaining to us the evils of religion and we are told that Christianity has been the worst of all. It is the intention of the Learned Elders to destroy all religion except for one, the religion of Lucifer! The Learned Elders themselves say *"NO ONE WILL EVER BRING UNDER DISCUSSION OUR FAITH FROM ITS TRUE POINT OF VIEW SINCE THIS WILL BE FULLY LEARNED BY NONE SAVE OURS WHO WILL NEVER DARE TO BETRAY ITS SECRETS."* What is the faith they are talking about? They all are Luciferians and worship their god Lucifer and want to force us to do the same!

PROTOCOL XV
RUTHLESS SUPPRESSION

The Learned Elders out right say they will kill anyone who stands in their way of global domination. Secret societies will be destroyed if they stand in opposition to the Zionist goals, even those Freemasons who "know too much", although they are in service to the Learned Elders, will be put to death. No one will stand in opposition to the Learned Elders and live!

The Learned Elders identify the Russian aristocracy and the Papacy as their two greatest enemies and we know what happened to the Russian Czar Nicholas and his family. I assume the Catholic Church is next!

SECRET SOCIETIES

The learned Elders make no secret of their promotion of Masonry and the Freemasons and how they are used as the main tool to rule over the Goyim. As we have discussed in an earlier chapter, men from all walks of life have become Freemasons and that they hold the highest positions in world politics, business and education. The influence of the Freemasons is felt worldwide as they are directed by the Illuminated Learned Elders of Zion. Unwittingly, we let them make laws and direct us, the Goyim, right into the teeth of the great beast they serve!

GENTILES ARE STUPID

Gentiles really are stupid! We have let ourselves be enslaved to a world that does not care about people or their welfare. We have been lulled asleep by distractions and the idea of freedom and wealth and, in the process, we have lost our freedom and our money is worthless! While the Learned Elders have been planning world conquest for centuries, we Goyim want everything here and now! We have trouble planning for the next year, while the Learned Elders are busy planning for the next century. While our children are watching cartoons on TV and playing video games, the children of the Learned Elders of Zion are studying law. It was commanded of the Jewish people to teach their children "from infancy" about the laws of God.

GENTILES ARE CATTLE

With the attitude that people are nothing more than a beast fit for consumption, that is how we are used. Even the Freemasons are not free. They follow the instructions of their trainers and are quick to lead herds of people to their death for any cause of war and we are quick to follow.

WE DEMAND SUBMISSION

As a people, we are glutted with new laws that are made everyday by our elected politicians and we are expected to follow those laws regardless if we agree with them or not. If we are found in violation of those laws, we could expect to be arrested and charged with a crime. In the United States, we are told we are guaranteed due process of law. This means that we will have a trial, and have a lawyer to represent us as our peers judge us for what we have done. We are also presumed innocent, until the Court proves our guilt.

You could expect this to change dramatically once the Learned Elders gain total control of their New World Order! In the judicial system of the former Soviet Union, you were presumed guilty and had to prove your innocence. If you could not do this, you would most likely be sent to a "gulag" or a state forced labor camp for years or possibly the rest of your life. Total submission is what the Learned Elders want and if they do not get it you could expect a very short live span!

WE SHALL BE CRUEL

The Learned Elders want to give the appearance that they are like our fathers and the government they want to establish for us will be for our own good and benefit. However, if you go contrary to the absolutism of their law, you will not just be punished, but you will be made an example of. Every communist government has had its purges where millions of innocent people were put to death for no good reason. I am sure that the 60,000,000 people who were put to death in communist Russia were not all guilty of death dealing offenses. The fact is that most were put to death just because of their education, or religion or social position in life.

PROTOCOL XVI
BRAINWASHING

By gaining control of the educational system, we are already being "reeducated" in the way of the Learned Elders. What is being taught in universities around the world is controlled and managed by professors that have called into question the accepted standards of the past.

As a nation, our children are becoming stupid and uneducated, even though they have been in the education system for years. It is a fact that the United States has fallen behind other countries in the education of our children. I have personally talked to college graduates who have less knowledge about basic education and could not answer simple questions about American

History that I learned in grade school, not high school, grade school! How do you develop world leaders that have little or no knowledge or real education?

When you have a nation full of children and young adults who cannot answer simple general knowledge questions, but can master the most sophisticated video game in a week, you have a sure recipe for social disaster!

WE SHALL CHANGE HISTORY

We have already seen this happen! The study of history deals in dates, facts and events so there is no mystery to history when you have all the facts regarding the event. I was almost shocked not long ago when I was watching a TV program where historians and archeologists were calling into question the existence of the Jewish King Solomon. What is this all about? How do you call into existence one of the most important personages ever to walk the earth? For almost three thousand years, King Solomon has been touted as the wisest man to ever live; now he may not have even existed. So when are we going to be told that the sun will rise in the west and set in the east? More worrisome than that I am sure some of our Goyim brothers are going to believe that the sun actually does rise in the west after they are informed of this change.

PROTOCOL XVII
ABUSE OF AUTHORITY

Currently the judicial system leans toward finding a defendant innocent. In the murder case involving O. J. Simpson and the death of Nicole Brown and Ronald Goldman, the evidence against Mr. Simpson was damning at best! The State of California lost the murder case against Mr. Simpson and he was found "not guilty" of murder, however, he did lose the civil case against him for the wrongful deaths of Nicole Brown and Ronald Goldman.

If this case had been tried in the courts of the Learned

Elders, Mr. O.J. Simpson would have been made an example of and most likely would have been publicly executed with no chance of appeal. The authority of the Learned Elders is meant to crush anything, or any person who is against the "State" in any way!

WE SHALL DESTROY THE CLERGY

There is no doubt that the Clergy stands in the way of Zionist goals. Not just Christian Clergy, but the Clergy of all religions. The Clergy of Christendom has been a thorn in the Zionist side for centuries! The hatred for Christians can be traced back to the time of Jesus Christ himself. With the Romans destroying Jerusalem and the Jewish nation, the Zionist had been plotting their revenge for almost two thousand years. When the Roman Empire became the Roman Catholic Church, the Zionist had even more reason to destroy it! Rome took the Jews captive and the Church persecuted them for centuries. Do you really think the Church will last long?

People today have given up on Religion! We all know that Religion has misrepresented God and lied to the people for centuries. Only in the Twentieth Century did people finally turn their backs on the Religious establishment. The Catholic Church is worried for its very existence. With the indifference of people today, the extremely bad press the Church has gotten over the years and the general knowledge that the Church is responsible for numerous wars and conflicts resulting in millions of deaths, people today just do not care what happens to religion. The vast majority of people do not attend a religious meeting on a regular basis. "Sunday go to meeting" is a thing of the past for most people and families.

The importance of the Church has been diminished. The role of the Clergy has little more importance than to provide a service for marrying people and burying dead loved ones, beyond that very few people really care.

We can see that the Learned Elders have set up the Church and religion in general for a fall and its destruction.

Chapter 11 ~ Commentary on the School

PROTOCOL XVIII
ARREST OF OPPONENTS

Throughout history, agents have been used to form conspiracies at every level. Politicians, world rulers and business leaders have all succumbed to this trap. The "Water Gate" conspiracy cost Richard Nixon his presidency and left his closest advisors in prison. Did Nixon's anti-Semitic comments and attitude have anything to do with this?

GOVERNMENT BY FEAR

The Soviet Union was a government that used fear to keep the population under control. At the first suspicion or wrongdoing, citizens were arrested and either executed or sent off to a forced labor camp, a gulag. Neighbors were spying on neighbors to gain favor with the Communist State. Can you imagine saying something negative about the government today out of frustration and being arrested tomorrow for crimes against the state, then executed the day after because you spoke your mind? Welcome to the New World Order, Comrade!

PROTOCOL XIX
RULERS AND PEOPLE

The intention of the Learned Elders is to encourage involvement of the Goyim in government, so they can inspect the attitude of the people and make adjustments in order to lay down greater controls. Anyone speaking seditious things about the government will be dealt with the same as a murderer would. Propaganda by the press and reeducation through the schools will keep us Goyim like cattle, or so they think!

PROTOCOL XX
FINANCIAL PROGRAM

Taxes and death are said to be the only definite things in life today. We are required to pay taxes on everything, from the land we may own to the money we work for and the food we eat. It almost seems that every time money changes hands, a tax must be paid to someone! Whose idea was this? Yes, the Learned Elders strike again!

In an effort to keep the wealth in their hands, we are taxed on any wealth that touches our hands. We may work and save our money for years to buy a house and property and then we have to pay the Government to keep it! Why does this sound like extortion? Because extortion is exactly what it is! Stop paying property tax and see how long it takes the local police to throw you out of your own home! We are not even under the rule of the new world order and already our money is being taken from us. The goal is for the State to own everything and us, the Goyim, to be totally reliant on the state for our existence.

WE SHALL DESTROY CAPITAL

If you read this part of the Protocol, you will understand where our tax system comes from and why we have to pay taxes. The saying "the more you make, the more they take" must have been coined by an agent for the Zionist tax plan. The plan is to remove you from your money! Remember, we have to work five months just to pay taxes. What if you had to work six or seven months to pay your taxes? Really, you would be working for the Government and that is exactly what the Zionist plan is, for everyone to be working for the good of their Government. "

WE CAUSE DEPRESSIONS

In 1929, the world was thrown into the "Great Depression".

Chapter 11 ~ Commentary on the School

When you do the research, you will find that the same events that caused the depression in 1929 were used again to cause the worldwide depression we have now. People lost their homes and their jobs at record rates and while the governments of the world were quick to borrow more money from the Federal Reserve Bank to stem off depression this time, in 1929 it took three years of problems and heart ache before the Federal Reserve gave the cash for President Roosevelt's New Deal. Make no mistake, the Learned Elders planned this!

GENTILE STATES BANKRUPT

Do I even have to comment on this? The whole world is in debt to the big banking families. The Gold Standard for money has been done away with and now there is nothing backing the money of the world but air. The only thing that separates our money from toilet paper is time. Before long, the United States will not be able to pay the interest on the money we owe the Federal Bank of New York, let alone the principal itself. When that happens the United States will fly the flag of the New World Order, we will have no choice!

TYRANNY OF USURY

At one time, it was illegal to charge interest on money that you borrowed. The Knights Templar found a loophole to get around this law; they charged "rent" on the money one would borrow. After the Templars were outlawed and banned, they disappeared, but what appeared after they were gone was our modern banking system.

Usury is still illegal in the United States, unless you are a bank. How does the United States allow a private bank to adjust the nation's interest rates? Maybe it is because that private bank almost completely owns the United States!

PROTOCOL XXI
LOANS AND CREDIT

Finances and banking are always at the center of the Learned Elders plot to gain control of world affairs and world governments. Naturally, you would have to believe that the Learned Elders are owners of the world's largest banks.

When you examine our banking system, it is based on "credit" money that is not there or does not really exist. Yet, we personally and as a nation, borrow money for one reason or another and it costs many times the amount that we have borrowed.

Several years ago, standing in the check out line at a super market, I noticed the person in front of me used a credit card to buy their groceries. I wondered just how much those groceries were going to cost them by the time they paid off their credit card bill. Yet, today most people will live off their credit cards and we enslave ourselves to the scams of these "Learned Elders"!

It is not just the people, it is the governments of the world who have enslaved themselves to the scams of the Learned Elders and the banks they control such as the Federal Reserve Bank of New York. Our government, already being in massive debt is forced to live on credit! To help pay their bill they raise our taxes. We, the people, are enslaved to the Learned Elders twice. Once by our government and worse, we enslave ourselves! Really though, what choice do we have? We ca not do anything without having a bank involved. So yes, we borrow one dollar and have to pay three dollars back and the Learned Elders get their way again!

PROTOCOL XXII
POWER OF GOLD

We have repeatedly talked about gold and the power it has. Why is that? Because we live in a time where "he who has the gold makes the rules", who has the gold? As the learned elders say,

"IN OUR HANDS IS THE GREATEST POWER OF OUR DAY - GOLD: IN TWO DAYS WE CAN PROCURE FROM OUR STOREHOUSES ANY QUANTITY WE MAY PLEASE." Remember, this was claimed before President Franklin D. Roosevelt forced the people of the United States to give the Learned Elders five hundred tons, more than what they already had at the time the "Protocol" was written.

PROTOCOL XXIII
INSTILLING OBEDIENCE

This Protocol maybe the most fear inspiring of all. The Learned Elders intend to have their One World Government! They will install a totalitarian king who will be willing to kill all those "societies" who are perceived to be against their government! A good example of this on a small scale was Joseph Stalin, who is responsible for the murder of possibly more than fifty million people under his rule of the communist Soviet Union. How many hundreds of millions of people will be murdered if this rule were carried out on a worldwide basis?

Maybe the most terrifying thing about all this, is that the Learned Elders believe it is "God's will" for them to install a ruler over the world and slaughter all Goyim who may breathe a word of protest! Do you really have to ask who their god is? If Jehovah is a god of love, then it is obvious that Lucifer, the god of this world and this system, is the bloodthirsty god of Zion!

Yes, we can expect concentration camps and gulags to be installed as execution centers for the defiant Goyim worldwide! Every flag in the world will fly the "Star of Moloch" and Lucifer will have the whole world under his control and everyone worshiping him and his installed king! All those who oppose this rule will die and the ones who Lucifer and his Zionist king want dead most are those good-hearted people who really want to have a relationship with the true God, Jehovah!

PROTOCOL XXIV
QUALITIES OF THE RULER

The king that the Learned Elders are talking about is their "Messiah". The man Jesus fulfilled all the prophecies of the Hebrew Scriptures regarding the Messiah. However, he did not fulfill the needs of the Learned Elders of Zion in the first century so they killed him! The learned Elders of Zion of the First Century were under Roman rule and they were looking for a man to lead a revolt against Rome, defeat the Roman Empire and install a Zionist World Empire. When Jesus said, "my kingdom is no part of this world", he signed his own death sentence.

Now two thousand years have passed and still there is no "Messiah"! What there is, is control of the world by the Learned Elders using the banking system against us to take our wealth and drive us into submission by way of taxation and usury and by making us an "I want it now" society.

So where is this king? Maybe a better question is, who is this King? The world stage is set for his coming! We are all in debt and so is our country. We have no gold, no power and no say!

The Learned Elders want a descendant of the Hebrew King David. This is going to be almost impossible to prove because the records were destroyed by the Romans along with everything that was not taken back as "spoils" from the conquest of Jerusalem. The Romans razed the city of Jerusalem to a smoldering mass of rubble!

So how are they going to prove that their king is a descendant of King David? There may be a way to do this. There is another line of King David that comes through his son, Solomon, and the Quean of Sheba. The "Messiah", the "King of the Jews", may come out of Africa!

The King that the Learned Elders want to install as ruler of the world is someone who the people of the world must love and admire. He must be a man who can mingle with his subjects and have their confidence. At the same time, he must be able to make decisions to destroy all opposition to the One World Government.

Most of all, he must appear to be above all reproach to the masses, both Jewish and Goyim, and be a good and loyal puppet to his Zionist masters!

LAST COMMENT ON THE PROTOCOL

If the Protocol of the Learned Elders of Zion is a hoax, or a forgery, the person or persons who wrote it had an uncanny ability of prediction and prophecy. Somehow, they knew every move that was to come during the Twentieth Century to gain financial control of the world governments and the people in those governments. They knew about the death of the Czar and his family and the world wars that would come. The writers of the formation of a world government, first the League of Nations and then the United Nations, will both soon be replaced by another "One World Government", the "New World Order"! There are predictions yet to be fulfilled, but the world stage is set for those predictions to take place. Then we will see the complete fulfillment of the Protocol of the Learned Elders of Zion come to pass, and we the people will be under the yoke of an oppressive Zionist government that will see the death of millions and millions of Goyim around the world!

CHAPTER 12
PROPHETS AND PROPHECIES

KNOWING THE FUTURE

As far back as you can go in civilized history, there seems to have been a great desire to know the future. What is going to happen tomorrow is valuable information. If you knew what was going to happen tomorrow, you could make some very safe investments and not have to worry about losing anything. You could see disaster coming and prepare for it. Just think how many lives could be saved if you knew about the Tsunami on December 26th, 2004, before it happened and could have warned all those who were at the mercy of this disaster!

To know and understand something before it happens would be a great gift. To use this gift for the benefit of humanity would be truly noble! Yet as we look through history, it seems that every ruler that ever was relied on some kind of foreteller of events to make decisions in ruling over their people.

The desire to know the future has spawned a whole industry. To tell one's future is an industry that goes back as far as civilization itself. To predict the future by reading the stars, astrology, had its start even before the flood of Noah's day. The book of Enoch tells us that the fallen angels taught astrology to their wives.

The ancient Babylonians became experts in astrology; remember, it was the "Wise Men from the East" who read the stars and came looking for Jesus. The knowledge of astrology is 5000 years old. It is interesting that astrology is as old as religion itself and they both had their start in ancient Babylon. In fact, astrology was central in Babylonian religion.

It would only be logical to think that if the fallen angels gave this special knowledge to their wives before the flood, their counterparts, the angels who did not come to earth but took the side of Lucifer, would want to guide people too. Remember, this was all about the control of the human family and people have let astrology control their lives for 5000 years. Even in a day and age of science and fact, you can open any newspaper in America, read your horoscope first thing in the morning, and then plan your day. Sure, you let someone who reads the stars control what you are going to do with your life! You just gave up control and your right of free will, you lost some of your freedom and you lost choice.

I really do not know enough about astrology to give a comprehensive overview about how it works and really, I am glad about that. I would never let it rule my life, but that is not so for hundreds of millions of people today. Astrology is alive and well! In a world where interest in religion is dying, people all over the world still rely on their horoscope to guide their lives. Sure, you can open any newspaper and read your horoscope, but when is the last time you saw a newspaper run a column that gave you helpful advice from the Bible? Really, would you read it anyway? Most likely, if you wanted advice you would just turn the page of your newspaper and read the "Dear, Whom Ever" column.

Here is something to consider. One of the most notorious men of the Twentieth Century, Adolph Hitler, used astrologers to guide his actions. Do you really have to wonder if demonic alien forces guided Adolph Hitler, who was responsible for deaths of more than fifty million people worldwide?

As civilization left the plains of Mesopotamia, astrology left with it. Every culture around the world has some type of astrology that it uses or has used to guide their future. From Stonehenge to the Mayans, from the plains of ancient Mesopotamia 5000 years ago to the streets of New York City today, people of the world have let their lives be controlled by astrology and other means of foretelling the future.

While astrology is most likely the oldest method of forecasting future events, it is only one method used to divine the future. People have used many methods to try to know the future; they have used palmistry, looked into crystal balls, tarot cards and other devices. Really, where is their knowledge coming from? It is true that many foretellers of events have no special connection or knowledge at all; they are frauds just looking to make money on people whose lives are out of control.

There is one major problem with using these technologies of foretelling the future; these technologies were given to pagan peoples who worshiped Lucifer as god! Remember government, religion, astrology and fortune telling all had their start on the plains of Mesopotamia in the cities that Nimrod built. He was king over all the then "civilized world". Nimrod was opposed to Jehovah and obviously blessed by Lucifer. This is the start of the "seed" or "offspring" of Lucifer.

WHAT IS OUR FUTURE?

Is it possible to know what is going to happen in the future? To an extent, yes it is possible to know future events. However, someone or some group plans most future events. Here we just considered "The Protocol of the Learned Elders of Zion" as a book that while written over one hundred years ago, explains how world conquest would take place, not only in the Twentieth Century, but events that have not taken place yet. So in fact, if you studied the Protocol, you would have a good idea of future events. When you consider the world events that have happened since the writing of the Protocol, you can be sure that the rest of the events planned for the future of the world will also happen.

Were the writers of the Protocol fortunetellers? Did they have special knowledge of future events? Maybe in some cases they did, but over all the Learned Elders of Zion are great strategic planners and they have an endless source of wealth accumulated. Really, what can stop their plans?

Because we live in an "I want it now" society, we fail to plan for the future and therefore, we can only be at the effect of future events. There is a saying that sailors have used for years, it is "Red sky in morning, sailors take warning! Red sky at night is a sailor's delight!" What does it mean? When there is a red sky at night there is going to be fair weather, but a red sky in the morning was an indication of stormy weather and it was time to 'batten down the hatches" and secure the ship for bad weather.

The human race is facing a morning with the reddest sky ever and we can see the warnings all over the world! Yes, we are headed for a very difficult future to say the least. In every sector of life, we are facing disaster. Global warming, pollution, food shortages, terrorism, war, diseases with no cure such as AIDS, and the fear of global epidemics and financial crises are all problems that are facing the population of the world. Yes, we face these things everyday now and no one can escape these problems.

There is a bigger problem that faces us as the people of earth. Some how we know it is coming, but again we are powerless to stop and that is "God's" war of Armageddon. What exactly is this war of Armageddon? Many people have wondered about this and have different theories about what it is. We are going to examine this subject in length and look for the prophecies that apply to the time that we are living in.

We really do not need the stars, crystal balls, palm readers, or fortunetellers to let us know that we live in very difficult times and people are going to have to come together just to survive the damage we have done to the earth. We cannot afford war anymore! Health care issues and costs have gotten out of control in most countries. Disease, food shortages and the lack of clean water affect almost twenty-five percent of the earth's population and we have all the makings for a major worldwide epidemic like the Spanish Influenza did, which left more people dead around the world than the First World War.

You and I and everyone on this planet we call Earth, are on the edge of a major global disaster and the state of the economy is going to be the last thing on peoples minds, survival will be the first! I know that those are grim words, but take a serious look at the world around us and then think, what is the world going to look like when my kids are my age?

Can we really stop the ocean levels from rising? Ask the people who live in the Fiji Islands, or should I say who used to live in Fiji. Can we stop air pollution? Maybe the people in Los Angeles, California can talk to the people in Beijing, China and figure out a way to clean the air in their cities. Do you really think we will ever see an antidote to the AIDS virus, or the elimination of cancer, or a vaccine for the next new strain of bird flu brewing in the far east that scientist believe will devastate earth's population? Can our governments cure or fix these problems?

As the earth continues to warm and the population continues to grow, the system we live in comes under more strain. The need for energy increases, food needs become greater and the need for clean drinkable water is paramount. In addition, the chance for disease on an epidemic level grows as well and the death toll along with it. If we are not close to the breaking point, we will soon be there. Evidence shows we are not far from the brink of collapse. We have already seen another economic collapse on a global scale, with banks failing in almost every country on the planet, what system will fail next?

If you had the answers about how to fix this global problem, which we the people are facing, would anyone really listen to you? No, most likely they would not. It is difficult enough to change your own habits and now you want to change the habits of everyone in the world? It is going to take a major disaster to get people to change the way we do business and live on this planet. The process it would take would kill millions and the poorest people and countries always suffer the most.

Still we want to know what we are going to have to face in the future and we always hope it is good and we will prosper, at least that is what a fortuneteller is most likely to tell you. However, the reality is far from the fantasy at times and you would be hard pressed to find anyone to tell you that things have gotten better with time. If they did, no one would ever talk about the "good old days". So where can we find a reliable source to learn what is going to happen in the future?

There is only one place we can look to find reliable answers about "God's War" or Armageddon, and that is the Bible. After all, it is "God's" book and his war!

PROPHECIES

Prophecies in the Bible are given by God to men through some kind of communication, either directly or through his messengers, the creatures we call angels, or by visions or dreams. These men were called prophets and had to deliver to the people the message given to them. In most cases, "God" sent prophets to the nation of Israel, but there were also other nations sent messages from "God" through his prophets.

The very first prophecy was told by "God" himself at Genesis chapter 3, verse 15 and it is a prophecy about none other than Lucifer himself. Really, what happened was Jehovah told Lucifer what he was going to do and what was going to happen. Fact is, Jehovah always told people what he was going to do before he did it! In Genesis 3:15 Jehovah told Lucifer, "...you and the woman will be enemies, and your offspring and her offspring will be enemies. He will crush your head and you will strike his heel."

Jehovah told Lucifer that his "woman", or Jehovah's wifely family, would be enemies with Lucifer and would raise children that would be enemies with the children that Lucifer would raise and one of Jehovah's children would be hurt in the heel by Lucifer, but this child would crush Lucifer's head in the end. That child became the man Jesus, the Messiah, or Christ, whom Lucifer made sure, was put to death, when he, Jesus was on the earth two thousand years ago. So when are Lucifer and his offspring going to get their head crushed and who are the offspring whom belong to Lucifer? Primarily the offspring are all who worship him, either directly as the Luciferians do, or indirectly by deception. Most people are and have been fooled and tricked, into blindly following the dogma of whatever church, mosque, or temple they attend. Remember the symbols, idols and teachings we discussed previously and their origin. They are mostly pagan and were used by pagan nations to worship their gods.

While "God" gave many prophecies to his people, we are only concerned about the ones that apply to our day here and now. What happened two thousand years ago, does not matter as much as what is going to happen tomorrow, or next year or whenever the world conditions hit their critical point and Armageddon strikes. What is important for us to know, are the prophecies that apply to us today, if we are to understand and survive Armageddon!

UNDERSTANDING ARMAGEDDON

Armageddon comes from the Hebrew Har-Magedon, meaning Mountain of Megiddo. This term is directly related to the war of Jehovah God. However, there is no literal Mountain of Megiddo, only the ancient city of Megiddo. The plains of Megiddo saw some very significant battles throughout the centuries and these battles always seemed to be very decisive and one sided, so to will be the battle of Armageddon.

Why is this battle going to be fought? The answer is quite simple. Lucifer refuses to give back what he stole from the human race. When Jesus died two thousand years ago "for our sins", his death was a ransom for the lives of all people ever on this planet. Jesus has the legal right and ownership of the lives of all people. Even with the ransom paid, Lucifer refuses to let "God's" people go. The Battle of Armageddon is really for the lives of we the people, by supernatural forces that we do not understand!

This is not some "Good verses Evil" psychological battle. This is a war, a very real physical war, using technology that we have little, if any, concept of. The thought that we humans are caught up in not just an inter-galactic war, but are involved in an inter-dimensional war, is very difficult to conceive. Maybe the world leaders have somewhat of an understanding of what is coming. President Ronald Reagan referred to an "alien force" in his speech to the United Nations and how quickly the nations of the world would unite "if we were facing an alien threat from outside our world". That is exactly what Revelation says is going to happen in chapter 16, verses 14-17. "The kings of the entire inhabited earth would be gathered to the place that is called in Hebrew, Har-Magedon."

This is a war to take back ruler ship of the earth! Again, this may be difficult to understand, because we have rulers, presidents, kings, dictators and other political officials who rule over us and they are humans. We see their faces in the news almost every day and they are real to us. What we do not see are the forces behind the faces. We get to see the puppet show and the puppets, but we never see the puppeteers! In his speech to the United Nations, President Reagan also said, "Is not an alien force already among us?" What did Ronald Reagan know that we do not? Is there really an alien force among us? Yes, there is, make no doubt about it and they are preparing for war! During his presidency, Reagan initiated the "Star Wars Program", a space based weapon system. The program died with the end of the cold war, but it was quietly reinstated under the Bush administration, funded with over fifty billion dollars. The Star Wars program is suppose to defend the United States from nuclear missile attack, at least that is what we are told, but when is the last time the government told we the people the truth about anything?

Let us face the truth here. This planet is in trouble; there is no doubt about that! Even if the Learned Elders of Zion get their "One World Government", they are going to be powerless to change very much. In fact, we can expect nothing but problems. What they are doing by establishing a "One World Government" is gathering the kings of the earth together to the place that is called in Hebrew, Har-Magedon!

IDENTIFYING THE BEASTS OF REVELATION

The book of Revelation talks about some strange creatures; wild beasts that seem to have been dreamt up while on some psychedelic trip. However, each beast has great significance and can be easily identified, if you know what to look for. The first beast that we want to examine is the "Great Dragon" in Revelation 12. We find here a fiery-colored, seven-headed dragon. This dragon has ten horns and on its seven heads there are seven diadems. This dragon's tail drags a third of the stars from heaven and hurls them toward the earth.

Chapter 12 ~Prophets and Prophecies

The next wild beast ascends out of the sea and also has seven heads, ten horns and seven diadems. On its seven heads are written blasphemous names. The body of this beast is like a leopard, its feet are like a bear's with a mouth like a lion. The Great Dragon gives power, a throne and great authority to this wild beast. The third beast that we want to identify is also found in Revelation, chapter 13 in verse 11. This beast has two horns and ascends out of the earth. It looks like a lamb, but it speaks like a dragon and it can perform great signs, even calling fire down from heaven.

These beasts of Revelation are all with us today! You may wonder where in the world these beasts are hiding, because if they are real we should see them right? They are hiding in plain sight. They are with us today and we do not even realize it. Why is that you might ask? It is because these beasts are so large we are like the fleas on the beast. We do not see the beast because we are living on it.

THE GREAT DRAGON

The "Great Dragon" is easy to identify; it is Lucifer himself. Revelation even tells us that. In Chapter 12 verse 7, we are told that war broke out in heaven and Michael and his angels battled the dragon and his angels. In verse 9, the dragon is thrown out of heaven and down to the earth along with his angels and he is called the original serpent, the one named Devil or Satan. Lucifer is depicted with seven heads, seven diadems and ten horns. Let us look to history for some support here. From the time of Egypt, there have been seven world powers to rule over the world. Each of these world powers were pagan and sun worshipers, they were Luciferians and ruled by the might of their armies. These seven heads or world powers had ten horns. The ten horns are the ten seats of power that ruled over the world. Egypt has one horn, Assyria has one horn, Babylon has one horn, Medo-Persia has two horns, Grease has one horn, and Rome has two horns, one for the capital in Rome and one for Constantinople. The last head or world power, the Anglo-American world power, also has two horns, one for England and one for the United States of America. This dragon represents Lucifer and his history of world domination by his seven blessed world powers. The stars that the great dragon drags from heaven are Lucifer's allies, the angels, whom he convinced to join in his rebellion.

SEVEN-HEADED TEN-HORNED BEAST

The next wild beast is not as easy to identify. Revelation only tells us what this beast does, where it comes from and that it gets its power from Lucifer. To identify what or who this beast is, we have to look at the actions it performs as well as what it looks like.

First, this beast is a composite made from the parts of three other beasts. The leopard, an animal that pound for pound is one of the strongest on earth; the bear, which has paws that can rip apart almost anything; and the lion, whose bite force is one of the strongest of all land animals and this beast has seven biting machines to tear apart and devour any prey! Again, the seven heads represent the seven world powers of history starting with Egypt. Upon the seven heads are ten horns, same as the "Great Dragon". Again, the horns representing the ten seats of power that ruled the world, but the diadems or crowns are on each of the ten horns. It is no surprise that this beast has the same number of heads and horns as the "Great Dragon", because it gets its power and authority from him. There is one more very important thing about this beast. In Revelation 13:3, one of the heads gets a death stroke and almost dies, but somehow recovers and is admired and followed by the whole world!

This beast comes from the sea where nothing is stable, constantly shifting and moving by the changing tides and winds. The same is true with public opinion; it is constantly shifting and changing depending on the needs of the people! Could we the people have created this beast? No, that is not the case exactly; the beast was and is an idea supported by public opinion.

This "beast" first tried to make its appearance out of the turmoil of the Napoleonic wars in the formation of the Congress of Vienna in 1814, but it was not the appointed time for this beast to show its head. It was not for over a hundred years later that the beast would finally show up on the world stage. Out of the turmoil of World War I came the beast called League of Nations! The League of Nations was the forerunner of the United Nations and the United Nations is the forerunner of the One World Government, which waits for us in the near future.

The League of Nations represented the then world powers under one political organization. The Rothschild family already had economic control of the countries of Europe through their banking system. In 1913, the United States allowed the Rothschild's Federal Reserve Bank of New York to start doing business in America, but it would not be long before America would fall to the Rothschilds too! It would not be the political pressures and rule of the League of Nations that would force the United States into submission. The United States was still too financially independent to be forced to join the League of Nations and the League seemed to be a European political power more than a world political power. However, Great Britain would be a major supporter of the League of Nations and a head country member.

The League obviously received a death stroke when World War II started in 1939. Adolph Hitler and the Third Reich, backed by the Catholic Church, did their best to destroy the Zionist influence and the One World Government they had planned. However this was not to be, the death stroke is healed and the League of Nations carries on stronger as the United Nations, with its headquarters in New York City, USA. Now the United States would take the role as major supporter of the United Nations and join England as a head country member.

Revelation 13:4 reads, "They worshiped the dragon for giving the beast such power and they worshiped the beast. "Is there anyone as great as the beast?" they exclaimed. "Who is able to fight against him?" "

There is no doubt that no one can fight against the United Nations, not even the United States. The United Nations supported by its member nations of the world, indeed rules over the people of those nations. Many people have called the United Nations "God's" representative organization for peace on earth. Even the religions of the world submit to the will of the United Nations and turn to it for peace on earth, not "God". We can see the words at Revelation 13:5 come true "The beast was aloud to speak blasphemous against God." In fact, the United Nations does not represent the interest of "God"! It represents the interest of world leaders as they submit their power to the United Nations. Revelation 13:7 goes on to say, "The beast was allowed to wage war against God's holy people and to overcome them." Is religion not under attack all over the world? It is really a case of submit or die and there is no doubt that religion is dying all over the world as people themselves become more beast like in their attitudes and actions.

Many world leaders say and have said that the United Nations is man's last hope for world peace. If the United Nations is a Luciferian supported and backed form of world government, are the people of the world not saying that a one world Luciferian backed government is the only way to peace?

By itself, the United Nations does not have any real power, but the seventh head or world power of this wild beast does! Remember, that seventh head has two horns or kingdoms which are the United States and Great Britain.

THE TWO-HORNED BEAST

Revelation 13:11-13 tells us about another wild beast. The Apostle John says, "And I saw another wild beast come up out of the earth. He had two horns like those of a lamb, and spoke with the voice of a dragon. He exercised all the authority of the first beast. And he required all the earth and those who belong to this world to worship the first beast whose death-wound had been healed. He did astounding miracles, like making fire flash down to earth while everyone was watching."

Remember, we are talking about representations of world governments when we are talking about these beasts. Where do you find a world government that speaks peace like an innocent lamb yet speaks as a dragon? What government can call fire down from the heavens? You may want to ask the people of Germany and Japan who suffered the fire bombing of city after city and the deaths of hundreds of thousands of innocent civilians during World War II. Maybe the people who survived the atomic fire rained down on Nagasaki and Hiroshima could tell you what government is responsible.

When the world saw the destruction of the atomic fireball on the cities of Nagasaki and Hiroshima, there was no doubt that the United States had emerged as a world power! For two hundred years, England had ruled the seas and had colonized much of the world, but after World War II, the power of the seas, land and sky belonged to the United States of America! If there was any question about the power of the U.S. after 40 years of a cold war with the Soviet Union, the world watched as the coalition forces led by the United States during the war Desert Storm destroyed the fourth largest army in the world. After that war, the United States emerged as a "Super Power" no longer a just a world power.

If the League of Nations and now the United Nations is the seven headed, ten horned wild beast, and the United States and England are the two-horned lamb speaking as a dragon, we can see how the United States and England "exercised all authority over the United Nations in both attacks on Iraq and on the attack on Afghanistan.

President George W. Bush, backed by Prime Minister Tony Blair, took the lead in telling the member countries of United Nations, in fact the whole world, that either they were with the United States in stamping out terrorism in the world or against the United States and therefore an enemy of them.

The United States and England, backed by the authority United Nations, forced all other countries in the world to take a stand against the perceived foe of terrorism. Remember that the reason for the second invasion of Iraq was that Iraq had "weapons of mass destruction", poison gas that could kill thousands. Remember too that Iraq claimed they did not have any weapons of mass destruction and the Coalition Forces, after months of searching, never found any either. Therefore, the United States and England forced a war that has lasted over 6 years now and between the wars in Iraq and Afghanistan, the U.S. taxpayers have spent almost 2 trillion dollars.

When it comes to peace, the United States and England claim to be the peacekeepers of the world. The United States, because of its military might, really takes the lead in this area. The United States has claimed to keep peace by having the strongest most technologically advanced army in the world. Yes, the appearance of a lamb in peace and the words of a dragon in war and the ability to call down nuclear fire from the heavens.

THE IMAGE OF THE WILD BEAST

There is one more “wild beast” we have to learn about and it is an image of the seven-headed, ten-horned wild beast that comes from the earth. The fact that it comes from the earth gives this beast a stable foundation. The image or statue of the seven-headed ten-horned wild beast is constructed by the orders of the two-horned wild beast. Revelation 13: 14 and 15 tell us, “And with the miracles he was able to perform on behalf of the first beast, he deceived all the people who belong to this world. He ordered all the people of the world to make a great statue to the first beast, which was fatally wounded and then came back to life. He was permitted to give life to this statue so that it could speak. Then the statue commanded that anyone refusing to worship it must die.”

There is an interesting sequence of events concerning these symbolic creatures from revelation. The dragon gives the seven-headed, ten-horned wild beast his power, throne, and great power. The dragon, or Lucifer, gives his full support to this wild beast and allows it to rule over the world on his behalf.

This beast has no apparent power, but after the death stroke it gives the people of the world admire and worship this beast. However, its power is more symbolic than actual, as it only seems to wage war with "God's" people. The two-horned lamb-looking beast has the real power. This beast forces the people of the world to worship and build a statue to the seven-headed ten-horned wild beast. Something incredible happens with this statue; it gains power and acts on its own and then wants to kill all those who do not worship it.

If the seven-headed ten–horned wild beast is the League of Nations, which becomes the United Nations after World War II, and the two-horned beast are the powers of the United States and England, who or what is the statue of the wild beast? The answer to this question is found on the back of every United States Dollar! Under the pyramid written in Latin, you can read "Novus Ordo Seclorum", or New Order of the Ages, better known as the New World Order, the One World Government of the Luciferians!

The statue of the wild beast has domination over all the kingdoms and peoples of the world and that is the goal of the One World Government, to rule over every people in every land on the face of the earth! This is outlined in the Protocol of the Learned Elders of Zion and those who oppose this rule would be put to death, just as was done in every totalitarian or communist government. We have already talked about the millions of people who lost their lives because of religious or political differences with the ruling governmental power. Once this statue of the wild beast takes its place as the One World Government, the killing fields of Cambodia will seem like a picnic. One third of the population of Cambodia lost their lives, extrapolate that on a worldwide level and you are looking at a death toll of more than two billion people. Revelation 13:16 and 17, tells us that the statue "required everyone great and small, rich or poor, slave and free to be given a mark on the right hand or forehead. And no one could buy or sell anything without that mark which was the name of the beast or the number respective of that name." It was common practice in Biblical days for a slave owner to mark his slaves on either the hand or forehead to prove ownership. Obviously, those who receive the "mark" of the statue become its slaves and they belong to the statue.

We further read in Revelation 13:18 "Wisdom is needed to understand this. Let the one who has understanding solve the number of the wild beast, for it is a number of a man. His number is 666." Yes, we are talking about the fabled Anti-Christ, but it is not a man that we are looking for as the Anti-Christ. The number is a man's number and this would indicate that the One World Government is established by men who are imperfect, and the fact that it is the number 6 repeated three times, is evidence that this government is severally limited and grossly imperfect.

THE ANTI-CHRIST

The number 666 identifies this statue of the beast, so where in the world would you find evidence of the formation of this beast? Revelation gives us the answer, but it also says, "Wisdom is needed to understand this". It is like playing the game of "Jeopardy", we are given the answer but we have to know the question and wisdom is needed!

Where in the world do we see the number 666 printed to represent a government or political power? We do not and yet it is there! We see the "question" to the answer on a regular basis and yet most do not even see it, because it is like the nose on our face! It is so close to us that we do not realize whom the Antichrist really is.

Their banner with the number plainly displayed, was placed on the earth to show a political presence. It is the emblem of the Rothschild's and their Zionist cronies who seek to destroy all that stands in their way to rule the world. It is the flag that displays a 6-sided star with 6 triangles and 6 points, the same emblem that was used to identify the god Molech, or Moloch, the god whom required child sacrifice! The Rothschild's and the Zionist, in their ambitions to control the world, cost the lives of almost 200,000,000 people in the Twentieth Century from war and war related deaths!

Chapter 12 ~Prophets and Prophecies

PEOPLE OF THE WORLD,
I GIVE YOU THE ANTICHRIST!

Now before anyone starts the protest that I am anti-Semitic, or that I am making an anti-Semitic statement, stop! I am not anti-Semitic! I am anti-Luciferian and I am pro-Yahweh, Jehovah, "The Almighty", "God", "He who causes to become"!

When the flag of Israel was presented, a voice of protest went up from the religious leaders of the Jewish people and the real nation of Israel and the Hebrew people around the world. Really, they had no choice, since the Luciferians had been planning to regain Judea from the time General Titus took them into captivity and made them slaves of Rome.

The Rothschild family, who were moneychangers long before they took the name "Rothschild", plied their craft to become the greatest moneychangers of the world and took control of the economy of one country after another to the point that they now almost own the world, or at the very least control the world economy.

Without the Rothschild family, the country of Israel would not exist. The country of Israel is really the Luciferian country of Rothschild and so displays the emblem of the old Rothschild family. If Jewish religious leaders had established Israel, most likely the flag of Israel would display the Arch of the Covenant, the most holy and sacred religious icon ever.

When the nation of Israel was given its laws by Jehovah, or Yahweh, through the Prophet Moses, He told the nation of Israel in plain words, "And you must not allow the devoting of any of your offspring to Moloch. You must not profane the name of your God that way. I am Jehovah." Leviticus 18:21. So why would Jewish religious leaders allow the Star of Moloch to be their national symbol? Most likely, they had no choice! The Jewish people of the world, are no less the pawn then the Gentiles, they just have a better seat, or position under the suppression of the Luciferian Antichrist.

Remember, in the Protocol of the Learned Elders of Zion

two enemies are identified, the Czar of Russia and his family and the Papacy, or Catholic Church. As we all know, the Czar and his family are no more; they were murdered at the hands of the Zionist backed Bolsheviks. The Papacy, which represents all Christianity, is next to be destroyed! The goals of the Learned Elders and what they have carried out and intend to accomplish, also fits with Bible prophecy in the book of Revelation.

THE STATUE TAKES CONTROL!

For years, people have been writing about conspiracies concerning something or other. By the end of the Twentieth Century and down to today, there is a glut of accusations of one group or another, for doing something to gain world supremacy, or at least domination. Every one of those accusations has some part of truth in them. Some people hit the mark very well, while others have spun a thought into the obscure. Nonetheless, the picture is becoming clearer and people understand that the world is in trouble from many different points. In order to solve the problems that face the world today, there is no doubt that major change has to happen. That change will happen and it will happen shortly as the Statue, or image of the wild beast, takes control and a One World Government becomes a reality for we the people.

We are told a little more about the Statue or image of the wild beast in Revelation the 17th chapter, in verses 11- 14, we read "The scarlet colored beast that was alive and then died is the eight king. He is like the other seven and he, too, will go to his doom. His ten horns are ten kings who have not yet risen to power; they will be appointed to their kingdoms for one brief moment to rein with the beast. They will all agree to give their power and authority to him. Together they will wage war against the lamb..."

The Statue is given a color, scarlet red, symbolic of war. This Statue becomes a world power in itself and is called the "eight king". So, we can expect the Statue to be a world power, coming after the first seven world powers counting from the first, Egypt, through to the seventh, England and American as a world power.

The ten horns or kings did not exist when Revelation was written, but they do exist today. While we do not have too many kings with us today, we have many kingdoms or countries, 195 currently at the time of this writing. The number ten gives itself to mean earthly completeness, so the kings of the earth, or the countries of the earth, will support the Statue and rule with it.

Let us look at the facts here. The learned Elders of Zion have been working to attain a One World Government for two hundred years, starting with the Congress of Vienna. After the First World War, they succeeded with the League of Nations. The League of Nations, the Zionist beast that comes from the sea, gets a deathblow by Adolph Hitler and the Catholic backed Third Reich. It recovers from the deathblow and becomes the United Nations with the United States of America and England being the strongest supporters and being able to force other countries to submit to United Nations Rule as we saw in the Gulf War and the War against Iraq to over throw the government and replace it with democratic rule.

The Protocol states that any country that does not submit to their rule will be ruined economically. The world just had a taste of this with the worldwide banking crisis we experienced in 2008. Here in America, we owe the Federal Reserve Bank $11,000,000,000,000.00 and rising fast! As you look around the world, democratic countries are slowly becoming socialist in an effort to survive the growing problems facing all people of the world.

Revelation tells us that the Statue will gain power, supported by the two-horned lamb looking beast that can call fire down from the heavens. We go on to learn that the Statue gains its own power and becomes an eight world power, supported by the kings of the world. Both Revelation and the Protocol of the Learned Elders of Zion are congruent in what has happened in the 20th Century. Revelation, written over 1900 years ago, and the Protocol, written over 100 years ago are both saying the same thing!

Revelation tells us that we are headed for a one-world

government and do not doubt this! The world is getting set for the Luciferian New World Order and One World Government. The kingdoms, or countries, will submit or face economic destruction, because the Zionist-Luciferian moneychangers control almost all the world's wealth! Make no mistake; we will all live under a One World Government soon!

The rouge states or countries that still exist in the world such as North Korea and Iran, need to take a lesson on what happened in Iraq, because if they do not give up their extremist ways they will not exist as we see them today. The Statue of the wild beast, the Luciferian One World Government, will kill all that stands in opposition to it as it prepares to do battle with an extraterrestrial force known as the "Lamb of God" at the place that is called Har-Magedon, or as it is more widely known, Armageddon!

FIVE SIGNS LEADING TO ARMAGEDDON

There are five events told to us that must happen before the battle of Armageddon:

(1) The nations must declare "Peace and Security"
(2) The One World Government, the eight king must be established
(3) Religion as we know it will be destroyed by the one world government
(4) A "Great Tribulation" brakes out worldwide which, if not halted, could destroy all people alive.
(5) Evidence in the heavens of the coming battle of Armageddon, most likely a comet, and it will hit the earth!

PEACE AND SECURITY

In the book of First Thessalonians, chapter 5, verses 2 and 3, the apostle Paul wrote, "For you yourselves know quite well that Jehovah's day is coming as a thief in the night. Whenever it is that they are saying "Peace and Security" then suddenly destruction is to be instantly upon them just as the pang of distress of a pregnant woman; and they will by no means escape."

The declaration of peace and security starts the beginning of the end. When a woman starts to go into labor, she does not just pop out a child on the first contraction. There are a series of contractions, which become closer in time and stronger in intensity until a child is born. This process takes several hours and I am sure it must feel like days to the woman who is about to give birth. The declaration of peace and security is the first of many contractions that will move this world closer to Armageddon. Just as the first contractions of a pregnant woman, they start far apart, but with each contraction become closer and more intense. So to, will the events that shape the world become more intense and quicker as the contractions of the "Great Tribulation" starts to take over and gives birth to Armageddon.

With the world in the turmoil that we see, you may wonder, how is it possible to have "Peace and Security"? Right now, we see war and financial collapse. The Peace that is declared does not have to be a real peace it is the "declaration" of peace, so the world has to acknowledge an agreement of peace. The one place in the world where peace is lacking is the Middle East from the formation of the State of Israel in the land of Palestine. That part of the world has seen little if any peace from that time until now and will not for the foreseeable future. We mentioned earlier that every American President from the time of Jimmy Carter has tried to bring peace to the Middle East and failed! Both Presidents Bush brought war to the Middle East in the name of "Peace", hence the two-horned wild beast, which looks like a peaceful lamb, but speaks as a dragon of war! George W. Bush in response to the attack of 9-11 made the remark in front of every major news camera in the USA that America was in a "crusade" against terrorism. What kind of response would you expect from the people of the Middle East when they heard they would be facing a "Crusade" aimed at Islamic terrorist?

It is obvious that you cannot send a "White Christian"

President of the United States and have success in bringing peace to the Middle East. Now the United States does not have a white president. In fact, the President is both African-American and Caucasian and he has a Arabic name and Islamic relatives. Is it any small coincidence that now in this time of world unrest, the President of the United States has these qualifications and background?

Barack Hussein Obama II has been touted as the most popular president in the world since Franklin D. Roosevelt. We learned earlier where Roosevelt's true loyalties were, but we have yet to see where Barack Hussein Obama's loyalty is and how he is used in world affairs. There is one thing for sure, President Obama and his family have also been likened to President John F. Kennedy and his family, bringing children to the White House and the debonair presence that Kennedy had. We too know what happened to President Kennedy and I know so does President Obama!

Eight weeks before he took office as President, Barack Obama started to release plans to bring peace to the Middle East. Senator Hillary Clinton, wife of President Bill Clinton and now Secretary of State, was charged with the mission to begin to lay the groundwork for peace in the Middle East. The U.S. policy is for a two-state solution and would have a Palestinian state living in peace alongside the Jewish state of Israel. Could this be possible? Yes, it is more than possible; it is likely probable! Once the money to buy arms is shut off, the Palestinians will be forced to accept what is given to them and Israel will fight not to give them anything, knowing they too have no choice but to settle the issue of a State of Palestine.

I have great confidence that President Obama can succeed in bringing a peace deal between the Israelis and Palestinians and I am sure that the "declaration" of peace will go out to the world! When that happens, when the nations of the world are declaring peace that will be the sign of the start of the Great Tribulation!

There is no doubt that if President Obama succeeds in bringing peace between Israel and Palestine, his popularity will sky rocket around the world. The people of the world will love him more than any world leader ever! You would have to go back to the legendary days of King Solomon to find a ruler so liked by everyone in the world!

You have to consider the world response of President Obama being able to bring peace to the Middle East. The United States would be looked at very differently, because it would have a President with worldwide appeal and a desire by people of all nations to broker peace throughout the world. Again, I point to President Jimmy Carter who, after leaving office continued to work toward world peace, wrote the book, "We can have peace in the Holy Land". On January 26, 2009, in an interview on the Daily Show with John Stewart, President Carter said, "We now have a man that can bring peace to the Middle East, Barack Obama!" President Carter also recommends a strong US presence to influence the outcome. Yes, the world is getting ready for peace to come. The question is, if President Obama does bring peace to the Middle East, what would he do next? Where would the people of the United States, nay the people of the world follow President Obama too? Could it be a world peace under one government, a One World Government? Could the guise of peace be a ploy to further the ambitions to attain a One World Government, led by a man who seems honest and promotes peace? All indications would imply yes! Does this mean that Barack Obama is a Luciferian? No, not any more than Franklin D Roosevelt or John F Kennedy was. At best, President Barack Obama is a Masonic pawn of the Luciferian Zionists and has no real idea of what is going to befall him, or the rest of us!

THE ONE WORLD GOVERNMENT ARRIVES!

Both the Protocol of the Learned Elders of Zion and the Bible book of Revelation agree that a One World Government is coming. Revelation foretold this event 1900 years ago and the Luciferians have been planning it for even longer and have formulated their plan in the Protocol, published just over 100 years ago. There is no secret that a One World Government is coming, only denial. The closest as we have to a one world government is the United Nations, a world organization that appears almost powerless and next to useless.

We identified the United Nations as the seven-headed ten-horned wild beast. This beast does not do much; it is the statue or image of this beast that has real power and forces the people of the world to worship it or die! The statue or image of the wild beast is the One World Government that will take control of all the governments of the world.

We all know that people give in to mob action or reaction and we know that the Learned Elders are experts at influencing the population of the world, using the news media to rally people for or against anything or any issue. In order to get anyone to do anything, you first must get their attention and then convince the people that it is the right thing to do.

Under the premise of peace, if you can get nations to lay down arms and give up warfare in a place that has not seen peace in years and is the central point for three of the world's major religions. Is it possible to get nations all over the world to support peace? Yes, it is, but you are going to need more than the idea or promise of peace to get the people of the world to agree to submit to a world government.

Every normal person in the world, regardless of where they live or their social status, are programmed, actually "hard wired", to flee from pain and danger and move toward pleasure and safety. Almost everything we do is a response to finding something pleasurable or painful. If having a large amount of money is very pleasurable to you, you are going to find a way to get more money, possibly by working longer hours or getting a better education and finding a better occupation. If you find you like to spend time with loved ones, you are going to arrange your life to be with the people you love the most. This is just very basic human psychology. Create a painful problem and people are going to be motivated to react, at least those who survive will react.

The people of the United States reacted to the events of

9-11 and gave up vast freedoms in the name of the "Patriot Act". Not many years later, the world found itself thrown into financial crises, fueled by bad bank loans and high-energy prices. Again, people reacted; unfortunately, many people lost everything they had. However, here in the United States in order to stop a repeat of the "Great Depression" and suffer many years of economic downturn, the government did not wait three years to step in and borrow money from the Federal Reserve Bank of New York for social programs and to bail out the banking system. Instead, the decision was made to move quickly and borrow trillions of dollars more and putt the country deeper in debt.

So here is the question. What has to happen to make the people of the world react to support the idea of a One World Government? Is it going to take a global disaster such as an act of terrorism on a nuclear level? Will religious extremists acquire a nuclear weapon, detonate it, and force the countries of the world to unite as one government to address the problem? Could it be an economic problem that forces the world into a single currency or just a few currencies based on geographical location like the "Euro"? With the world in debt to the banking families who control the world economy, we could be seduced to join a One World Government to forgive the national debts and reissue new currency. There is already talk of the Amero Dollar, a currency for the United States, Canada and Mexico. It really is hard to say exactly what will happen, but something will happen to bring all the countries of the world together under a One World Government.

When you examine what is written in the book of Revelation, the two-horned lamb looking beast, the United States and England, somehow "order the people of the world" to build a statue to, or an image of, the United Nations. This is clear support of a One World Government! We are also told that the kings of the world or the countries of the world will submit their individual rule to the One World Order, so that they will rule as part of the Statue of the wild beast, or be supporting and enforcing members of a One World Government.

What may be the most logical thing is a spin-off of a peace treaty in the Middle East. If President Obama can get to the point of bringing peace between Israel and the Palestinians, the people of the world would most certainly support and hail him as a great man and a world peacekeeper. However, not everyone will be happy about seeing peace in the Middle East. No doubt religious extremists are not going to stop and with advances of the Taliban in the country of Pakistan, the world stage is set for another dramatic problem. Remember that Pakistan is a nuclear state and has about 60 nuclear warheads; how many have to get into the hands of the Taliban to create a problem?

With peace finally established between Israel and Palestine, the world will not let this peace be broken easily and it is possible that all countries will unite to keep the peace and stop the world from sliding into a nuclear holocaust.

Also, another uniting factor we need to consider is the LOST treaty that the United Nations has wanted all countries to endorse and obey. We talked about the Law of the Sea Treaty (LOST) earlier; this would give the United Nations, or the image of the United Nations the Statue of the beast, dominion over all the oceans of the world. With tens of billions of dollars lost every year to high sea piracy, NATO or the United Nations can form a navy or order member nations such as the USA to patrol the seas and enforce the law.

When you combine the problems of the world that could be eradicated by a one-world government, the incentives to be part of that government could be very large. The incentives could be both a combination of the proverbial carrot and stick, the pain or the pleasure response. It would make logical sense to use the promise of peace, the threat of terrorism and the elimination of world debt, to seduce the people of the world that a One World Government was in their best interest! Use the news media to promote this idea with all the positive things a United World Government could bring the people of the world and I am sure that mob mentality will take over and we will let ourselves be convinced that this is a good idea!

Chapter 12 ~Prophets and Prophecies

RELIGION IS ABOLISHED AND DESTROYED

To think about a world with out religion is almost impossible. It seams from time in memorial religion has always been part of peoples lives, controlling king and peasant, politician and voter. Nations and people have been conquered in the name of religion and "God" and when you look close enough, religion has been at the heart of many wars and conflicts through out history. Still to walk down the street and not see a church or religious building is a concept many of us just do not have. Churches are among the most prestigious of buildings in almost every city and town in the world.

It was not until after the Second World War that religion started to loose its grip on the people of the world. As more and more people became collage bound and attained a higher education, the more religion was replaced with science. The courses being taught in our higher places of learning actually call into question the very existence of "God" himself.

When you look at all of the problems that can be related back to religion, you have to really wonder is religion worth all the problems? Still we in the United States of America are guarantied freedom of religion and the right to worship, as we want to. Nearly everyone, when asked what religion they are, will give an answer of some denomination, usually the religion of your parents or family, even if you do not practice that religion. However, there are many billions of people around the world, who take their religion very seriously today! Even if you have not been in a place of worship for years, there is a certain comfort level we have knowing that we the right to do so when ever we wish.

As we discussed in a earlier chapter, the 20th Century started with almost all people going to church and no one believing in aliens and flying saucers and by the close for the 20th Century, more people believe in UFOs than go to church here in the United States. Regardless to the reason, through education, or maybe better said, re-education, "God" has been reduced to a myth and really, only the uneducated need religion. At least that is what "they" tell us!

If religion is to be done away with, how will it happen? It is the goal of the Learned Elders of Zion to promote a "state religion" and destroy all other religions starting with the Papacy or the Catholic Church and the rest of Christianity. If anything can be learned from the Bolshevik Revolution and the establishment of communism, one of the first things that were done under the new communist rule was to close the churches and impression the clergy. The people had no place to meet and no one to lead them either in prayer to "God", or to protest against the government and revolt. In a very short time religion all but disappeared under Soviet rule.

Complete devotion to the government was what was demanded from all people, under Soviet rule. As we discussed earlier, non-compliance with the demands of the government ended with the deaths of countless millions of lives. Is it possible that the same thing could play out today on a worldwide level? Yes, it is and it will happen!

Back in the book of Revelation this time in chapters 17 and 18, we learn about a woman, a great prostitute who sits on many waters. In Chapter 17: 1 & 2, we read "...And I will show you the judgment that will come against the great prostitute who sits on many waters. The rulers of this world have had immoral relations with her and the people who belong to this world have been made drunk, by the wine of her immorality." From the days of ancient Babylon and the Tower of Babel, religion has tried to control the governments, starting with Nimrod's wife Semiramis down to the clergy's influence in politics today.

Maybe the most obvious of religion's involvement in politics today, is the influence that Islam has over the Arabic governments and the on going threat of terrorism and war, by religious zealots. Long before this was a factor in our lives, the Christian and Jewish religions have been doing the same thing. Let us not forget the Third Reich, the extension of another thousand-year reign of the Catholic Church as state religion. By means of secrete deals and pacts; religion has been like a prostitute, whoring herself out to every government possible, in order to remain in control of the people.

Historically this is an interesting scenario, because some historians believe that Semiramis may have been a prostitute before becoming consort and Quean to Nimrod. As queen and goddess, she controlled the people through the different religions of Nimrod's kingdoms. Remember she set her self up as goddess of the earth, "Mother Earth" and then Goddess of the moon heavens and stars. Some historians also say that Nimrod was ripped apart at Semiramis' command.

Revelation 17: 3 goes on to tell us "...I saw a woman sitting on a scarlet beast that had seven heads and ten horns..." verse 5 and 6 reads "A mysterious name was given her on her forehead: "Babylon the Great, Mother of all prostitutes and Obscenities in the World." I could see that she was drunk-drunk with the blood of God's holy people who were witnesses for Jesus."

Picture what is going on here, a woman who has the name "Babylon the Great", a religious prostitute, is sitting on the seven-headed, ten-horned wild beast, the collective world governments. She has the pleasure of riding the beast where ever it may take her, even to war and so she is drunk on blood all those who died because of her. What happens next?

Revelation 17: 15 – 17 reads, "...The waters where the prostitute is sitting represent masses of people of every nation and language. The scarlet beast and his ten horns – which represent ten kings who will reign with him – all hate the prostitute. They will strip her naked, eat her flesh and will burn her remains with fire. For God has put a plan into their minds, it is a plan that will carry out his purposes."

The very beast she is riding destroys this woman Babylon the Great or religion. The nations evidently turn against religion, strip its wealth, confiscate its land and business holdings and kill or destroy her clergy to the point where there is nothing but ashes left. The amazing thing about all of this is that "God" wants religion destroyed too! Remember, "God", or Jehovah did not want to be worshiped, He wanted to be loved by his "children" or "family"!

Religion is an invention of Lucifer and there for needs to be removed and destroyed.

When you consider that the Zionist have been under the rule of Rome from the time Rome was a world power over two thousand years ago, you can understand that they want to see Rome and the remnants of the Holy Roman Empire destroyed. Evidently, the Zionist will get their One World Government, the scarlet seven-headed ten-horned wild beast with the number 666 given to it. Exactly how the One World Government is established is not told to us. However, it does have the support of ten kings, or the support or the countries and governments of the world and it is established after the nations declare "peace and security". World events are going to be shaped, so it appears that is good idea for the nations of the world to want to give their up their right to self rule and become state members of the New World Order.

Most likely, there will be protests by militant fundamentalist and Para-military groups around the world, over the establishment of the New World Order. It would not take much of a stretch of imagination to think that religious leaders around the world could be encouraging protest to the New World Order. Whatever the cause maybe the wild beast of the New World Order, will turn on religion and destroy it!

Religion is already weakened in "Christian" countries to the point that most people do not care if they go to "Church" or not. Regular church attendance for most people today, means going to "Church" at Christmas, Easter, and attending weddings. Scandal and the tremendously bad Press in general have weakened religion over the years. Many religions have had to settle cases of child molestation and other wrongdoing, costing millions and millions of dollars!

Because people have lost interest so less attendance means that there is less money collected in the "plate" and churches have closed their doors on their own. Should religion loose their tax-free status and have to pay "income tax", this will be a great financial blow and no doubt, more churches will close, as religious organizations try to try to keep from going bankrupt.

Chapter 12 ~Prophets and Prophecies

Exactly how religion comes under attack and outlawed by the New World Order is not explained, either in Revelation, or in the Protocol. However, when you consider all the freedom that Americans willingly gave up after the attack of the World Trade Center on 9-11, what would it take for the world to give up its freedom and unite under one government? Could terrorist getting there hands on and detonating a nuclear device do it?

When President George W. Bush declared a World War on Terrorism, he told the rest of the world either you are with the United States against the war on terrorism, or you are against us! There was no middle ground. If a group of religious fanatics did detonate a nuclear device, this could scare the governments of the world to unite under a One World Government and it could set up the destruction of religion as we know and understand it. If you do not have any religion, you cannot have religious fanatics can you!

THE GREAT TRIBULATION

In the book of Matthew, in the 24th chapter, Jesus' disciples ask him what would be the sign of the end of the system of things. As with most all prophecies of the Bible, they have a duel application, one application for the current time they were spoken for and a second application for the last days of the system we live in today. We will consider key points of the 24th chapter of Matthew, for application in the times we are living in today and the near future.

Matthew 24: 7 & 8 tells us "The nations and kingdoms will proclaim war against each other, and there will be famines and earthquakes in many parts of the world. But all this will be only the beginning of the horrors to come."

Matthew 24: 9 reads, "You will be arrested, persecuted, and killed. You will be hated all over the world because of your allegiance to me."

Matthew 24: 21 & 22, "For that will be a time of greater

horror than anything the world has ever seen or will ever see again, In fact, unless that time of calamity was shortened, the entire human race will be destroyed. But it will be shortened for the sake of God's chosen ones."

Matthew 24: 29 & 30, "Immediately after those days end, ***the sun will be darkened, the moon will not give light, the stars will fall from sky and the powers of heaven will be shaken.*** And then at last, the sign of the coming of the Son of Man will appear in the heavens, and there will be deep morning among all the nations of the earth..."

In these verses of Matthew, Jesus points out some very specific things that we would see happen. The 20th Century has already proved to be the bloodiest ever recorded due to wars between nations. We have seen the world wracked by food shortage, mostly in third world countries, but we even see food shortage among poor people in every country.

Earthquakes have constantly been in the news, highlighted by the earthquake in Indonesia in 2004, setting off a tsunami killing over 200,000 people. According to the USGS, the year 2000 saw twice the number of earthquakes having a magnitude of 6 or greater than any other year in the 20th Century. From 2004 on we have seen a tremendous increase in major earthquakes world wide. Geologists contribute this sudden rise in earthquakes do to global warming and the redistribution of water weight on the earth's tectonic plates. No doubt, until global warming is under control, we can expect many more earthquakes around the world. Christians, those believing that Jesus was the Christ or Messiah and refuse to give up their beliefs or faith in him, will be arrested, imprisoned and killed! There is no reason to believe that any group, religious or not which stands in the way of the coming New World Order will die. Remember revelation says that the statue of the wild beast commanded that anyone refusing to worship it must die! The Luciferian New World Order, commands the same thing, anyone resisting the New World Order will die in the killing fields of a One World Government.

As protest goes up against the destruction of religion, no doubt world conditions will become dyer. The news programs we see at night showing the war in Iraq and the urban door-to-door combat will not be confined to the streets of some town under insurgent control in a country we care very little about. The news will one day show clips of the fighting in your city or town. There are numerous gangs and militia groups virtually in every community across America and in most towns or cities of the world, these groups will fight and kill to keep control of their territory and their way of life.

We have all seen the nightly news showing pictures of refugees leaving war torn areas. We have seen videos of people, mostly women, children and the old, gathered into large camps where clean water to drink and food to eat are scarce, if there is any at all. Many people do not leave these camps and die due to the disease that brakes out from unsanitary conditions and over crowding.

Most of the time we see pictures like this taken from some country in Africa and while they are unpleasant to say the least and I am sure that many people feel regret and sorrow for people who must under go such treatment and living conditions. However, Jesus told us that things would get so bad that if those days were not “cut short”, no one would be left alive! Those pictures we see of destitute people in refugee camps may be us one day!

Really, how do you think the “Religious Right” of America is going to react to seeing their churches shut down and closed by government law? Yes, we will se our neighbors fighting New World Order troops in the very streets or our towns. We will see a brake down of social order and food shortages will take place in one place after another, along with food shortage you have malnourishment and sickness. Now the world is set up for a real pandemic, with the world population weakened by food shortage and civil war, the latest designer virus will devastate populations more quickly and efficiently and there will be no place to get medical attention, so death will follow quickly and mass graves will become a common sight for those who survive.

Those days will be cut short, or reduced in time, because of one group of people, "The Chosen Ones". The days of the great tribulation are not allowed to just run their course, but they are stopped by the next and final sign of the last days before Armageddon.

EVIDENCE IN THE HEAVENS OF THE COMING BATTLE OF ARMAGEDDON

The final sign before Armageddon comes from the sky. Jesus gives hint of this when he says in Matthew the 24th chapter that the sun and moon would not give their light and powers of heaven will be shaken. We get a little more insight of this if we consider the book of Acts. In the 2sd chapter of Acts, verses 19 & 20 we read "And I will cause wonders in the heavens above and signs on earth below – blood and fire and clouds of smoke. The sun will be turned in to darkness and the moon into bloodred, before that great and glorious day of the Lord arrives.

Another Bible translation reads "And I will give portents in heaven above..." a portent is "evidence" of" an event or "proof" of something. Evidently, we will have proof in heaven that "God's" day is coming. Then we read "...and signs on earth below, blood and fire and smoke mist..." We will also see evidence of the coming War of Armageddon on the earth with the signs of blood, so people are going to die. Fire and smoke mist, what can cause fire, smoke and mist here on earth?

After seeing the impact of the comet Shoemaker-Levy 9 on the planet Jupiter, it became obvious that the same thing could happen here on earth. Geologist and archeologist, tell us that comets and meteors have hit the earth many times before and we can see evidence of the impacts on our planet. As we have learned, it was an impact with a space object that killed the dinosaurs and many other species over millennium. According to what we read in the book of Acts and from what Jesus him self said, it seams that some kind of space body is going to have an impact with the earth, halting the great tribulation and giving the people of this planet something else to contemplate.

A comet is most likely the "evidence" or the "wonders in heaven above" that is talked about in the book of Acts. You can a comet coming long before it gets to where it is going and it is seen by the naked eye very easily, because of the long tail it has. A comet, being made up of dirt rock and ice, would create smoke and mist just by its very composition. The big question is, if there is a comet coming to impact with the earth, where is it going to hit?

If you were "God" and wanted to get the attention of the world's population, but you did not want to destroy the earth, where would you send a comet? What part of earth would you chose to hit? The book of Job gives a hint to where "God" may choose. Job 38: 22 & 23 refers to "Storehouses of snow" which are saved for the "day of fight and war". We talked about these "storehouses" before and the fact that the ice all over the world is melting and raising ocean levels and disturbing the weather patterns, causing problems all over the world.

What if a comet of the right size impacted with the "storehouse of snow" at the South Pole? The ice reaches 2 miles deep there, so the comet would have to travel through 2 miles of hard surface before it hits the earth. The heat generated by the comet would be enough to melt most of the ice turning it into water vapor and dispersing into earth's atmosphere along with any ejecta generated from the comet and earth. Because it hits a continent covered in ice, the likely hood of a fireball incinerating earth would be small, if any at all. The comet only needs to be big enough to melt the ice and release a tsunami headed for every coastline in the world!

Government officials will know the place and time of the impact long before the general public does. How much time is going to be given to evacuate the coastlines is the real question. Will there be any effort move people to higher ground? Eighty percent of the world's population lives with in 90 miles of the coast. How do you evacuate 400,000,000,000 people? Where do you put them if you could evacuate them? Where do you put the people of Bangladesh? How do you move the people off the island nations of the Pacific, then where do you put them? My guess is that very little warning is going to be given by the government of the New World Order.

Cities cannot be moved but the valuables, the priceless artifacts in museums and such can and most likely an effort will be made to get them to a place of safe keeping, it hat has not already happened due to world protest over the rule of the New World Order. With the world at a point of great turmoil, if the government officials of the New World Order knew that the coastlines would be wiped clean by an impending tsunami, they would order their troops back to higher ground and let the people, the Goyim, be wiped of the face of the earth too! You could almost guarantee that there would be no regard for human life, by our One World captors.

What would happen if a comet did hit Antarctica and melt the ice? What would be the impending result? A good part of the ice is going to be vaporized instantly or with in seconds of impact and become part of our atmosphere. As the rest of the ice becomes liquid, it will rush off the land, crashing into the sea with a violent force. This could add enough water to make the ocean levels raise over a hundred feet by it self, with out considering the initial cascade of tsunamis, which could reach as much as a thousand high in some places as it crashes on to apposing coastlines.

When the tsunamis reach the other end of the planet they will crash together over the sea ice of the North Pole and return back south, this action will recur repeatedly until the wave action subsides. As the weight of the water moving over the earth shifts, from one tectonic plate to the next, earthquakes will shake most of the earth causing the infrastructure of many country-states to collapse. As the tectonic plates shift, anywhere that there is volcanic activity is sure to see eruptions of unprecedented magnitude pouring ash and smoke into the atmosphere. Between the water vapor generated by the comet impact and the smoke and ash from volcanic activity, there will be enough suspended particulate mater to block the sun from giving its light and the moon will look as red as blood if it is seen at all.

There is no doubt that the New World Order, the Statue of the wild beast, is never going to survive this earth wide disaster as a functioning world government. Non the less there will be forces that are going to regroup and salvage what ever power they can to face the battle of Armageddon and their final destruction.

We cannot be sure what kind of supernatural power is going to show up on earth's doorstep, but whatever intelligent force does appear, they will be ready to do battle with the remnants of Lucifer, his agents here on earth and the survivors of the great tribulation. Whatever kind of super natural forces face off against each other is yet to be understood, but one thing is for sure!

The words spoken in the book of Ezekiel in the 39th chapter and in verse 7 it says, "...I shall no more let my holy name be profaned; and the nations will have to know that I am Jehovah..." there will be no doubt in anyone's mind that this is Jehovah God's War of Armageddon and he will win!

CHAPTER 13
YOU CAN SURVIVE ARMAGEDDON!

We know that the time we live in has more problems than the world has ever seen before! During the cold war between the United States and Soviet Union, the people of the world were worried that our planet would be destroyed by thermo nuclear war. Humans would be gone with everything else, rats and roaches would be all that would survive. Wile that seams unlikely today, the fear of either "rouge states" such as Iran, or North Korea manufacturing atomic weapons and either deploying them or selling them to terrorist is a great concern to both the nations and people of the world.

While atomic war or the detonation of a thermo nuclear device is uncertain, it does remain a possibility. However, there is complete certainty to the fact that our planet is in peril from our own hands. Humans are in the process of destroying the ecology of the earth in a way that we have threatened our own survival and the survival of our children. Pollution, global warming, over population, lack of clean water to drink, food shortages, diseases that can not be cured or controlled and a bleak economic outlook for the majority of the people in the world are all problems that face us today. The governments of the world spend the equivalent of almost $25,000.00 US Dollars for every man, woman and child on this planet and we do not feel any safer or secure in our daily lives.

We all know that this way of life cannot go on very long before there is a major collapse, or brake down in society! While there have been people through out the years to proclaim that "Doomsday" is near, there is no doubting that now in our lives Doomsday is near!

The change that the world needs for people to live in, in true peace and security, can never come by the hand of those who are running, or running, the world today! There is no major business that is going to say "Let's give up profits, because we can not keep destroying the planet we live on." We are never going to see anything like this on a "voluntary" basis.

We live on a planet dedicated to using fossil fuel and we have all been educated to the effect that burning fossil fuel creates greenhouse gasses. We also understand that we must reduce greenhouse gasses, if we are to return our planet to a stable environment and put the issue of global warming to rest. We also do not like to think about it, because we know that the world we are going to leave our children is destine for failure and collapse, just from the issues related to the environment and global warming. However, there is hope! The book of Revelation says in the 11th chapter and the latter part of the 18 verse that God would "...bring to ruin, those ruining the earth", so we are going to see Jehovah God, bring to ruin those companies and industries that are destroying our environment. When this happens, our way of life is going to change!

ARMAGEDDON IS COMING

Over the years, the general consciousness of the world has been awakened to the belief that Armageddon or at least a world calamity of some kind is coming our way and we will see it! No doubt "Hollywood" has capitalized on dooms day, Armageddon type movies. World ending calamity has been the theme of many movies, it stimulates our thinking, and makes us reflect for just a moment and ponder, "This really could happen...", but what action can we take?

On a more realistic note, we look at the world around us and we do not like what we see, we know that God must do something soon! The consciousness of the world has come to understand that we are living in what the Bible calls the "Last Days" of this system. We can probably thank Jehovah's Witness for allot of this. Who has not gotten a knock on their door on a Saturday or Sunday morning, only to open the door half asleep and find a bright cheery smile and a cheerful "Hello!" and then the message that world is in trouble and Armageddon is coming! "Yes, thank you, good morning to you too!" Regardless of what you think of these people, they have been dauntless for over 100 years telling us the same thing over, and over again! Maybe they are the Paul Revere of our day and Armageddon is really coming! We can all agree that the world has not gotten to be a better place to live in.

We cannot believe everything we hear, or read for that matter, we need proof, scientific proof! How do you get scientific proof about a future event? We need to look for evidence from as many sources as possible. People have looked to many sources to see if we really are heading to Armageddon. Occult prophets such as Nostradamus has been looked to for information and his writings, his quatrains have been investigated and calamitous events are suppose to be headed our way. From what we are told by Nostradamus "During the appearance of the Bearded Star the three great princes will be made enemies. The shaky peace on earth will be struck by fire from the sky..." Many have wondered, could these words be telling us that a comet will be hitting the earth? Yes, it does sound like that!

Many people from the archeologists to the conspiracy theorist have made a study of the Mayan people and their calendar. Everyone agrees that the Mayans had advanced knowledge of astronomy and movements of the stars and our galaxy. The Mayans predicted the future by their calendar and according to what the Mayans say, 2012 will bring an alignment of our solar system and galaxy and marks the end of one time-period and the start of a new one. Many researchers believe that this system will end on December 21st 2012 and calamity will change the world as we know it.

Isaac Newton, long believed that the Bible had a secret code in it and tried to prove this. His connection to Freemasonry may have given him some insight to what Hebrew mystic Kabbalist had claimed during medieval times that a code existed with in the Bible, which will foretell the future. The Bible Code, or Torah Code, is dated back to the 13th Century; some say it is more than two thousand years old, which would mean that the scholars of Jesus day were working on deciphering this code. It would also mean that the Bible Code was being worked on, when Rome destroyed Jerusalem in the First Century. If the Bible Code existed, could it and other secret documents, such as the Kabala, been buried under the Temple in Jerusalem? Is this what the Knights Templar was looking for, when they started digging under the Temple Mount in the 12th Century?

Many scholars and Hebrew historical researchers have taken up the search for a code written with in the Bible. It was not until the computer age that they were successful and their findings are astounding to say the least. By braking down the first 5 books of the Bible known as the Torah and using equal letter spacing, a program is run using a name, date, or event and a matrix is sometimes formed, with additional information about the subject matter.

The Bible Code has reviled some astounding historical events, but it also reveals events into the future and this is where true controversy starts to question the validity of the Bible Code. The question is raised "Should we know the future and can we trust what the Bible Code has to say?" Opponents of the Bible Code claim that they can find codes written in other books too, okay, that is nice, but we are talking about a code that is written in the most holy book in the world. That must carry a little weight to what we find encoded about past, current, or future events.

The Bible Code does not have very good things to say about the future, but then again neither does the Bible! The Bible Code foretells plague and disease, earthquakes, terrorist attacks, atomic devices detonated and comets and asteroids hitting the earth. Well guess what the Bible in the Christian-Greek scriptures says the same thing and it is not "encoded" in anyway!

There is a great question of if the Bible was encoded who encoded it? The first response to this would normally be Jehovah God himself. However, I am not so sure. You see the Torah has been copied many times over the centuries and as the Hebrew language developed, so did the wording in the Torah to a degree.

It is still Hebrew and carries the message of God, that did not change, but the Torah is no longer the identical document written by Moses in his hand as Jehovah dictated to him. So while the Bible Code says the same major events will befall mankind as the Bible does in the Christian-Greek Scriptures. Maybe this is proof that putting faith in Jesus, as the messiah is what the nation of Israel should have done!

There is no doubt that if the Bible is encoded, it could have been the work of Lucifer himself. Why would this be? The answer is very simple Jehovah God would not have to put any secret code in the Bible. There is no need to hide what he is about to do. The Bible has accounts of prophet after prophet, sent to the nation of Israel, to tell them what God was going to do. They did not have to look for the answers in any secret code, there were prophets on the street corners of Jerusalem telling the people what was going to befall them, or what they needed to do, to remain save and protected. The Prophet Moses told the nation of Israel to paint the blood of a lamb over the door and on the posts, the night before they left Egypt as free people. This date and event became known as the Jewish holiday "Pass Over". The Angle of Death "passed over" their houses in his search for the first-born children of Egypt he was to kill. The point is that God does not cover-up or hide things, he makes them plain and easy to see, or rises up prophets to warn the people of impending disaster!

Jesus, the Christ, or Messiah was the greatest prophet that lived. Almost the whole of the Hebrew Scriptures pointed to the coming of the Messiah. It gave signs and prophecies that pointed to Jesus as the son of God and the Messiah. Jesus himself told his apostles what to look for and what we should look for as the "Last Days" approach. In the book of Matthew Jesus is explicit about what things would happen in the "Last Days" and we see those things starting to happen today.

With all the evidence, we see before us today and from so many different sources, we must be in those last days before the great battle of Armageddon! After all, if you listen to all the "Dooms Day" prognosticators, we are all going to die in 2012, when a giant comet hits the earth and destroys civilianization, as we know it. Well this is not going to happen; at least not like people believe it will. Jesus told us in Matthew 24: 36 "However no one knows the day or the hour when these things will happen, not even the angles in heaven or the son himself. Only the father knows." Armageddon is going to happen on Jehovah's timetable, not the predictions of some occult prophet, or the timing of a pagan people's calendar, or a code that has seamed to magically appeared in the Bible and found with advent of the computer. However, make no mistake Armageddon, Jehovah's War is coming!

THE WAR TO END ALL THE WARS!

What exactly is the battle of Armageddon about? To put it plainly and very simply, 6000 years ago the human race was kidnapped by the alien entity we have come to know as Lucifer. Even God's Word the Bible tells us that Lucifer owns and rules over the earth and he is an "Angel of Light", so why should we have any doubts about who is ruling over our world today.

Lucifer wanted the human race as his own "children" and the deception started. It is very much like someone kidnapping a baby, or small child and then raising the child as their own. If you were the parents of that child, would you ever give up searching or hope that one day you would find your child and be together again? Really, what Lucifer did was much worse; he kidnapped and enslaved part of Jehovah's family, the babies of his family, the humans, we the people!

Look at the historical evidence and you will see the pattern that forms. From the start of civilization on the plains of Mesopotamia, down to today, the human race has been enslaved to ridiculous religious ideas all revolving around sun worship and ruled over by self-centered, egotistical, maniacal, idiots, who are ready to kill all those who appose their rule!

We the people are facing the biggest "wake-up call" the world has ever seen! History, the Bible and the evidences we see around us in the world today show us that indeed civilization as we know and understand it, is doomed. The human race for the first time ever is about to be rescued from our "kidnapping" and we will have the chance to live the life that was intended for us to live. A life truly free of oppression and dictation, a life that is based on love and family, not rules and laws that carry a death sentence. Think about the complete human race brought together in peace! It almost sounds impossible, but when you remove the satanic influence that Lucifer has cast over the earth, remove the religious and political difference between people around the world and you remove what has kept the human race at war for 6000 years. Think of the hate that has developed between religions over the centuries. Christians, who are supposedly follow Jesus' teaching of love, hate the Muslims and the Jews. The nation of Israel has been battling the Arabic nations from the time of their ancestral father Abraham. The fighting between Abraham's sons, Ishmael and Isaac, was so bad that Abraham sent Ishmael and his mother away into the wilderness. The nations that those sons of Abraham produced are still fighting today!

No one has to talk about the fear terrorism that the world lives in because of the Islamic Jihad carried out against both Christian and Jew; we see and hear this every day as the media reports the news from all over the world. The Jihad that Islamic extremist carry out does not stop at religious enemies but targets the political and the innocent.

The political hatred we saw between the Soviet Union's communistic governments and the Democratic Block of Nations in the 20th century, kept the world sitting on the brink of nuclear destruction for decades. However now that the "Iron Curtin" has fallen and we are all friends, the world breaths a bit easier. No longer fears a nuclear exchange as we did in the 1950's and 1960's. Nuclear weapons are still a very big concern, with North Korea developing atomic weapons and long range ballistic missals, Iran having an atomic development program and terrorist doing their best to obtain a nuclear weapon, the world governments and intelligence agencies have their hands full trying to keep any of this from getting out of control. Yes, the political and religious differences that Lucifer and his agents have fomented upon the world really do need to end! The human race must be rescued by an entity that cares for and loves us.

The thought of the human race being rescued by aliens might almost be laughable, but what is even harder to grasp is the human race being rescued by God's angles or messengers, led by his son Jesus Christ as a "Warrior King" as described in the Book of Revelation. Nonetheless, this is what is going to happen! Somehow when you take the "religion" out of the Bible and you look at what is being said from a scientific viewpoint, it changes your perspective a little. Let us face facts, the gods of our ancestors have become the "alien encounters" that are reported more frequently around the world. What did President Ronald Reagan mean when he said before the members of United Nations, "...is there not an alien force already among us?"

We already discussed the destruction of religion as we know and understand it, by the New World Order, the "Image", or "Statue" of the "Wild Beast". We can pretty much figure that Lucifer will force the gods of religion to take their place along side him as the War of Armageddon draws closer. We told that the "Kings of the Earth" or "Nations of the Earth" would support the Statue of the Wild Beast. Those nations "will be gathered together to the place that is called in Hebrew Har-Magedon!" Remember Har-Magedon is not the physical location; it is the point of world condition and timing. The War of Armageddon is not just in one place, it is a "Global War"! It is literally a war against the physical government New World Order!

We had a vision of this as Adolph Hitler allowed Germany and the German people be destroyed by the Allied Forces during World War II. Adolph Hitler's final hours, took his own life as he sacrificed the lives of his last supports and defenders. The same thing will happen here on earth as Lucifer makes his last stand, he will sacrifice all that he has controlled for the last 6000 years. Yes, this alien we fondly call Lucifer, who has been an "Angel of Light" for the world, would rather see all of we the people of this planet die, than give us back to our rightful father Jehovah.

Just as those faithful Nazi solders, gave their very life for Hitler in his final hours, so to will the nations of the earth as they defend their Luciferian right to rule over this planet and we the people.

Exactly what will face us is not totally revealed in the Bible, but one thing is for sure, earth will be a battleground and it will be very one-sided battle in Jehovah's favor! The forces that Jehovah controls will destroy the Luciferian leaders of the New World Order, their government officials, their armed forces, their supporters and followers! There will be no existence or last vestige of any of them. The only ones who survive the War of Armageddon are those who Jehovah recognizes as his children or those who want to be his children.

HOW DO WE SURVIVE THE WAR OF ARMAGEDDON?

Make no mistake the War of Armageddon is a real war! Think of the two world wars that the human race has seen in the 20th Century, the nations of the world were gathered together to do battle with each other. The book of Revelation tells us that the nations are going to be gathered together to do battle with the army of the entity who calls himself Jehovah. In the Book of Isaiah chapter 37 and verse 36, we are told that just one of Jehovah's angels killed 185,000 Assyrians in the camp of King Sennacherib, in just one night! The armies of the world are going to be facing hundreds of thousands, if not millions of these alien forces. What ever military might the world armies can muster, what ever technologically advanced weapons earthly armies will display, they will have little if any effect on the Army of Jehovah!

Remember we the people have essentially been kidnapped by the alien Lucifer and are ruled over by his followers and supporters. They have told us what to think, what to do, whom to worship, how to live and that we should support the government and be good citizens. They have been telling us this for 6000 years now, we know that there is something wrong with religion; we know that the government is corrupt, we know that we are lied to by almost everyone, we are just not sure how. Most of we the people of this planet, earn just enough money to live on. We are slaves to this system, not the children of it. The Children of this world are the Luciferians who control the governments and big business and for the time being, religion.

Yes, religion is included as long as it is a supporter of sun worship, remember the three major world religions promote the worship of the sun or the symbol of the star god Remphan also spelled Rephan. This star god represents Lucifer himself. The "Star of Remphan" has become the "Star of David" and is displayed proudly on the Israeli Flag. The winter holiday that the Jewish community keeps is a "festival of lights" known as Hanukah, this is not one of the festivals given in the law of Moses, it was added on as a tradition. Remember that Lucifer means "light bearer", so who is this festival held in honor of?

The Romans called this same star god Saturn and the holiday to honor this god is Saturnalia, we call it Christmas today. It is a happy time of the year and as we know, it is celebrate it all over the world. Even people who are not Christians keep the holiday of Christmas. It is also interesting to note that the central figure in the Catholic religion is the Holy Mother, Mary the Mother of God is the one whom the Church holds as immaculate and most perfect of all women, for if she were not she could have not given girth to God, in the mind of the Catholic Church.

Lucifer, represented as the star god Remphan, is now incorporated as the "Star of Islam". The Star God Remphan is born from the womb of the "Crescent Moon". During the time of ancient Egypt, the "Horns of Isis" and the sun disc in between the horns symbolizes this. The birth of Islam was a birth of a new religion, but not the birth of a new idea. The representation of Lucifer is loud and clear in Islam. The teachings of Islam nullify the blood of Jesus, which is needed to pay for the sins of people and the perfect life that Adam and Eve lost and were tricked out of, by Lucifer. According to the teachings of Islam, Jesus was just another prophet of Jehovah, or Allah and never died for the sins of humans.

This would leave all of we the people of this planet, with out any hope for the future.

The three main religions today represent the first rulers of the seat of all pagan false religion ever to be cast upon the world by Lucifer himself. The first king of the world was Nimrod, his wife Semiramis and her son Nimrod incarnate, Tammuz. The "Tower of Babel" was built for these three rulers to control the world from. As we learned, the Tower of Babel was to be the capital of the world and the seat from where Lucifer would "rule" over and control the world's population as it grew. As history has shown, Jehovah was successful at stopping this from happening.

Today those first three Luciferian rulers of the pagan world, Nimrod, Semiramis and Tammuz, are represented well by Judaism, so called Christianity and Islam. The teachings of Judaism no longer just follow the Law of Mosses, but also include the teachings of the learned elders of Zion. There is no doubt that the Learned Elders of Zion and their teaching has permeated the world, its business, its governments and most of all the financial system. They have planted their flag with Remphan's Star on it in their homeland and have left little doubt that they are controlling the world governments. Nimrod set himself up as the god of the sun giving life to his people and their lands. The Pharos of Egypt modeled their rule on Nimrod's example. Nimrod was king of the world and the main god to his people. The Learned Elders of Zion are controlling the world events by controlling the world currency; hence they are as a group, king of the world and guard their religion with all means possible from Holocaustic sacrifice to out right warfare.

Christianity, represented primarily by the Catholic Church, holds the "Holy Mother" as dear and so Semiramis lives on with us today. Semiramis first became the goddess of the earth, then she added the moon and the stars to her god ship and controlled the people with pagan religion and holy icons which are still used today with in the Church. The Catholic Church venerates anything they deem holy, from men of faith, to icons recovered from the Crusades, to crying or bleeding statues and shrines.

If the Catholic Church did indeed covertly started the teaching of Islam to destroy other Christian sects through out the area of the Mediterranean Sea the Arabic world, then indeed Semiramis did give birth to Tammuz in the sense that the Catholic Church gave birth to Islam. The sigh of Islam is the Star of Remphan being born from the crescent moon, or Tammuz being born from Semiramis' womb. So to whom does the nation of Islam really render worship to?

1st John 5: 19 explains the problem we face here on earth very well when we are told, "...the whole world is lying in the power of the wicked one." The Bible never seams to run out of scriptures that tell us this. We are told over and over that Lucifer, Satan, the Devil, the Angel of Light, has control of this world and the system that we live in, so why should we doubt this?

People of the world, we are in dire times and it is time to examine what you believe! Look at and question the world around us do not take anything at face value! You cannot hope to survive the War of Armageddon if you are on the wrong side. You will positively die! If you are part of Lucifer's world in any way, shape, form, or fashion, you are going to be destroyed along with the rest of this Luciferian world. I know that these are strong words but it is the truth. You cannot expect to practice or believe teachings that are founded in a Luciferian world and expect to be considered a child of Jehovah God.

No one can make judgment on what you find acceptable in your life and what you do not. What you do is between you Lucifer and Jehovah God. What it will all come down to is your attitude and your relationship with whom ever you make your god. We are already at a disadvantage because we live in Lucifer's world and are influenced by him and his agents everyday! This world does everything to distract us away from getting to know our real spiritual father, Jehovah and his purpose for we the people. In fact almost all new Bibles omit the name Jehovah and replace it with terms like "God Almighty" or the "Lord God" or some similar expression. How can you ever develop a close relationship with someone whose name you do not even know? The reality is that you cannot. This Luciferian world has done its best to cover up any attempt to learn the truth about Jehovah and yet it is essential if we are going to live through Armageddon!

In order to survive the War of Armageddon we must make Jehovah our father and abandon any kind of Luciferian teaching that influences our life! We need to develop a relationship with an entity that we hardly know and have been misinformed about. It is not going to be easy by any means, it is going to take a deep desire and research. The Bible book of John 17: 3 tells us "This means everlasting life, their taking in knowledge of you, the only true God, and of the one whom you sent fourth, Jesus Christ."

Knowledge is key to building a relationship with Jehovah God, not just knowledge, but accurate knowledge is essential! The Bible book of 1 Timothy 2: 4 tells us that God's "will is that all sorts of men should be saved and come to an accurate knowledge of the truth." How do we find out what is the truth, where do we start? Book of Matthew chapter 7 verses 7 & 8 give us the place to start, it says, "Keep on asking and you will be given what you ask for. Keep on looking, and you will find. Keep on knocking and the door will be opened. For everyone who asks receives. Everyone who seeks, finds. And the door is opened to everyone who knocks." The first step is to start looking for the truth about Jehovah and start to build a relationship with him! If you are sincere in building a relationship with Jehovah God, start by making it a matter of prayer. The answers you are looking for you will find and you can start to build the personal relationship that is needed to be considered one of God's children and survive Armageddon.

A great place to start building a relationship with Jehovah is to learn about the things that Jesus taught his disciples and his twelve Apostles, most of which is recorded in the Four Gospels, Matthew, Mark, Luke and John. The religious leaders of Jesus day stopped teaching the truth about their God Yahweh and took up teaching the traditions of Zionism. God's name became too holy to say in the eyes of those religious leaders and was eventually was omitted. The truth is that God's name Yahweh, or Jehovah, became painful to hear in the ears of the Luciferian religious leaders. Their descendants today still find the name Jehovah painful and they have done their best to eradicate Jehovah's name so no one will learn the fact He is our true spiritual father.

When he was asked, what the greatest commandment was, Jesus answered, "you must love Jehovah your God with your whole heart, your whole soul and your whole mind." Then he said the second like it was "you must love your neighbor as you do yourself." Jesus said that "on these two commandments the whole Law (the Law of Moses) hangs and the prophets." In Jesus words, these were the "greatest commandments". The Law of Moses given to the nation of Israel was gong to be replaced by the Law of Love at Jesus death; this is because Jesus was the fulfillment of the Mosaic Law and his example of love for the human race and Jehovah is an example for us to imitate.

If you intend to build a personal relationship with Jehovah and hope to survive Armageddon, you are going have to be motivated by either your desire not to die, or your desire to be part of Jehovah's family. Many people feel they are "connected" to a "higher power" in some way and indeed, we are. It is something that is almost "hard wired" in to our psyche along with the need to be loved. We can use this feeling of a connection to a "higher power", to inspire us in the search for the truth about Jehovah. It is a natural process and when we start to look we will find.

A great resource to use in learning about Jehovah and the truth that has been obscured about Him is the internet. Research the teachings of your religion, research the origin of the icons and symbols used in the worship of "God" and see which god or gods they were originally used to worship. Research the things written in this book and see where they lead you. We all need to examine what we believe and do our best to build a personal relationship with the God who calls himself Yahweh, or Jehovah if we have any intention of surviving His War of Armageddon.

Humans, we the people of planet earth can all survive the worst problems and the final judgment facing this worlds system of things, if we become part of Jehovah's family. Jesus told us in the book of Matthew, in the 24th chapter, verse 22 that there would be "Chosen Ones" saved from the great tribulation facing the world. In the book of Acts in the 2sd chapter and the 21st verse "And everyone calling on the name of Jehovah will be saved." How will you know to call on God's name Jehovah if you do not know who Jehovah is? With the desire to be part of Jehovah's family and developing a personal relationship with Him, we will know enough to call his name in time of need. Not just at the time of Armageddon, but when ever we need him. When a young child is having a problem or is hurt, what is the first thing they do? Do they not cry for mommy or daddy? We need to have the kind of relationship with Jehovah; we need to know him so we have to confidence to call on him when we have problems in our life.

If we can develop this kind of relationship with Jehovah now, it will not be as difficult for us to have faith in him helping us as the problems that face us increase and this world system starts to fail and collapse. Our faith and trust in Jehovah will only become greater and our personal relationship with Him will take on a power of its own. Jehovah will know that you want to be one of his children and will treat you as such as he exacts judgment of this world the Luciferian powers that are ruling over it!

WE THE PEOPLE SURVIVE ARMAGEDDON!

The many things we have to face between now and God's War of Armageddon. We will have more than just our faith tested. Most likely, we will face our own mortality! Jesus said that in the Last Days, things would become so terrible that if those days were not cut short, no life would be left on earth. It is because of the "Chosen Ones" that the terror and brutality of this world will be finally done away with. Honest hearted people have wanted to live in peace for thousands of years, but there is no peace in a world where Luciferians rule over and oppress the people. For the very first time in the history of the civilized world, the Luciferian influence will be gone and peace will finally be established worldwide.

Revelation 21: 3 & 4 tells us "I heard a loud shout from the throne saying, "Look the home of God is now among his people! He will live with them and they will be his people. God himself will be with them. He will remove all of their sorrows, and there will be no more death or sorrow or crying or pain. For the old world and its evils are gone forever." "

When you contemplate this scripture and the world that is spoken about, is a direct opposite of the world we live in now. Why, you may ask? There is no more Luciferian influence! In fact, the world is under the influence of Jehovah! The human race will finally be back with our true father Jehovah and we will have his direct love, caring and attention!

This will be a very exciting time in our life, because not only we be reunited with our father Jehovah, but there is a whole family that we know nothing about that we are going to meet! From a study of the Bible, we find that there is a whole family that has been created, before the human race was created. The life forms that the Bible talks about are God, Arch Angle, Seraphs, Cherubs, Angles and Humans. Of all these intelligent life forms, the only ones we know about are the Humans and allot of them are really not very nice! Obviously, the Humans that are not nice must be part of Lucifer's family. Seeing that Lucifer and his agents are done away with, that will only leave Jehovah's family left here on earth. Congratulations, it is time to meet your family!

The earth it self is going to be pretty beaten up, after all the whole planet just had a war waged across it. We know that after every war and after every natural disaster, the clean up starts and rebuilding usually follows. We can believe that the same thing will happen after Armageddon, we who survive the war of Armageddon will be charged with cleaning up the mess and rebuilding civilization. However, we will not be rebuilding to the Luciferian standards used in today's world. No doubt, we will have very close direction and help from our new family in the rebuilding process.

Chapter 13 ~You Can Survive Armageddon!

THE PURPOSE OF JEHOVAH

A little over 6000 years ago, a new genetic species, placed in a garden or park like home on the planet earth. Jehovah gave a command for this new species to "multiply and fill the earth and subdue it". This new species was the start of the human race and as the population grew the garden was to encompass the whole earth. So all earth would now be filled with a human family, who were created perfectly and would not suffer the bodily brake downs, failures and sickness and death we know all too well today. We would mature but not age, we would grow old and never die. If Jehovah's purpose were carried out, we would all be in perfect health and would know our whole family here on earth back to our first parents, Adam and Eve. Jehovah's purpose has never realized in the last 6000 years due to Lucifer's interference. Once Lucifer and his followers both earthly and alien have been removed, Jehovah's purpose will start to be realized.

Over the next thousand years after Armageddon, with the help of our alien brethren, our "heavenly family" under the supervision of Jesus Christ, the earth will be reformed into a paradise type garden and we today can be part of making this happen! We the people can be part of Jehovah's purpose and family. We can have access to knowledge and technology that is yet unknown to us. Better yet we will have Jehovah's spirit directly upon us, this is something that only one man has had from the time of the first two people until now, that man being Jesus. Could you imagine having the perfect mind and body of Jesus Christ? How enjoyable would that make our lives? Do you think we the people could live together in peace as one family? Yes, there is no doubt of it!

While this all sounds wonderful, there is allot of work that needs to be done in order to get there! First, we have to do work on our spiritual side, coming to know the person of Jehovah and doing our best to be part of his family, one of his children. Then we yet have to face the great problems that lead to the War of Armageddon and we have to be one of Jehovah's "Chosen Ones" who are found fit to be part of His family. Lastly, we need to be rescued, and saved through the War of Armageddon as part of Jehovah's family. It is only then that we can start to reap the benefits of being out of Lucifer's world and part of Jehovah's world.

THE RESURRECTION

Something talked about in the Bible and greatly misunderstood, is the resurrection of those who have died. The religions of Lucifer all teach that there is life after death some place and to a point, there is. It is not to heaven or hell or some place of limbo where you go, your body goes to the ground and your spirit, which contains your personality, goes back to Jehovah. The book of Revelation, chapter 20 verses 12 & 13 tells us "I saw the dead both great and small, standing before God's throne. And the books were opened, including the Book of Life. And the dead were judged according to the things written in the books, according to what they had done. The sea gave up the dead in it, and death and the grave gave up the dead in them. They were all judged according to their deeds." Those of the human family, who died and paid the wage of sin, are going to get a second chance. They will be resurrected, brought back to life to this planet earth. Remember that Jehovah is now reestablishing his purpose here on earth, so his attention is here, not somewhere else.

It would not be too difficult for an entity such as Jehovah to recreate a human that has died. Jehovah could create, or genetically engineer a woman from the tissue sample of a man, could He take your genetic information and build another you? Remember, when you die, your body, your genetic information is either buried or reduced to ash, depending on your wishes or customs. Your life force, along with your personality your spirit, is reabsorbed by Jehovah and you stop being you. It would not take too much effort for Jehovah, to genetically reconstitute your spirit and DNA together and build another you. So, it should be easy to imagine that it is possible for Jehovah to bring back to life anyone whom He wants to. Yes, we will be able to welcome back dead loved ones and before long the whole human family will be alive once again.

Keep in mind that this will be a process and is not going to happen all at once. Everything that is done, or accomplished, is done so on a timetable and under the best supervision we could ask for. Finally at the end of the thousand years, Jehovah will have a perfect earth with perfect people on it, all of whom what to be his children, but before this happens there is one final test.

THE FINAL TEST

This is going to seam like a bad joke, but Lucifer is still alive and well at this time and so are his fallen angles. Lucifer and his hoard are only captured at Armageddon, they are not destroyed. They are used one final time to test the human family at the end of the thousand years. Most likely Lucifer will start just as he did 6000 years ago and cause divisions between people of the world and then raise up rulers to dominate over the general population. Remember if "great and small" are to be resurrected, we can expect former world rulers to be among the people brought back to life on earth. The Pharos of Egypt, the Caesars of Roam, Alexander the Great Attila the Hun and the bloodthirsty sun worshiping rulers of Mezzo-America are all going to be common people, not the infamous demigods they thought they were. It is possible, even probable that if these world rulers from history are resurrected, if given the chance for another kingdom, or to be a rulers over the people of the world again they would take advantage of opportunity!

Lucifer will gather his followers out of the world's population and try to make himself god of this planet again. Lucifer will have success and he will weed his followers out of Jehovah's family. When the people of the earth make their choice to back what ever type of government Lucifer tries to cast on the earth and try to establish it, then those Luciferian followers, along with Lucifer himself and his fallen angles will all be destroyed once and for all time. The human part of Jehovah's family will have been restored 100% and Jesus will give is authority over the reconstruction of the earth and the purification of the human family, over to Jehovah God! It is at that point that we truly become children of Jehovah and he our father. Never again will a test of Jehovah's authority be made or ever be even questioned, because he is the father of all those intelligent life forms, both human and nonhuman, who what to be part of His family.

Earth and all life forms on this planet, will be restored to the way Jehovah purposed it. Everything from we the people to the very ground we stand on will be blessed by God. Our minds, bodies and lives will be perfect, this is a concept that we can hardly fathom at this point in our lives, but one day it will be the reality!

BEYOND THE FUTURE

We have an idea of what the future holds for the human race, because of the words recorded in the Bible for us. We are told what will basically happen up to a thousand years into the future. After that we are told In Revelation 20: 12 that scrolls or books are opened along with the Book of Life. Those, whose names are written in the book of life, will get to know what is written in those other books that are also opened. As to what their content is, we can only guess, but science today may have given us a clue.

With new technology in space exploration and new telescopes placed both on earth and in space, we can look back billions of years in to the past of our universe and in fact the processes that took place in order to create our own solar system and planet earth. Astronomers have been looking for what maybe considered other "earths", planets which are in a sweet spot from their sun and about the same size as our earth and capable of having life on them. Fact is they are finding them. Planets about the size of earth and the same distance from their sun are now being discovered.

Just by the pure numbers, scientist and astronomers believe that there must be millions of other planets just like our earth. There are billions of galaxies just like our Milky Way, which have billions of suns just like ours and now we are finding that there are planets revolving around those stars. In the Bible book of Isaiah chapter 40 verse 26 we read "Look up into the heavens. Who created all the stars? He brings them out one after another calling each by its name. And he counts them so see that non are lost or have strayed away." If Jehovah has names for all the stars, he must have a purpose for them too. How many stars have earth type planets capable of supporting human life? I am sure Jehovah knows all their names.

Have you ever wondered what you would if you never died? Would life become boring for you? Also with the reproduction system that humans have, if we lived forever and used that reproductive system to its full design capabilities, each set of parents could produce 400,000 children. It would not take long for this planet earth to become over populated and we would be not much better off than we are now. Jehovah is a God of Love and He gave us that same capability, it would be logical that if he wanted to and it was part of his purpose, that he would spread that love over the universe. He could use us, the human race to populate the stars and galaxies across the universe. How quickly would you get board if you had your own planet filled with your children, your children's children and so on? Your family would grow and you could watch generations of the family you created, fill the planet you which you choose, or were asked to populate.

Really, the possibilities are endless when you think that we are part of a family that is billions of years old. Jehovah's purpose for us has not been totally revealed. We do not know the whole story, just the part we need to survive the War of Armageddon and become part of Jehovah's family. We know that it does not end there but that is just the beginning of the rest of our lives!

YAHWEH, JEHOVAH'S WAY, OR NO WAY

There is much information to consider in this book. There are many new concepts and different ways of looking at the world around us to think about and ponder. Please take the time to think about the logical case made here for our future, for the future of our children and the future of the human race.

We know that this system is doomed to massive failure if drastic measure is not taken quickly. We also know that big business is not going to stop polluting the planet. The captains of business are not going to abandon ship and give up profits for the benefit of the environment. The world rulers are not going to give up their power, but they will all unite behind the beast looking One World Government. We know that this world runs on greed, power and wealth and every one wants their share!

Our world is in constant fear of global terrorism, global pandemics and disease and in Third World Countries food shortage. The ice is melting, earthquakes are becoming more numerous and serve, weather patterns are changing, the magnetic poles are shifting and the prophecies of 2012 are quickly coming. The uncertainty of our future is of great concern to all intelligent honest hearted people of the world.

We know we have been fooled by the establishment of this world, we are just not sure how exactly. Or now, maybe you have an idea how this lie we call life has been trust upon we the people. If you have any questions or doubts, investigate the information written in this book! Make an effort to study the Bible and learn what is written about Jehovah and his son Jesus. If needed find small Bible study groups which operate outside of Church dogma and the Luciferian teachings of men.

I am not endorsing any religion or way of life, nor am I making judgment on what you believe or do in your life. This is not just a religious matter we are facing, it is a matter of life and death, ours! It does not matter what your religious beliefs are or what political group you chose to support. What is going to matter is if you identify yourself as a member of Jehovah's family and build a personal relationship with him. We are all going to have to take sides in this war we cannot remain neutral. We are going to have to put our faith, trust and love in a god we hardly know, a god that calls himself Yahweh, or Jehovah, "He Who Causes to Become!" if we are to survive the coming problems that are facing the world, and Jehovah's War it self Armageddon.

We must all examine our faith and what we believe in. We are all intelligent life forms with free will to do as we please and want to do. It is time to invoke your intelligence and look at our world from a logical stand point and ask your self, "Do I want to be a child of Jehovah, or do I want to be a child of Lucifer". The choice is plain to see, because it will be Yahweh, Jehovah's way or no way at all!

THE END

CPSIA information can be obtained
at www.ICGtesting.com
Printed in the USA
LVOW10s0834050417
529687LV00015B/543/P